Dates to Remember or Wish You Could Forget
"Getting it Oh So Right"

Gabrielle Anna

Brighton Publishing LLC
435 N. Harris Drive
Mesa, AZ 85203-7303

Dates to Remember or Wish You Could Forget
"Getting it Oh So Right"

Gabrielle Anna

Brighton Publishing LLC
435 N. Harris Drive
Mesa, AZ 85203-7303

First Edition

Printed in the United States of America

Copyright © 2014

ISBN 13: 978-1-62183-210-2
ISBN 10: 10: 1-621-83210-4

ALL RIGHTS RESERVED. NO PART OF THIS PUBLICATION MAY BE REPRODUCED OR TRANSMITTED IN ANY FORM OR BY ANY MEANS, ELECTRONIC OR MECHANICAL, INCLUDING PHOTOCOPY, RECORDING, OR ANY INFORMATION STORAGE RETRIEVAL SYSTEM, WITHOUT PERMISSION IN WRITING FROM THE COPYRIGHT OWNER.

Dates to Remember - Gabrielle Anna

Author Notes

To the reader: The names and details of the characters in this work have been changed to protect their identities, and the dates are not in necessarily in chronological order.

Acknowledgments

I am both excited— and somewhat flustered— to have this privilege. I've always admired those giddy individuals who get to give shout-outs and thank yous. I am in bliss to make my list, and apologize beforehand because I know I'll forget someone or something. I'm fortunate to have so many inspirational people in my life. Those owed gratitude, all the more ambition for a second thank you page... in a second book—yes!

Thanks to all the busy cafes that kept me fed and caffeinated in my times of power-writing or procrastination. I learned to appreciate the atmosphere, energy, and ambiance provided in these places. It is a blessing for writers—not so much for a writer's wallet, however.

Thanks to the characters in this book, whether you do or don't identify with these pages. Whether you deny your contribution altogether, I thank you regardless. I appreciate you being a part of the novel and its inspiration. Your real identities are not included. *Just mine.*

To my brother Adam: May this inspire you the way you inspire me! You are such a strong and loving little being, who is, in fact, not so little anymore. Love you always.

To Jay: This book may have been significantly delayed if not for you. After a laptop vigilante stole the first laptop I ever bought and loved, you were there for me. When I was filing police reports, and watching hours of camera footage to catch the perpetrator— you were supportive and gave me a laptop to aid in my detective work. Though lost chapters were never recovered, and my investigation went stale, you were the first person I laughed with after my three days of trauma. Thanks for your generosity. You are a kind friend whom I'm flattered to have shared so many laughs with, Karaoke battles, gay bars, and labyrinths. Details excluded.

To Mr. Jones: Thank you for inspiring me! My optimism doesn't come close to your belief and compassion. I wish there were words big enough to express my gratitude. Your support for everyone is admirable. Love you!

To B: A once-true soul sister who was with me through adolescence and into womanhood. We made it! Thank you for showing me it's beautiful to embrace my emotions, whether they are tears, laughter, or my deepest thoughts. You helped me find my voice when I didn't know I had one, and you helped me embrace writing beyond my scattered journals. You are family, and thank god for that because you know my immediate relatives are insane. While we have since gone separate ways, I'll never forget the paths we did walk together. All girlfriends deserve to meet their soul sister, and I was lucky to have spotted you so early.

To Danielle: Thank you for sharing your talents, and helping me in the initial stages of this book. Our hours of amusement, recollection, titles and "research" are cherished, matcha girlfriend. My days of camping out in cafes were much more fun with you.

To Andy: Thank you for being many firsts. The first person who helped show me how to love me, and helped me be at ease in loving someone else. You were so patient with any transition I went through. It never fails to make my eyes swell up when I think of the unconditional love and friendship I have felt for you. While you resist reading your chapter and now outright resist me after my many pullbacks, you were able to experience it with me firsthand, and you have the many emails to prove it. Some women take a lot of pictures, some women scrapbook—we have dated and documented memories. Some of those memories are now published.

To Nana and Grandpa: With all you've done for me, I am pleased to be able to dedicate anything and everything to you! In all of our best interests, I don't recommend you read beyond this page. This the one time in a book where skipping to the conclusion is suggested. Nonetheless, thank you for your continuous support and love. To the two people in my life who have never and could never disappoint me. I love you unconditionally. Please key in on the "unconditional" in case you decide to read the following chapters. Genetically you are tied to me, but I won't hold you responsible for any of my soon-to-be exhibited behaviors. Just my good manners. Looooovvveeee yooooouuuu.

Thank you to Don McGuire, my acquisitions editor, and Brighton Publishing. I am in gratitude for your confidence and dedication to my word. Also, for taking a chance on my crazy story. The pep talks are always memorable and inspiring.

Dates to Remember - Gabrielle Anna

Introduction

Through observations of my own and contributions from other females and males, I have created a list of bachelors to be cited or at least provide some warning. Read and meet at your own risk.

Types of Bachelors to be Suspicious of:

1. Pretty Boy—self-sufficient + or self-obsessed.
2. Mr. Entitled.
3. The Only Child—reference to birth-order theories.
4. The Charmer—one of my favorites to observe.
5. The Pessimist—to be or not to be…paired with optimists.
6. The Bromance Lover—typically travels in packs.
7. The Over Eager.
8. The Bad Boy—we are exempt from one of these in our lifetimes.
9. The Sugar Baby or Sugar Daddy—choose your fix wisely.
10. The Challenge—our egos love these.
11. Mr. Woe is Me—do not give any attention.
12. The Serial Cheater—often has a highly presentable alter ego.
13. The Insecure.
14. Mr. Boss.
15. The Intellectual.
16. Mr. Foreigner—look beyond the accent.
17. Mr. Sarcasm—sarcasm is for humor, not for language.
18. Mr. Mixed Signals—they are in their glory with texting these days.
19. The Creep—just falls short of stalker/stalking.
20. The Enabler.

Dates to Remember - Gabrielle Anna

21. The Romantic.

22. The Woman Hater—easiest to identify.

23. The Penny Pincher—perhaps most compatible with other Type A's.

24. The Glutonous.

25. The Baby Daddy—Baby Mamas are likely not far behind.

26. The Reformed Man Whore.

27. The Friend—questionable territory.

28. The Flirt.

29. Mr. Independent or Dependent.

30. Mr. Status—progressive or suppressive?

31. Mr. Athlete—playing the field + or playing you.

32. Mr. Comedian—comedy routines are great until he's only acting.

33. Mr. Nurturer—hugs may take one back to the womb state. Hate-love relationship may develop.

34. Mr. One Upper—you make dinner, he hires a chief. You start walking, he runs a marathon. You get pregnant, he gets the symptoms.

35. Mr. Homie—has no aspiration to leave home… ever.

Foreword

According to the mathematical theory, we should date a dozen people before choosing a long-term partner; that provides that best chance that you'll make a love match.

—Laura Shafer, 25 Funny Little Facts about Love

Such news is both elating to me and exhausting. I've never been any good at math, but on these terms I understood. Who comes up with such "mathematical theory"? Could love and all its layers simply be summed up by a protocol? The following is relationship quotes, facts and stats to consider… again read at your own peril. Ignorance may be bliss!

Partnership helps her get good night's sleep. University of Pennsylvania researchers claim that women in stable relationships get better shut-eye than single woman do. (Does this mean single woman are having all the sex? If we had to compromise sex or sleep, what would be the consensus? I will say confidently, after sex with a partner, I sleep like a blissful baby.)

One in three men and women are completely satisfied with their sex life. (This stat I find completely disappointing.)

Research suggests that men use gifts as symbolic gestures to accelerate sexual encounters with women.

Relationships are now governed by the 'principle of least interest.' The person with the least interest in continuing the relationship has more of the upper hand or power.

Romantic love and addiction share many of the same neurological pathways. When love is lost, and we endure a breakup, the symptoms mimic those of withdrawal.

Very few people actually manage to find a relationship in a bar, which is one of the most favored methods used when trying to meet someone.

Dates to Remember - Gabrielle Anna

(Suggestions anyone... the work place? Grocery shopping? Online dating?)

If your relationship has just broken up and the person involved says that you will never get another like him or her, feel lucky. This is a good thing because you are broken up hence you would not want someone like that individual anyway.

Some female penguins engage in prostitution. Believe it or not, in the wild, certain females will exchange sexual favors with strange males for pebbles they need to build their nests. According to Dr. Fiona Hunter, zoologist, 'It tends to be females targeting single males, otherwise the partner female would beat the intruder up.' On some occasions, the penguins trick the males. They carry out the elaborate courtship ritual, which usually leads to mating. Having bagged their stone, they would then run off.

It's a lot easier to treat each other as equals when you are dating someone of the same sex.

(Old fashioned gender rules need not apply.)

Traditional dating, places men in control of the date, and women in the position of paying off the date with physical intimacy. This pattern has been argued to be perpetuating the double standard of women, the sexual exploitation of women, and the economic exploitation of men.

Research has found that men actually value cuddling more than women do.

If a woman offers to pay for everything, chances are she isn't that into the date. There is an unspoken understanding that a man paying for everything is a form of a 'copulatory gift' which is almost universal in all animal species.

On average, there are 86 unmarried men for every 100 unmarried women in the U.S, although the actual numbers vary according to region.

Research shows that men know they're falling in love after just three dates, but women don't fall in love until date fourteen.

The vibrator, a common sex toy for women, was originally designed in the 19th century to fight the anxiety-related symptoms of female hysteria.

(I'd like to bring this back for research purposes—therapy anyone?)

If you want to create an instant link with a date, say his or her name at least twice in conversation. This shows attentiveness and connectedness.

(Side note: Can be easily overdone!)

In the online dating world, women are afraid of meeting a serial killer. Men are afraid of meeting someone 'fat.' According to Ann Rule, about 3% of men are psychopaths.

☙

Beyond facts and stats, now for some beautiful suggestions and food for thought…

Practice love in your relationships. The key to this is avoiding expectations. It's expectations that makes most people miserable in love—the return on the investment.

–Rama

In terms of spiritual development, it's not a big deal whether you have sex or not, the issue is who you have sex with, and what their energy is doing to you.

–Rama

I think men talk to women so they can sleep with them and women sleep with men so they can talk to them.

–Jay McInerney

Dating is about finding out who you are and who others are. If you show up in a masquerade outfit, neither is going to happen.

–Henry Cloud

Dating is not only a wonderful time of life, but also a context for enormous spiritual and personal growth. You learn so much about yourself, others, God, love, spirituality, and life through dating. Done well, it can be fulfilling in and of itself.

Done well, it can be one of the most fun and rewarding aspects of your life. Done well, it can lead to a good marriage.

—Henry Cloud, *How to Get a Date Worth Keeping*

I profess not to know how women's hearts are wooed and won. To me they have always been matters of riddle and admiration. Some seem to have but one vulnerable point or door of access; while others have a thousand avenues, and may be captured in a thousand different ways. It is a great triumph of skill to gain the former, but a still greater proof of generalship to maintain possession of the latter, for man must battle for his fortress at every door and window. He who wins a thousand common hearts is therefore entitled to some renown; but he who keeps undisputed sway over the heart of a coquette is indeed a hero.

—Washington Irving, *The Legend of Sleepy Hollow*

When you're looking for someone, you're looking for some aspect of yourself, even if you don't know it… What we're searching for is what we lack.

—Sam Shepard, *The Observer.*

The key to successful dating is, rather than focusing solely on finding and winning over that one and only right person, use this time in your life to learn about yourself and about relationships and to become a better partner. Being single can offer a unique advantage in the pursuit of good relationships. You have the opportunity to step back, take an inventory, learn and grow, and be far more ready for a healthy relationship. Instead of leaping headlong into the next romance, slow down and make some personal discoveries that will increase your chances of having your future relationships be more successful.

—Nina Atwood, *Be Your Own Dating Service*

Dates to Remember - Gabrielle Anna

The Beginning

NOVEMBER 28, 2008 — FIRST COLUMN

I'm sick of rhyme schemes so I'm just going to write. No more emotional poetry, no more riding around in my car highly caffeinated and singing to angry females. I've evolved. I will not let this experience allow me to doubt myself, or declare myself asexual. It's not going to sound perfect, I may not even make sense, but if Carrie Bradshaw can talk about her Sex & the City, then I can talk about my sex—right? I may not be having the sex she is, or living in the great city of New York; however, I am a young female searching/stumbling for a compatible companion.

I'm fortunate enough to experience glimpses of the nearby cities, however, I live in quiet suburbia. In the act of reflection, I hope for a revelation. Perhaps some understanding in the other sex, if that's possible. In finding that person to listen, to laugh with, I seem to have only found a clearer encounter of... me.

Speaking of encounters, I do have a counterpart. It sometimes scares the crap out of me. She gets me so much, and at the same time we're opposites. Her name is Rosy. When I was born, my nana told everyone my name was Rosy. We always say that's a sure sign we were meant to be friends. If I were a lesbian, we'd have quite an explosive romance. That stands as a possibility for our future. We determined awhile back, if our soul mates were not found later in life, then we'll be one another's lover.

I feel us growing apart, but I could never turn away from her. She is one of the few people who truly appreciates me and doesn't demand I explain myself. No, she just kind of writes it off as, "Oh that's Gabrielle!" and although it's sometimes condescending, I appreciate such freedom. I have my mom too, but that can seem a cliché. Cliché or pathetic, I haven't decided which yet. At the end of the day, she is my "mother," and I can only go to her with so many ridiculous stories. We're close now, but that doesn't mean I've completely erased everything she's done to me. The blessing of birth, the curse of a parent.

Dates to Remember - Gabrielle Anna

After last night I need to vent. F**k. I'm cursing a lot but we all take up bad habits. The word f**k was the most appropriate to start with last night's reflection. For bad habits, I'd rather drink a coffee a day or curse excessively for emphasis than other bad habits people swear they can't live without, or can drop in a second. I'm not going to swear about either—I'm just going to swear.

First things first —mother nature is actively testing my patience. Yes, I'm talking about my nonexistent periods, and it's fine to talk about them. Five months! This leads me to believe clearly my hormones are out of whack, thus I'm only partially responsible for my actions and or attractions. I've got all these little hormones parading around in me and my little body doesn't even know what to make of them.

Am I intrigued? Annoyed? Funny or peculiar? Gentleman or Man-whore? There tends to be such idiosyncrasy in trying to decipher my interaction with the opposite sex. My doctor tells me it's fine to get one period a year. One period a year? Tricking my body into being pre-menopausal does not sound like a solution to my mood swings. Why do we listen to the crap we're spoon-fed without question?

I met Riley a little while ago. I'd like to lie and say it's been longer than two weeks but it hasn't. What a short lived almost-romance. I thought potentials are on their best behavior—at least in the early months. It all started when I wanted a Blackberry. Post-breakup trauma can easily lead to new material goods, a haircut, or self quizzes in the self-help section. I was vulnerable when we met, so he had an advantage from the start. I had been single for the past three months since my last boyfriend cheated on me with his ex. When I say cheated, I mean "found-her-panties-in-the-bed" kind of cheated and I still didn't react. Don't feel sorry for me or yourself, it happens. Particularly in naïve love. My new motto is, "Why get even when you can get even better?" When breakups fuel creativity and motivation, one can be the ultimate female fatale.

I have no problem being single, so it was easy for me to walk away. I've never been relationship-driven except around the holidays. There's just something about the holidays—I don't know if it's because you feel obligated to be cheerful, or because it's that much easier to tolerate your family when someone is there with you. I'll admit, after the incident with my ex-boyfriend, I was a little crushed. Prior to that ex, the one before him slept with my current best friend. I wasn't sleeping with him yet, so I don't know if that makes her case worse or better. I guess she did me a favor. She was truly kick-ass up until that point. The best friend of mine got a tattoo that read "loyalty and betrayal" supposedly in my honor when I caught them, but I think it was just an impulse of her binge drinking. The boyfriend later taunted me, stalked me, and then completely ignored my existence all together. First, he claimed he wanted me back—but, when that failed, and I was just contemplating forgiveness for my broken heart, he then exclaimed I was a whore, anyway. This is often the scapegoat for failed relationships where men identify women as the cause. "You're right," I had to admit. "I'm the whore who caught you sleeping with my best friend while I was picking up the Finding Nemo DVD for me and your puppy on our detour to Petco."

To be clear for storytelling purposes, Ex #1 and I broke up after my whorish ways, and Ex #2 and I broke up because his ex-planted her panties intentionally for me to find. In his case, I had started to feel more like his babysitter anyway. He was the first person I was really having sex with. I thought I was being broken into womanhood at the prime age of eighteen, but sex at eighteen is about five minutes of bumping. No bump and grind as R Kelly had once promised, no singing with flash mobs as I had envisioned—just a mere, Bump! Bump!... Bump? Nonetheless, I was hopeful for my future as an almost-woman.

The whole "panties-in-the-bed" find mostly just burned my competitive side. Fortunately, while one half of me wanted to come back in full-blown costume—black-leather lingerie with a whip and leave him high and dry in some compromising position, the other half of me knew it was best to make my composed exit. I believe I said something along the lines of, "You know what you did!" and then walked out. Step One on the path of future guru.

After that, he was put in my phone as Never Pick Up. His mom still has half of my book collection, which makes the end of our relationship all the more disappointing. Now I was stuck wondering, *Do I seek belongings, call it a wash, or use it for leverage and reunion?* At the time, I had put in excess work to win his mother over as the ex-girlfriend, and had made great effort to stay in the picture. Her continuous drive-bys and drop-ins were a lot to keep up with. One day she'd show up crying, the next she'd show up with muffins. Fortunately for my relationship with his mother, our shared pleasure of reading was an easy joy to bond with.

Long story short—when this new guy, Riley, asked me out, I decided, *What the hell, I'll go with it.* I've spent three months in reflection. I've been broken up with for four. I'm ready to be let into the wild again... right? My self-talks aren't challenging enough, they just feel repetitive—it must be time. I was literally crying when I met this T-Mobile potential because it was such a hassle to get my new phone.

So when he handed me a tissue and offered me a date, I was suckered in. Suckered being the key word. He was cute. He was funny. He seemed comfortable with himself. He was older, which apparently doesn't grant wisdom or maturity. He wanted to cook me dinner—I'm not a picky eater. Speaking of that—I don't get it. The last guy who tried to get my attention was a personal trainer at my work, aka the Vortex. He cooked me dinner, he cooked me lunch, he bribed me with breakfast from DD, proactively bribed me with coffees on my early shifts, and I wouldn't even budge for a second. He ended up banging a couple of his clients, anyway, so it was a blessing in disguise because now I'd have to borrow a suit from ET's transporters before I'd embrace him.

Still, how is it that with Riley I dove in with high hopes and it didn't even feel right? I needed to stop denying the inevitable instincts that are known. I think he got me with the nice apartment, and the puppy. I really felt that if he could take care of a dog, he could take care of me, too—right? How sad. Not that I needed to be taken care of, but for once I wanted someone responsible, someone secure. I see it now. I was intrigued by Riley, but I then kept trying to reignite that initial feeling. I was projecting onto him my hopes, and they were fogging my vision. Before I belittle the poor guy in the following writing, I will say he was a good catch, but we simply weren't compatible. After last night, everything I first saw as "cute" wasn't so cute, and the potential I was convincing myself we had, suddenly didn't look so promising.

I slept over on the first date. Infatuation can seriously fog the clearest vision. Well—that and alcohol. We didn't do much because he felt so rushed, but even that I should have seen as a red flag. When we got back from the bar, he was insistent about me sleeping over. I should've written it off as desperation instead of caring, and called it a night.

"Honey, you absolutely can't drive, you have school in the morning, and you shouldn't have had a beer at the bar."

Where was this speech when he was buying me that beer? It was my own fault for being so trusting and comfortable with people. Despite my letdowns, I still seem to be trying to figure it out.

It seems to me that guys and girls can never be friends. Accordingly, my advice is that, when on a first date, especially when uncertain about the person, Rule # 1 is to bring a girlfriend; they can talk sense into you if necessary. Or if they encourage you to misbehave, both of you have made a bad decision, which makes for a good story and debriefing.

Now I'm going to conjure up some justifications for my ignorance. He cooked me dinner, he was on time, and he had a clean apartment with no visible, excessive porn stash—or something else that would give me a glimpse into his true character—the cute puppy, fun friends, and a good living location in Worcester. This is how I rationalize as a female. Maybe I was slightly jaded from being cheated on twice, thus anyone looked like a liberation. Maybe I missed the comfort of someone, and maybe I was biting at that first year of college freedom. Nonetheless, all of the above—at first—made me somewhat acquiescent.

The first date had somewhat convinced me we had a future. I texted my mom and said something silly like, "He's great, and even a good kisser." Usually, I'm not so easily swayed. It's rare that first dates of mine have ever even gotten to walk me to the door—and to think this one even got a kiss. After trying to convince him I was fine to drive, we settled on a separated sleepover. The next morning, feeling comfortable, I rolled out of bed, got my coffee as always, and conveniently went down the street for my two classes. He had even made me breakfast. I felt a little gaga. What male sleeps on the couch and still gets up to cook you breakfast? I was delighted. I did notice, during my first period class, he texted me rather excessively, but I overlooked it.

There should be more clear-cut guidelines and regulations in the rules of text messaging. I hoped he'd be like a sex messiah or something, and that we'd have this fabulous relationship. Me, him, and the little dog—wrong. Then, of course, in my second period class, this guy I'd been flirting with for an estimated three months finally asked me to hang out on the upcoming weekend. Life is so like that, isn't it? We've given each other googly eyes since September, and now it was like he could smell another male near me so he made his move. Ironically, they shared the same name of Riley. I haven't had much luck with Rileys in the past. Even more ironically, they graduated together in the small town of Millbury. Even more ironic, this Riley says that the other Riley has issues. I try to base my perception of someone on how they make me feel, but I should have at least considered this statement.

Friday night for our third date I was late... again. I think I was about two hours late, but it was news to me that we had plans. It was the sleepover so early on that set me up for disaster. We went from "date one" to "couple" within the span of twenty-four hours. With couple status comes expectations. It's not that I didn't enjoy dating, I think I had just become a little selfish. I needed to be! I was so used to getting burned, that when taking care of me became a priority, I may have gone a little overboard.

Also, not to make excuses for myself, but I'm an Aries. For anyone who read horoscopes, they would recognize I'm headstrong and need to ease into change. I'm also a little impulsive—all characteristics of being a ram. I go back and forth from ram to a lamb. Maybe I'll send him a copy of sexology for his future relationships—it could offer a little insight.

I met him at his house and you know what he said? "You're late again. You're the type of women who will be late to her own wedding."

That was strike one. I should've walked out right then. You don't tell a girl who played with Barbies until age ten that she will be late to her own wedding. A full-on conversation went on in my head as I stood there, stumped.

Are you crazy? I silently wondered as I looked at him. *Why are you mentioning marriage on date three, and then immediately follow it with an underhanded insult? I will not deal with passive attacks. My virginity dream has already been crushed, now you're telling me I'll be late to my own freaking wedding. At this rate, who says I'll make it there? According to you, I will, so at least one of us will be in matrimony.*

Dates to Remember - Gabrielle Anna

There should be a manual for dating. I sometimes feel thrown into these situations simply ill-equipped. He even leaned in for a kiss after that, but I wanted to blurt an obnoxious proclamation. So, instead, I just turned away. Some of the moments men deem as intimate make me question their sanity. He then goes for a hug, and I resisted. He picked me up in an attempt to be cute, but I really felt as though my ribs were being crushed. Still resisting the hug, he ignored that my boobs were being squished and I now have a genuine look of sheer fright across my face. Don't get me wrong, I can appreciate a hug, a bear hug, or even a protective comforting man hug, however, this one was not invited. Instead he was just over-crowding my space and aura.

When we walked upstairs and entered his living room, there were three individuals. Not just any—these three look like a grandma, a mother, and a father. All were here to meet on our behalf. For an hour, we all sat there and delightfully conversed, although bits of the conversation I missed by the loudness of my wandering thoughts. His mom just sat and stared at me, his grandmother seemed proud he had a new girlfriend, and his dad ran through actual knock-knock jokes. When the sudden family intervention ended, I didn't ask any questions.

After the family meeting, he finally took me on a mission to get my new phone. We were sitting in his fabulous car, so I excused his bad singing. He thinks he's the next white rapper. It took me a long time to accept that I wasn't Whitney Houston, so I didn't hold it against him. We get to the phone place and he now decides to tell me the Blackberry I want is an extra $30 a month. I appreciate the honesty, but that counts as withheld information. He got the date with a promise and bribery that he would help me attain the phone I wanted with ease, and no confusion or question. He offered to help me because he works for the phone company, and now here I am on date three confused and still phoneless.

Well, I browsed the store while he asked the salesperson about fifty questions. Spitting them out one after the other, "How's your store doing here? How's business? Did you meet quota today? What do you do in sales? What products came in?"

I wanted to yell, "Shut up!" and spare the poor man behind the counter from this 60 Minutes episode.

Strike two. I debated on intervening, but waited it out because I half-hoped that the conversation would tire him and spare me from further chatter and inquisition. On impulse, I got the phone that I didn't want in order to spare the poor salesman from Riley's conversation.

I got back into the car with the guy I suddenly didn't want either. He made me pick the green phone which looked like vomit. I wanted red, to match my heels of course. He didn't get it. Then he told me that we needed to stop by his friend's store. Glorious! I don't look my best. I was frazzled. I was already irritated and then I had to meet his friends.

Wasn't meeting the family enough? His friend owned a paintball store and lucky for him, I was a little intrigued. Enough to go at the very least. I'd recently tried to get my brother into paintball, and this could have been a good resource. His friend was a sweetheart, but I was a little taken aback when I found he's already heard all about me. Emphasis on all. Let me remind you this was only date three. We met Monday, it was now Friday.

Maybe I'm nuts, but I'd rather be labeled teaser or whore for sleeping over so early on, than girlfriend on day three to my not-so-compatible companion. I want to be recognized as Gabrielle, not as Mr. Mobile's girlfriend. Of course I say this now, and karma will punish me by sending me the love of my life, and I'll act cuckoo and then he'll write me off as overbearing. Karma has a funny way of coming back around.

I imagine I'll get love struck in the future and proclaim someone my significant other on date one, and then be looked at as ridiculous or over-emotional. Lucky for me, despite my instincts, I gave Riley a chance, so hopefully karma will be courteous.

Riley and his friend were practically high-fiving at what a catch I was. I wanted to say, "Come on!" Now I wonder what his exes before me looked like. True, I'd feel threatened if they all looked like Angelina Jolie, but I didn't mind if they were good looking. I didn't want to be deemed accessory wear when I was still deciding if we were going to date. I then questioned if he was only looking for a girl to pose as eye candy, a girl he could drag around for all his errands. I was way too far behind on my To Do list for this crap.

I didn't expect Riley—after a long day and the third date—to meet my friends and bat his eyelashes while shaking his ass as we made my rounds and fulfill my agenda. I didn't even know I'd be meeting friends that night, and by week one, I met the whole circle. I've already gone against every cynical thought and slept over the other night, and now here I was giving up my TiVo on a Friday night for this. I was being punished wasn't I?

They talked amongst each other, I pretended not to listen. His friend was so charming that I bought a hat I didn't need and will probably never wear. It was pink camo. I should have asked for a bodysuit to go with it. Then, I could make easier exits. In an attempt to distract myself, I picked up a magazine and there were pictures from teams paintballing at Huntington Beach. Suddenly, I was reminded of my ex-boyfriend who paintballed. Great. Maybe they know each other, too. Maybe that ex will even walk in right at this very second. Riley had already graduated with my crush from class, it would only be appropriate if he knew my ex.

We got back to his house, and he looked at me like I'm the Antichrist when I said I won't sleepover. Next thing you know, I was borrowing pj's and he's making me Ramen noodles. How did he go from gourmet chief on date one to Ramen noodles and Cheetos? What happened to the conscious cook he from our first night? I had too much pride to be looked at like I'm the Antichrist, so I doubtfully agreed. I'm a sucker for infatuation and second chances.

We talked. Last night's conversation was stimulating, tonight I just felt bored. He cracked two "yo momma" jokes and there's never any reasoning for that. Even worse, every time I said something he didn't agree with or he disapproved of, he went "waa-waa-waa" in a crybaby tone to mock me. "Riley I'm going to go take this call," "waa-waa-waa," "Riley I want to watch this movie," "waa-waa-waa". I was ready to say, "Okay, boo-hoo-hoo because I'm leaving and then you can waa-waa-waa as much as you like." Could I really deal with someone slaughtering the English language whenever we disagreed?

Next, he told me how his ex had called his grandma today, and his grandma told her he was dating someone new. A little surprised I said, "Wait—who are you dating?" Apparently, he was referring to me. I didn't know whether to be flattered or flustered. I couldn't breathe—and not the good loss of breath. Week one and grandma was ridding his exes for me. Why are exes still calling grandma in the first place? I couldn't meet those expectations.

Dates to Remember - Gabrielle Anna

My previous ex's mother has a good portion of my beloved book collection (Deepak, Jodi Picolt)—now this grandma has daily calls with girlfriends. I didn't know if I could even make it through that sleepover. So I said as sweetly as I could muster, "Maybe you should work things out with your ex. We just started talking and we can't rush into things. I'm sure she still cares about you." Then I got a look of disapproval. If a waa-waa-waa followed, I may have made my exit right then. I learned right here that the truth is the truth. Sometimes it hurts. That is my only regret in life, forever lying to myself for someone else's sake or lying to another for fear of my own truth. Relationships can't be built on guilt or pressure, so what happened to passion?

After we talked a little longer, he tried to set the moves. The other night I had been slightly aroused and overly hopeful, which may have been alcohol induced, but tonight I was as dry as the Sahara. I didn't want to cuddle. I didn't want to look into each other's eyes. I didn't want to spoon. I especially didn't want my hair played with, yet he simply didn't get this.

He took off my hat and threw it on the ground. I think that was an attempt at passion? He tried to kiss me and I was more interested in the TV screen. He did *not* notice that. I kissed him a little because I was hoping my body would get some kind of response—but, nothing.

He then went for my pants, as if he was trying to wrestle them off me. I could only laugh. I watched him struggle with the third button. It was too humorous to tell him to stop and sadly, too humorous to let him continue. He was still so persistent despite my laughter. Nothing. Nothing. Nothing.

The other night I had such high expectations, now I was more impressed with the looks the dog was giving me. Mac seemed just as entertained in this scene as I was. After no luck with me or my pants, Riley moved onto my feet. *Geez.* I smiled at him, but I shouldn't have because now he was encouraged. I said, "Let's just go to bed," in the least-sexual way possible. I like sleepovers, but man or boy, the opposite sex just can't handle sleepovers only.

We laid in bed, and I attempted conversation. I tried to develop some sort of understanding for each other, tried to dodge the inevitable. In order to see if he violated any ultimate dating deal breakers, our questions got more in depth and intrusive. I realized I needed to get down to the details. I finally said, "Listen, I don't know what I want—do you?" The conversation took a sexual turn and then he hit me with the final blow.

The premature man refused to go down—if you know what I mean. I think maybe I heard him wrong.

"Please elaborate," I said. Nope, I heard him right. Wow. I would consider myself an incredibly understanding person, far beyond my age level. You could tell me anything without judgment—but, if trying to sway me, this was simply not the right kind of pillow talk. I didn't want to listen to him boast about himself either.

At this point, I should've called it a night, but I was too polite. I tried to be respectful. "Why don't you do it?" I'm an instigator naturally.

He said something like, "I'm not into it."

I think he even referenced a previous bad experience. I wanted to say, "Man up!" I couldn't bear to beg a boyfriend for oral sex. That's outright foolish. If you've already pulled me in, fine. I'd deal. Week one and you deny oral sex in a relationship altogether? No deal. He acted as if to do it would be doing a grand favor, charitable even. I can most certainly respect boundaries. There are things I'm not comfortable with in sex, but those words were no less unsettling. One wouldn't necessarily give up sex after a bad experience; if that was the case, I'd be celibate for the rest of my life.

I didn't sleep well that night. I don't sleep much anyway. I just laid awake, stared at the ceiling, and talked to the little pup Mac who was lying on my tummy.

The next day, I was late for work. These were all obvious red flags I so foolishly ignored. Late for work because of stimulating conversation, excused. Late for work because of fabulous can't-get-out-of-bed sex, excused. Late for work because I stayed up and talked to your dog, not so much excused. I sacrificed two crucial years of my life to preserve other peoples' happiness. I've worked hard for stability and structure; I didn't want it to fall apart when it's not even worth it.

At work the next day, he texted me continuously and I seemed to be given a five minute window for response time. If I didn't answer accordingly, I got the worried card. "Just let me know you're okay, babe."

"Riley, I am doing sales in a gym, not hits for the mafia. I am okay and I am ALIVE. ... Listen, I won't see you tonight. I'm going to a formal black and white party."

He then invited himself and a friend.

I said, "No, you and your friend can go to Vegas for all I care — just don't come to anywhere I'm going."

He laughed.

Then I felt like saying, "Waa-waa-waa-waa."

That night, I went to my party. I even went to Boston with the other Riley, classmate Riley. *Shame on me,* I thought, *but I've been talking to and only talking to this Riley for three months now.* It was funny because I didn't notice him at first, then suddenly I wanted to stand on my head to get his attention. Few people make me want to stand on my head in the name of approval.

Amy came with me to Boston—I was smart this time and brought a sidekick. Boston was fun and we had a great Saturday night.

On Monday, I went to class. I worked my nanny job, which consisted of Rock Band and junk food with Ronny. Then I worked my cocktail job which consisted of food and drinks for the Greeks and Italians. I was convinced that my period was coming because I suddenly have that need for comfort, companionship, whatever. I suddenly thought, *Maybe I'm too stuck in my comfort zone.* Maybe it just took a little movement on my part to make space for someone to fit.

I agreed to see Riley after work. I told myself that maybe we could be friends—maybe I was too judgmental. Maybe he and Mac were going to be awesome. Maybe this, maybe that, as I tried to fix our incompatibility.

I got to his house at 1:00 in the morning because of work, and he was asleep on the couch. I was somehow sucked back in—into this false belief that maybe we could date. I lay down next to him and little Mac. I closed my eyes and thought, *Maybe it's just nice to know someone waits for you to come home, and maybe it's that much nicer to have them next to you when you wake up.*

Dates to Remember - Gabrielle Anna

Tuesday morning I woke up, but not in time for the spin class I'd sworn I'd take. Sorry, ass. Riley was up practically fondling his paintball gun, and I wondered what he took me for. Seemed since he couldn't fondle me, he'd busy himself fondling his other toys at 8:00 a.m. in the living room.

Even though I looked at him harmoniously in his sleep last night, this morning I couldn't look at him or escape fast enough. He was awake and not-so-harmonious looking. We said our goodbyes, mine was casual as usual. Mac got a kiss and a hug goodbye, Riley got a, "Call you later." I got my coffee to go, but Dunkins didn't give me happiness in a cup. Out of politeness, I sucked it down anyway in the name of caffeine.

It was pouring rain. I pulled out of price chopper after grabbing my groceries and this guy hit me head on. I was crying, shaking, sucking down my horrible coffee until I was awake enough to fathom what had happened. I got out of the car and found myself apologetic even though I knew it wasn't my fault. I looked down at what I was wearing—boots, a long t-shirt, and booty shorts. Just f**kin' lovely. I booked it out of Riley's so fast that attire wasn't a concern. My t-shirt was long enough so I could play it off, but as the rain started to soak through, I could tell today was going to be a bad day.

I blamed myself. I blamed Riley. I blamed my need which left me driving out of here for the sake of company. I blamed Dunkins. I blamed and I blamed, but it felt no different. I deemed this as a massive red flag. The cops came, and luckily, they were helpful.

Once I finally made it home, my neck was killing me, but I sucked it up and went to work at the Vortex an hour late and worked until closing. That was where every irritating thing hit me at once.

Amy had been texting me all day; she wanted go out with Riley and his friend to the bar. Suddenly, she became interested in Matt and I would have been a horrible friend not to set them up. To make her happy, I agreed. I was tired of telling people no. I'd rather stay home and clean my room until 1:00 a.m. listening to mellow music.

People started to catch on that Fiona Apple wasn't a real person whom I'm spending time with, but merely a voice on my stereo. People

Dates to Remember - Gabrielle Anna

dislike that type of rejection. Matt was excited because Amy had blown him off four times, and twenty minutes before I could leave this Vortex and pick her up, she canceled. I could have dragged her out of her house by her extensions, and unwillingly taken her there. I actually said this to her.

I listened to her excuses. "Oh Gabby baby, I wanted to come." This was not when I want to be Gabby-babied. I told Riley that we couldn't come.

"Damnit! Get out here—I miss you," was his text-messaged response. Don't tell me to get anywhere, I make a choice of my travels—and miss me? I saw him this morning pre-accident, and honestly I thought the only connection I had with him is his dog. He didn't even acknowledge the accident when I called to cancel plans. Not one word to its existence, he just said, "Ok so get out here."

I said I'd talk to him later and hung up.

I then went home and tried to tell my mom my life status but really I was talking in gibberish. She was standing in the kitchen with an absent expression on her face, probably just piecing together why I listened to Fiona Apple in my room most nights. I finally rationalized—the way any nineteen-year-old girl does—and I said, "Okay, I'll go out tonight. I'll break it off in person with Riley."

My mom wished me luck, but laughed with amusement.

I got to the bar and Riley met me in the parking lot. He hadn't even made it to my door yet and he was asking for a kiss. We walked. He stepped in a puddle and got wet. I was slightly irritated already, but then I thought, *At least one of us can get wet*. He seemed gentleman-like, opening doors for me, ready to buy me a drink and then I wondered, *When did girls start feeling grateful for these things? Feeling we owe something in return for cordial behavior? Is it really too much to ask for?* I refused the drink and decided that he is nice, and then I pondered which one of my friends could date him because despite my efforts—I couldn't.

We walked downstairs. He walked me right up to this guy who was about 6'3" and in a white hoodie. The guy turned around and I saw that he looked like Channing Tatum. Channing Tatum look-alike, are you kidding me?

Dates to Remember - Gabrielle Anna

The guy flirted with me and Riley said, "This is my girl, Gabby." Kill me. I'm not a shallow person, I don't even have a type, but at this moment I realized I was just wasting my time. Here I was in Celtics attire, talking to the Channing Tatum look-alike, missing the game. It was like a prelude to torture of incompatibility.

In my aloof state, Riley left me standing alone by the bar. I often found this scenario familiar. Perhaps this is why I find dating so undesirable. Regardless of their adoration toward me, I always found myself feeling inferior to my male suitor. Feeling that they see parts of me, but don't see me when I actually needed their attention.

Two guys came over and hit on me and Riley didn't even notice. I wanted to say, "Where is my introduction now?" I was his girlfriend before, now he was ignoring my blatant "please come help me" signals. Finally, when I walked over to his table, he just started rubbing me. Reminder, Riley—I'm not Mac. I didn't want to be treated like a puppy or a plush carpet.

I said, "Riley, I don't want to be petted. Please get me a vodka and cranberry drink. Don't let them jip you on the vodka." It was wrong of me to mislead him in that moment, but I had to buy time and rehearse my breakup material. Sending him on a drink mission kept him occupied for a few minutes, and bought my mind some time.

I looked around for my exit. The closest getaway was the girl's bathroom. I literally couldn't stand to be there any longer. No window, plan A was ruined. I called Rosy four times—no answer. Plan B was ruined. I decided to just find the courage, courage on the way to the exit door.

I walked right up to Riley and said, "This isn't working!" and then, high heels and all, I actually ran to my car. I hated to run, but the freedom in that statement came over me. Perhaps it wasn't as rational as I hoped our conversation would go that night, but I reacted on a binge of sudden energy. I got in my car and drove. My car was such a safety for me, a moving safety—and as I pulled into my driveway, it hit me. I thought of how often we ignore the blatant feeling or signal that sometimes even with sincere optimism—or ego—two people don't work, sometimes it was never meant to be anyway. From there we must stand tall, and continue on our search where we find that stranger—or just the very strange.

Chapter One

TO THE NORTH...

2009 was an expansive year for me—change, opportunity, confidence, and self-exploration. Amazing what a little dedication does for our self-esteem. What led Alexander and I to one another was perhaps unusual, but most encounters are, especially the ones which end up being quite significant.

Adorable, doll-faced Amy was asked to waitress poker games and needed another girl for the job. I uncomfortably agreed. Once we got the location, we did our share of spying before deciding the work was legitimate. Our boss, Teddy, was the typical Greek ever-loving, father figure. His name couldn't have been more suitable. His recruiter Patrice, was strange, fetish freak-type of guy, but Teddy kept a fair eye on us and everyone else's eyes off us. Our job was to serve coffee, endless food, and clean up for the poker games. Once we were comfortable, this meant us drinking coffee, eating food, and then venturing out of the kitchen with our bright smiles. Often it was just the regulars every week, still occasional new faces would pop up. We spent more time focusing on the poker cards rather than the faces.

Observing the male species may still leave you clueless, while observing gambling could at least get us hopeful for a win. When I first met Alexander, he was introverted and quite the gentleman. Reserved and careful even with eye contact. Amy and I would gawk at him and his brother from the kitchen, but his cool demeanor we couldn't quite read. It took him a while to become comfortable, but with sincerity, he asked me out. He even first got approval from Teddy. Loving Teddy approved, but he made sure to talk with me beforehand in the kitchen about dating.

Me? Typically dating males a few years older, the ten-year age gap made me unsure. I kept him at bay for a little, and then he put me on the spot. One to not shy away from a challenge, he literally played his cards right and I found myself in agreement. "What do you mean I won't go out with you? Of course I will!"

Our first date left me in awe. A drive to the city made me feel independent and anxious. We met at his North End apartment, and when I arrived late as usual due to lack of direction, he handed me a GPS.

Dates to Remember - Gabrielle Anna

"Gab, I felt you'd need this." The gesture was moving. Simple, but noteworthy. As my nerves started to subside, we headed out on our date. He brought me to my first Celtics game with floor seats, and as we cheered, a huge feeling of gratitude came over me. After the game we went out to dinner in Boston. He was greeted by everyone at the restaurant, and we ate in a cozy corner. *I could get used to this!* I thought.

After that, without question or pressure, he brought me back to my car, shook my hand, and let me go on my way. My ride home was filled with uncertainty and self-talk. "Does he like me?" "Am I boring?" "Why didn't he even try for a hug?" "Are we friends, are we more than friends? Do I want to be more than friends?" The ease in the date and his authenticity was new to me.

As time went on, he continued to invite and include me in multitudes of plans. Foxwoods where he'd have me signing off all bills as Mrs. Zola, social gatherings, nights in the city. It was all new to me. Our fall romance was rocketed by the excitement and mood of the holidays. Italian family dinners filled with love, affection, and wine, dining in the North End, karaoke—my weakness—with his savvy, talented sister.

I got swept up. I was infatuated by him, his lifestyle, and what it brought out in me. As sparks flew, I loved him more and more, but deep down I knew I wasn't ready to be in love. When our togetherness started to feel overwhelming, I could feel myself pulling away. He and all the others referred to me as his future wifey, but I had just found me. I couldn't fathom giving that me to someone else. I was outwardly selfish. I had just met myself, and I couldn't give her up without more discovery of who she was. The depth of me felt inhibited by the stigma of a relationship.

After many attempts, I tried to call it off, but he remained at arm's length. I was more so responsible for this. Patiently waiting for me to pull him back in, he wasn't fazed by my time away. Despite my honesty in our lack of a future together, I dangled him there. Could I give up so easily the first *man* I'd ever dated? Could I walk away from the secure life that would await me? He was not only the first man I had ever dated, he was the first boyfriend to get more than a minute's interaction with my family. I often avoided that for everyone's sanity. He beat my system. As the owner of a market in Boston, he showed up one night at my house with boxes of fresh produce—blueberries, greens, vegetables, and fruits, casually carried in by my doting Taurus. He later used a similar drop-in move again when he showed up for my brother's baseball game one day, and then another, and another. At the time, I was too crabby to appreciate such dedication.

He knew me and understood me, and the fairly simple camaraderie between us was a lot of fun, yet the thought of staying together felt too final. I was stubborn. I wanted to establish myself, not rely on my endearing-eyed bachelor. I knew he'd do anything for me, and that felt like too much freedom with someone's heart. I didn't want to be labeled anyone's girlfriend. I didn't want to fit into someone's life. I had ambition to make my own without distraction or compromise. Why does he love me so unconditionally? No one ever had done so like that.

Batting away gifts and adoration, I dug my heels into the ground and stopped us from moving onward. Despite my like for the pedestal he so effortlessly provided, I had too much pride and too big of a heart to lead him on. I knew my self-work was just beginning. I knew I had a personal, spiritual path which awaited me—I just didn't know its steps.

Just before our Miami trip, I coldly cut ties for his best interest. My heart knew the truth, but my mind talked me in and out of feelings. After our final end, I left him hanging on a stitch of attachment, though I knew its frailty. Following our breakup, though, those exes remain nearby (as long as it's not stalking distance, this is okay) and I swore I met my match. One can't contemplate getting back together with their ex when you feel you've met your husband.

I met Calvin shortly after Alexander and nonchalantly said, "That's the man I'll marry."

Calvin will be introduced shortly. After months of my own blatant stalking, he still didn't budge beyond friendship. While I tried to patiently prove myself, nothing worked. After that revelation, I felt I couldn't try to reconnect and start a life with Alexander, yet I received no interest beyond friendship from Calvin.

The following excerpts are the noted memories of Alexander post-breakup. I was often too busy with our dating and too happy during, to write about us. Our only documentation is after the completed breakup. Oh, the tangled webs of relationships!

Rose and Gianna

Last week I was sulking about my current relationship circumstance, and this week I'm elated. This next writing is both a follow up to the effects of Christian (Chapter Mr. OCD—you'll meet him soon) and further confirmation on Saint Alexander. Even though Alexander and I have been broken up for months, he remains on Saint Status, continuously prevailing as the lover I should be with.

Saturday for Halloween, Rose and I decided we'd venture to Boston. Our names for the evening would be Gianna and Roxanna. I proclaimed awhile back Gianna would either be my alias name—alter ego—or my future daughter's. I felt quite clever in meshing my first name initial with my middle name. Alter ego or future baby? Two very different extremes, but the name connects to me. Despite my recent desire to dress as and channel Lady Gaga, I stuck with the theme and went as Madonna. I have to keep some of my impulses in check.

Our original plan was that I would be the designated driver and only have one drink for the evening. Being under twenty-one, this was an easy duty to maintain. We later decided we should literally crash at my Alexander's house, my ex-boyfriend. One—because Rose still probes on why I broke up with her ideal bachelor. And two—because we know he's always reliable. We later decided that one drink for the evening would turn into three drinks for the evening. Had we thought rationally about the above decisions, they wouldn't have seemed so desirable.

It is hard enough to keep track of oneself while drinking, never mind a night when ninety percent of people are costumed.

As we later read, my text outbox was documented proof of why two Madonna's should not be out drinking together. Rose and I decided not to leave each other's tutu'd side! Locating friends, not for the drunken. Leaving sidekick, not for the drunken. Trying to tell my dating potentials how to find me, I thought for the drunken—not.

"No, I'm wearing a tutu! Don't you see me? I've had Hell raiser following me all night and I'm standing with the three amigos by that bar. You know the bar with all the people and 1...2...3... yeah the three amigos and OMG and Tupac! Shit! I'll call you later! What if it's really him?"

I learned many things even later that night. One—leave all technology in the car while drinking. Trying to decode messages the following day was quite humorous. Two—leave the camera in the car because drunken pictures are only funny until tagged on Facebook.

The night started around 10:00, typical for two single college girls on a venture to Boston. After parking in Alexander's lot, I was anxious and ready to take on the night. Anxious is probably an understatement. I was a caffeine pill deep, and I was either going to throw up or pee myself and the night hadn't even begun yet. Rose and I initially intended to park in Alexander's lot anonymously. They still left me my space, even though I was the ex-girlfriend. God, he's such a gentleman.

We then rationalized how can we park here and not say hi? Not at least call? As we walked over to his apartment we thought, *How can we not at least invite him for a drink?* By the end of the night it was, *How can we not at least sleepover?* We arrived at his apartment and, like usual, I made myself right at home. Did a quick bathroom check (not for creeping purposes, but for makeup), gave Rose a tour, helped myself to food in his kitchen (Bless Boston Cannolis) and then did our reuniting. It's funny how certain people can fall out of your life for months but when you're back together, it's as if you've never left.

We told him our plans, and explained our surprise drop-in, and as usual he didn't question or probe about anything. I really realized how understanding and patient he was with me. After everything, he acted like this scenario was totally normal; he was even excited. I left him months ago and here he was looking at me the same. I did care about him, but the bottom line feeling was still there. I wanted him to be happy; I wanted him to be with someone who could fit into his mold and ideals. I just wasn't ready.

A move to Boston for our relationship's future felt too big, too permanent. Before we left, I told him, "Don't let us hold you back tonight. If you've got plans, I won't drink so we can go home. If you've got a girl coming over, seriously tell us because we don't want to intrude on your privacy." He didn't budge, not even a flinch. His dedication to loved ones is noteworthy.

We all walked over to R2s together and the night began. My other half had her usual Sex on the Beach, and I was handed a vodka Stoli. Eww. I accepted it gratefully and sipped on it. At the time, I thought this would be my first and last drink of the night. Alexander and I used to go to R2s on date nights once a week, and the place felt just as welcoming and warm as before. Certain spots would always have an attachment or association with him. I remembered us in our usual seat by the window, eating pizza with his sister—and I was taken back in an instant. It took all my will not to look at him lovingly or order a pizza in that moment. I refused to have a heart lapse. I am Madonna. I am an icon for the night. I sipped my drink a little faster. The Monster Mash started playing.

Once we finished our drinks, Nick calls me. Yes, meet Nick—trainer, assassin, Dave-Matthews-obsessed Nick. He was at a popular bar with his friend who was involved with the Bruins, and for the sake of Rose finding romance, I agreed we'd meet them. I tried to talk her out of it at first.

"Rose you are Roxy tonight. You don't need a man. You are the like a prayer version of Madonna, we shouldn't be chasing down bachelors." She delivers a fair rebuttal. She knows my destination of the evening was chosen with my hopes to run into Christian, aka Mr. OCD, and she was right. It was only fair that I be her sidekick in meeting my trainer's friend who could possibly be a potential for her love life.

Before I knew it, Alexander had hailed us a cab so we could be on our way to the club safely. As we got into the cab, he handed me money—the usual gentleman. "Alexander, I don't want your money. We'll call you later. Go enjoy yourself!" I refused multiple times. Even in our relationship, money was never a priority to me. As I slid into the cab and shut the door, I saw Rose has taken the cash. *Oh Rose.* We got in the cab and I realized how lucky I was. Alexander let us park in his lot for free, bought us drinks to start the night, got us a cab, and then with no questions asked, sent us on our way in our like a virgin costumes.

Sitting with my best friend, I couldn't tell if it was the buzz, caffeine pill, or my heart—but, suddenly I'm looking at them both with lovey-dovey eyes. I had told the cab driver we were going to Telfi just to make sure Alexander didn't casually run into us, and as we pulled off I confessed our real destination. The cab driver laughed suspiciously, and said, "I wasn't going to take you girls there, anyway. That club is for lesbians. Damn lesbians, they're ruining my dating life. It's like all you girls have gone lesbian."

He said this to us hopelessly as were in the back holding hands and applying each other's lip-gloss. I offered him my usual dating advice. Somehow even on Halloween night, I found myself still offering guidance on relationships. Even when I wasn't trying to engage in psychology, it resurfaces.

As we jumped out of the cab, there was a line almost around the corner to the bar. We held each other in the line as it started to lightly sprinkle rain. In that moment, we saw an old girlfriend of mine, one of which I still love and another non-friend whom had become bitchy and backstabbing. While the bitchy one disregarded Rose and looked me up-and-down judgmentally, I heard my name. There was Nick in the front of the line with his Bruins bachelor, waving to us to cut ahead and enter with a body guard.

The moment was perfect. As we entered the club, I saw the sky open up and start pouring. We pranced in with our dry tutus and oversized bodyguard escorting us along. No wait, no cover, no frenemies. We high-fived each other and raced over to the bar in all of our glory. Drink number two in hand, and we made our way to the dance floor. Roxy attempted to take drunken action shots of us dancing, and we giggled as I did the bump-and-grind with one of the Ninja Turtles. Nick was watching us—he wasn't amused.

After thirty minutes of dancing, I got caught. I got targeted. Caught by my trainer, the non-boyfriend who apparently thought his "VIP rescue" partnered us for the evening. His grip on my arm was so tight when he pulled me off the dance floor; I deemed this as the last trainer I'll ever take up on a date. I tried lunging away to remind him he was my trainer only, but he wasn't impressed or smiling. As I lunged toward the sea of people, he pulled me in and pressed me against him for an attempt at a first kiss. When I finally get out of the embrace, I dragged Rose to the bathroom for evaluation.

"Rose, I hope you know this VIP cost me a kiss. We're leaving. A kiss and a trainer! Onto the next club! No trainer of mine is going to beat me down, cyber-stalk me when I cancel, and then off me from a dance floor all while being paid by me. I should have a Jennifer Lopez ass for all this work."

We laughed it off and made our exit to the front door. As we pushed past people, we saw the group of frenemies just getting in—soaked. I thanked Mother Nature for praising me on disregarding their judgmental stares outside. As we tried to track down our next destination, we couldn't hail a cab. Not one cab! Pushing past people on the drunken, busy streets of Boston, we attempted to navigate toward The Esta. On our journey, we stopped and asked a few bouncers how to find the club we were destined for. I literally used the word destined. They tried to lure us into their club instead. As chance had it, before we realized what was going on, we were suddenly being escorted on our feet via a huge black man in a fur coat. He was either a pimp, bouncer, or body guard—his true identity was unclear. He shouted and pushed past people, parading us block-to-block like celebrities. He sufficiently led us to the club and brought us yet again to the front of the line. We paid him for the time and deemed that service better than a taxi. Pleased with our night thus far, we showed our IDs to the bouncer. Denied. Denied? Denied! Whether it was intoxication or my fake ID, we were denied.

Our first roadblock of the night. We tried to compromise, we tried to reason. "If I was drunk, could I do this?" The bouncers were entertained, but it didn't get us any closer to the inside. After I confessed that I was trying to casually meet my friend Christian, the bouncer who knew Christian called him for us.

"Uh, yes, I'm meeting him but he doesn't know it yet!" Great, I'd blown up my own spot already. So much for unpremeditated run-ins with a recent ex. Christian walked out, his usual, sexy self-costume as a secret service guy. How f**kin' appropriate. Even in this attire, I found that he still managed to look prettier than me. He could get us in, but as he scolded us on our behavior and outfits, my agitation increased. I decided that we were better off on our own. I made some awkward slurs. We walked off and tripped over the curb trying to sexily regain our composure. Christian and the bouncers watched us sit on the curb compiling a new game plan. We looked back at them, and they, too, seemed to be awaiting our next move.

Dates to Remember - Gabrielle Anna

As if it couldn't have been planned any better, a limo pulled up beside us. We knocked on it as if by chance this could be our transportation. I wasn't one for smooth talking, so I expressed the honest truth to the limo driver. "Can we get in? That guy behind me in the secret service costume thinks I'm just a drunk girl in a tutu. If we leave with you, we'll at least be drunk girls in a limo" The limo driver was amused with my honesty, so he let us in and took us a few blocks over to Telfi. We felt it would be the most appropriate under these circumstances. As we walked over to the entrance, we saw lights flashing for club D. In the window, I saw someone waving to me. I can't quite make the bachelor out, so we went in anyway, curious.

As we got in, I realized it was Riley. Riley who I wrote off as gay or unavailable due to his lack of communication. Yes, that Riley from history class. Riley that graduated with the other Riley is standing in front of me. He invited us to his VIP table and we giggled about our luck for the evening. At that point, we were waving their bottles of Grey Goose, and suddenly my creative side got the best of me. I decided we should stand as statues in the window of the club, pose after pose we carried on clenching back laughter. This was successful for a short while until we got scolded to come down.

After being escorted back to their VIP table, I decided it was best we call it a night. My usual extremist self. I had no longer any desire to be out, and I certainly had no desire to be out with my once-upon-a-history-class crush. We left, and while drunkenly texting with Christian, Rose took away my phone to call Alexander for help. Being the saint he was, he somehow found us. Literally within ten minutes he was there with a cab to safely bring us home. No questions. Not one. No judgments. I was covered in sweat, body glitter, and shoeless—yet he looked at me with his typical regard. When we arrived at his apartment, I was convinced I was going to throw up.

I lay myself on the bathroom tiles and started making pleas to God, Jesus, Mother Nature—whoever I could get ahold of. I tried and I tried but I couldn't seem to throw up, and I couldn't seem to lift myself from the bathroom floor either. Roxy came in and she was already in a t-shirt and shorts of Alexander's. I, on the other hand, was tangled in my own tutu. She tried to helpfully hold my hair back like a good girlfriend. Nothing. She then thought it would be a good idea to feed me cookies.

So, there I was in my ex's bathroom floor, in a tangled tutu, getting cookies shoved one after the other into my mouth. By the seventh cookie I told her to leave me there. Saint Alexander came in and tried to peel me off of the floor, but I swear I was content and wanted to be left. He washed my face, brought me a blanket, and I napped there briefly. When I got up, Rose was on one side of the bed with Alexander—and, while I found this scenario odd, I brushed it off.

I carefully fell onto the couch and, in under a minute, Alexander was on the couch with me—spooning. Ready with a blanket and pillow, he offered to sleep with me and he cocooned me into the blankets. I told him to go into his bed with Rose, though the words felt a little uncomfortable—I insisted.

A few hours later, I tried to get myself out of the cocoon on the couch, and I managed to get up. It was 6:00 a.m. and I have to open up the Vortex in an hour. Ugh. With promises of Dunkin Donuts, I pulled Rose out of bed, and we each kissed Alexander on the cheek with thanks. We drove home and I showed up for work in my usual Vortex '80s-style attire. Through hangovers, we decoded my messages and laughed at our single lives. I called Saint Alexander and thanked him. Thanked him and promised to take him to Mike's pastry to replace his cookies. He said he didn't mind that his bathroom floor was covered with sprinkles and glitter. As we hung up the phone, I deemed while we were certainly over, it was only appropriate I see him one more time. For the cookies' sake, for manners' sake. It would be rude not to replace them... in person, no less.

Distracted Diva

Hall & Oats' Man-eater song feels somewhat accurate right now. If you were to ask the male species, I guess they would deem me one of those women. To clarify, I'm not actually eating men, I just dabble in my observation of them. Kind of like a mad scientist. They don't take kindly to women they can't figure out, and after years of our suppression, I want to say, "Yes, honey, there will be more man-eaters."

I should have seen this coming. It could worry me, but I think I'll just go with it. Where are the guidelines for playing the field? I read a book once about Aries women being these sexually unattached creatures, man-eaters until won over and I laughed it off as if it was completely ridiculous. Now I find the reading all too familiar.

    I almost wish I wasn't such an extremist. I feel horribly stagnant if I'm not invested in something all the way—and, if that's the case, I don't want to be in it at all. Why bother? Last year I went through a phase where I was relationship driven. Relationships, a union of two people—what could be more fulfilling, more satisfying to develop? What could be more intimate and encouraging? For a second there, I even started to get infatuated with thoughts of marriage and a family. That was until I became a post for all the married people I know. Having their views dumped on me was kind of a check. I didn't become a pessimist.

    Sometimes, after they'd reveal to me their infidelity, their boredom, their regrets, their lack of general interest, or their desire for too much outside interest, they'd look at me with guilt. "Not to ruin it for you or anything." A similar line would always soon follow their confessions.

    It didn't change or taint my views. I'd just take in what I could and learn from it. Following my relationship phase, I hit my single peak. Suddenly, I cut out all interest in guys and dating, wanting to focus solely on developing myself. Not that I wouldn't flirt, I naturally flirt with men and women.

    At the end of August, my single streak was broken. Altered by a casual first date, and now here I've evolved into a man-eater. While one side of me finds casual dating to be exciting, another side of me finds it unmanageable and is truly desperate for *The It* romance. The one that inspires and overwhelms. Casual dating is simply arduous. When dating "casually," if there is such a thing, you can't truly progress. I've developed a problem here. A problem in my experimenting with saying yes. Yes to first dates. Yes to crushes. Yes to almost-romances. Yes to myself. I gave myself yesterday as my last hoorah — it's always easier to start being our best self tomorrow, and then I will act sensibly and use my feminine powers for good.

Let's Reflect

I made plans with Alexander—I know, I know—but he continued to put up with my shit. He was so patient that it startled me a little. The way he waited for me to come around, I couldn't help but half-question if he was on to something. It was baffling to have someone love you so completely despite your neurosis, despite your withdrawal, and still be looked at in the same angelic light. I don't know if he was addicted to the challenge or actually feels that deep of a connection with me.

On my drive to Boston, I got this strange feeling out of nowhere. I was singing and suddenly had an urge to say something to Calvin—my friend whom I longingly admire. We talk on the phone frequently for hours before bed; sometimes I think we're having a breakthrough. I don't know if I just felt confident, but I wanted to, yet again, confess my love to him.

This is an odd sensation that comes over me from time to time. When I'm sure of something, I don't give it even the slightest question or doubt. When I'm sure of something, I want to express it no matter how insane it makes me look. He is the only man I've ever met in my life where, with no thought at all, I could see us married. Now he's always close by as a devoted friend, which would be fine if I wasn't viewing projections of our future together.

Contemplating conversation with Calvin, I pondered the socially appropriate way to tell someone you love them without all its attachments. Of course I rationally talked myself out of it, and quieted my impulses. Was I simply feeling pulled in two directions? Driving to meet an ex with an attempt to be friends, and driving away from the friend I see as so much more?

I caved a little and sent Calvin the hello text. A chance for communication with lack of actual communication. Shortly after I arrived at Alexander's. As much as I adore him—even now with the small pinch of me that wants to see us work, my gut knows the inevitable. I can feel already our friendly dinner is just another failed attempt at rekindling. I think I like to hold onto a small part of us because it was so special to me—but, what past lovers can successfully manage a friendship? I hate that a break up has to be so definite. "Due to our failed relationship, I'll see you never." Ugh. I need to get better at accepting the shift of relationships.

I know how busy Alexander is, all the busier when trying to not seem available. Men love that card. Once they don't know what the hell to do with you, those hard workers become engulfed in work. For myself, it's writing or caffeine, and if I'm really overwhelmed, emotional binge eating. For men, it's their success. I get there and he's got phone call after phone call. It's sexy for businessmen to be busy until overdone. When this tactic is overdone, I get to a point where I want to start taking calls from the president and making business plans of my own. My wonderful friend Steven says it best, "Some men live to work, and others work to live." I am the work to live. A work to live woman who is enthralled by the live to work man within set limitations.

So it stands, left to entertain myself in the North End apartment. Not that I needed all of this attention. When I was getting it, I didn't know what to do with it. But after a forty-five minute drive, I would have appreciated not being neglected. For the first half-hour I texted. I don't even like texting, but it seemed appropriate. The next half-hour I watched the news, which I loathe to do, and by the third half-hour, I was doing fitness on demand. There I was, in five inch stilettos, black leggings, and a girl's dress shirt that oozed a certain sex appeal, and Alexander didn't even look at me. Had I known this shirt would have made me feel like such a sex goddess, I would have kept it away in my closet only to be used for exceptional occasions.

There I am yoga posing in his living room on the hour that I thought we would be catching up the way exes do. Actual exes, not booty-call exes. I was in the mood for a red wine kind of evening. At that point I was ready to kick off my shoes and order sushi for us. That's another thing with Alexander—he's never disappointed me, still I often feel on the edge of discontent. I've had girlfriends who would revel in this. I can't bear to blend into the background of someone's life.

Relationships are funny. There are those few people I'd bathe in the blistering sun for, just to be around, and others any heat with them can feel all too hot. With Calvin, for example, I used to work overtime at the gym just so we could carry out our conversation. If I was on the rare occasion actually working out at the gym, I'd walk that stair master until my legs were on fire and my body was trying to circulate oxygen. All for our usual conversation as passing gym partners.

I looked over at Alexander to release me from all these thoughts, and I decided to refocus my wondering brain. I turned my gaze to loving lenses and could then appreciate the fact that we're comfortable together.

Ahh. My brain and heart are content for about two minutes. Does comfortable matter when neither is on the same page? I could have been running naked laps around his living room and he'd leave me alone. I could be painting the walls, I could ask to take his car for a joy ride around Boston and he'd go with it. "Yeah, Gab. Okay, Gab." Yet here I am psychoanalyzing why the above couldn't keep me satisfied. The answers are often there, as humans we seem to torture themselves to accept that. Is it wrong to need someone who calls you out a little, rather than justifies your insanity for the sake of staying content?

As my thoughts run off, I am brought back with a text from Christian. Alexander is my now ex-ex. Christian is the ex. I swear he senses whenever I'm with another guy. That's the usual time I'll hear from him. Whenever I'm alone, embracing boredom, and mentally willing some companionship, I don't hear from him. I could be having tea with my Nana most days of the week and he's MIA. The second I venture off my usual grounds, there he is.

In this text he asked me, well, *tells* me to be at his house at 9:00 p.m. God he's good. He always has a way of being annoying and incredibly sexy in the same moment. The way he bosses me around I find both hot and womanizing. I guess my response back depended on what my mood was and my mental state of the evening. After this weekend I felt truly disconnected from Christian almost to the point of no attraction, yet I outweighed the options for going. A total of two-and-a-half hours have already gone by, and the most I've done was catch up on world news. I decided, *Okay, I'll hang out here awhile longer and if the night continues like this, I'll stop by Christian's on my way home. Just a drop-in. I'll go in, remind him how sexy and confident I am after our breakup, and then I'll leave. I'd like some appreciation in this outfit. Most of the time my look is no makeup and a bun, but today I did my hair and the cat eye.* Hair and makeup efforts are dangerous. I believe this is why I so often dress down, understated. It keeps me grounded.

Dates to Remember - Gabrielle Anna

As I was formulating my plan for the evening and quite pleased with my justifications, Alexander looked over at me. Hi...? Suddenly, he was ready for dinner and to bask in each other's company.

"Well, I have to leave around nine," I say responsibly. I'm an awful liar and the second I said it, I felt the heat rise within me. Oh I hate to lie. It was on my face right then. I could already feel its weight and my body temperature rising. I had thought I'd show up shortly after 9:00 at Christian's—his apartment is on my way home. Despite his disapproval in my tardiness, I'd show up fashionably late just to rile him a little.

Alexander tried to outsmart me. "Let's just go to dinner and if you need to leave you can." My darling, passive man.

I gave a rebuttal, "No I'm not even hungry anymore, so let's just hang out while I am here."

I was tempted to just tell Christian I was busy, but I also knew if I stayed too late at Alexander's, he would find leverage for trying to get me to stay over. I knew this game. After red wine, after dinner at Trescts, after our conversation, my willpower wouldn't be so strong. Here it came, another lie. I said something about having to pick up my brother from the movies later. I don't know why I lied, because we aren't dating. Maybe it was me who didn't want to hear the truth. My voice of reason knew I was lying to aid my own discomfort. If only I had a better poker face as I tried to bullshit the poker player in front of me.

We made it to dinner. He knew everyone as usual. Such a Bostonian—kisses, hugs, and drink offers anywhere he goes. He made the city feel so small when I was next to him. We sat at a beautiful table by the window —I hadn't even had a sip of wine yet and I could feel my willpower sliding. I could feel myself trying to mentally compartmentalize our future. Wait, why did we not work again? What crazy bitch broke up with him?

As I looked around at all the stylish, coupled girls, I thought, *Why am I not one of them? Why am I at dinner with my ex-ex with a detour scheduled for my other exes?* The owner came over and asked me what I wanted to eat. This was how wonderful they were to one another and one another's significant others. I could be that significant other. I was and I...?

Dates to Remember - Gabrielle Anna

We ordered, cheered to life, and luckily he started to make some ridiculous comments or I would have slipped into oblivion. I text Adam, my brother, and tell him to call me at 9:00. God love him—age thirteen and he's already getting me out of dates. My little buddy since we were younger, and I'd dress him up for tea parties, choreograph our dance numbers, take him for trail hunts on our more tribal days. As I got older, and spent more time with friends, he became quite the little gentleman. Bringing my girlfriends flowers from god-knows-who's garden, writing love letters. I like to attribute so much of his diversity to my mood swings. I'd do anything for him, and I hope he senses that. 10:00 p.m. and Adam was on the phone pretending to be at the movies. He knew what I was up to, and still he remained so well-adjusted. Alexander and I left, but I admit I felt rude for leaving on the run, but it was that or negotiating on when I'd see him again just to be able to leave later. I was usually very honest with him. The moment my heart and mind weren't connected and committed to us, I told him. I never wanted to take advantage of his feelings for me, or have him miss an opportunity.

On my drive home, my avoided-personal trainer texted me. What has happened to people's work ethic lately? Once hired and paid as PT, he was now not only stalking Dave Matthews, he was text-message-stalking me. The other day, he had me squatting all over the gym with his eyes that were beaming. It was apparent that it was punishment for not returning his calls. I could have been foaming at the mouth, and he would have added weights. I first had to avoid him as trainer once he got gaga-eyed with me, then I had to avoid his vengeance. His text message read that he was moving and if I ever wanted to see him again, tonight was my last chance. It was all too dramatic for my liking.

I said, "Best of luck" and continue on my detour to Christian's house. As I got close, I could already hear his wrath about my tardiness. Thank you, Mr. Punctual. I could see him now, opening the door as sexy as ever, greeting me with a simple "Do you know what time it is Gabby baby?" I then would say something clever, and he'd reply, "Is that the time you said you'd be here Gabby?" With the scenario in mind, I contemplate not getting gas but decided it was better to be late than to break down.

Dates to Remember - Gabrielle Anna

I finally made it to his house, and he answered the door, sick. Another person who caught the swine flu; this was now my fourth encounter of trying to dodge it. I weighed my options here—was this karma? Was this fair warning for me to stay away? I hadn't even fully entered his house yet and he got me taking off my shoes—my really fabulous shoes. One should want to do me in these shoes, but OCD prevails. Alexander flickered in my head. I could show up at his house with war paint on and he'd simply ask me what I felt like doing. *Sigh*.

As I settled into Christian's, I realized I hadn't been here in just about a month. Is a month long enough to realize you miss each other, or long enough to remember why you broke up in the first place? This time he was a little more lax, he didn't make me wear a hoodie on the couch so oil from my hair doesn't get on his white furniture. Perhaps this was a step in the right direction.

Where was such flexibility when we were trying to give us a shot? It felt comfortable, but I noticed he talked differently to me now. I could feel it. While he'd say I didn't let him down, it was obvious by his demeanor. He used to be so affectionate. Looking at him, I marked us off in my head as friends. We laughed so much together. Just because we failed as companions didn't mean we had to give up what lead us to each other in the first place. Right as I was picturing us in friendship, he insisted on cuddling. I should've run then, or at least used his sniffling as a valid excuse to go home. He started to put on the moves, usual protocol when the guy goes for it and I'm too curious to stop it. I put little emphasis in looks, but when he's looking at me straight in the eyes with *the* look, my inner female perks up.

The impulsive one had been triggered. He turned me on in five seconds but then it'd be a very confused arousal—on, off, on, off, no wait, on, okay, no seriously off, on, dancing on the on and off line, flickering on. Then—we did it. For the first time! How ironic. After months of dating and we'd only kiss. Now, two months after our break up, we do it. The good, dirty-sex kind. It wasn't mind-blowing, it was more awkward, yet for the first time in my life—it clicked. I thought I'd felt it once before as I've been with two guys before him but this was different. I finally got sex. He kept making me stop every eight minutes, and I actually wanted more. I had never truly wanted more. We needed to work on his timing, but I felt like Lance Armstrong. I wasn't going to give up until my leg muscles literally rejected me. When we finished, I politely asked, "Are we done here?" I finally realized the fuss over sex.

I finally felt ready to let go of my past experience, perceptions, and mixed emotions surrounding the three letter word. As I got out of my own head, I tuned into the sound of his rambling. I believe his word of choice was *awesome*.

Guys are so simple. He just kept saying the word "awesome" as if that was the only vocabulary he knew. I tuned out his talking because I was so wrapped up in my own thoughts and revelations. I even rolled over and fell asleep while he was carrying on.

7:00 a.m. and I was up and ready for coffee and oatmeal. He looked at me like I had five heads when I refused to roll over and go back to sleep. How could I sleep at a time like this? Three hours of sleep and I'm ready to take on the day. I had far too much evaluating to do.

I wanted to absorb this energy of feeling like a sex goddess. I've just been reacquainted with my vagina, after years of its denial. I've just taken interest in the penis for myself as opposed to the feeling of obligation. I raced out of there and, after getting my usual coffee, I call my friend Steve so we can discuss last night's events over sushi. I don't have a gay male best friend, but he's a suitable substitute. I can talk about my waiting on the future husband, my first time sex with my ex, and my trying to be friends with the man who loves me ex. Only a true friend can appreciate this insanity. After I give my share of drama, Steve can then confide in me on his psychotic girlfriend, thus we make for great companions. We both experienced sexism in our relations and interactions. It gives me great perspective to hear from him.

Ex-Lovers
Ex-Amination

I've just experienced a buzz kill. Not a literal buzz. It's only 10:00 a.m., this was a happy buzz. I hate it when one has to schedule in things that no individual would want to endure. It's questionably torturous. "Oh yeah doc, put me down for that unmedicated root canal you're telling me about on the 25th. Also, when you're in my mouth, ask me some life questions so I can attempt to answer them." My GI doctor just called and I've got a colonoscopy now scheduled. I'm not even going to Google this one because, for once, I don't want to know details, no thanks. I booked it despite my reservations. We are at such mercy to certain things in life without knowing. Before I became proactive in my life, I was left to be reactive to whatever doctors, government; or "medical experts" threw at me. I had to accept their generalized norm as my own.

My mom was still on a kick after my first appointment, so she was surely looking forward to this for entertainment. In my first meeting with this doctor, I had to unpreparedly drop my pants. I went to take my jeans off and realized, as usual, I had gone commando. I said something like, "Oh no, I'm not wearing underwear... how convenient."

Dr. Garb remained professional, composed. Then, I had to turn over and say when I ready, ass in the air.

"Ok I'm ready!" He still didn't flinch. My third response was a fairly appropriate reaction, I felt. "Doctor, I'm sorry my ass is so tight right now. I'm clenching because I'm nervous and I can't see you back there." I thought my mom was going to choke from laughter. Still, he remained nonchalant though his cheeks turned pink. I imagine he's experienced much worse.

Following the examination, I got his personal number. My mom had a field day with that one as we left, putting on our best English accents. "We've got to call him," she said so optimistically. What was the protocol and boundaries for dating your one-time GI doctor? Excusable if it's not an ongoing relationship, correct? I had no intention of calling other than to confirm all was well with stool samples, but I had to entice my mother. She was infatuated with his English accent, and kept insisting I call. What a great way to tell the story of how you met your partner. Could this make for a more or less comfortable relationship? "Well we met with him exploring my ass... now we're dating." Not a conversation I wanted to have.

Let's talk about ex-lovers. I have two I'd like to mention. While I like to limit my time on Facebook, on the rare occasion I go on, it's easy to stumble across what we typically *don't* want to see, it's even easier to end up creeping. Today, it was Christian who popped up. Damn. Mr. OCD ex-lover. A single picture staring right at me. He would never do such thing like actually put himself on Facebook. Someone else had tagged this beauty. He looked so smoking hot, it was painful. Pretty, cherubic, and masculine. Here I was, gawking at the picture, fixated on the pop up on my computer screen. Why wasn't I more loving while we were together? I should have been finding out beauty tips, toting him around, yet I was awkward and became a word vomit liar. As much as I was tempted to start this one up, there comes a time when an ex must remain in ex territory. At some point, we can't continue to drag them out of there, brush them off, and give them a new title. Right then, I was in a place of wanting dating potentials only—suitors for the future, not have-beens, not almost-was and, in Alexander's case, a should-be. Perhaps he, Rose, and I could date merrily. Ideally, Christian and I have different viewpoints, which would ultimately overshadow our connection. I knew evolving happens in relationships—we grow as people, as partners, but certain red flags kept me in check. Beautiful man-boys aside.

Ex-lover Number Two

For learning purposes, I'd like to reference my talk with Alexander on Saturday. Good ol' Saint Alexander. Forgiving, patient Saint Alexander. About three weeks ago, he managed to annoy me. I was disgusted. We had a nice dinner, catching up as friends, then the night felt ruined later on. He was so persistent in convincing me to stay, convincing me we were meant to be together, meant as lovers, bringing up our future children—and this is not the first time. I felt flustered. Sometimes it was like he didn't hear me at all, and I wondered if he was simply devoted or, maybe, delusional.

After going back and forth, explaining myself, trying to justify our break up, I was just as confused. While I thought we could remain friends, he was patting by belly and asking me when I'd have our babies. I went for a pee break in his bathroom to collect my thoughts while trying to get out of there safely. When I opened the bottom cabinet, there were two boxes of tampons. Unopened Tampax? Who was preparing for a flow? I opened up the bathroom door, said goodbye, and fast-walked to my parking spot without looking back.

Since then, he called me every day to make plans, each more elaborate than the previous. He tried to lure me into Boston, but I refused,-no comment. I almost anticipated the Italians coming after me, or banning me from the city altogether.

On Saturday, after his many attempts, I finally came clean. "Alexander, the last time I saw you, you had two boxes of tampons in your bathroom. After a whole night of trying to convince me we should be together and you're hiding Tampax under your sink. If you've got a girlfriend, seriously, move on. I can excuse a Hula-Hoop at your door, but Tampax? We didn't work out, you two might—there's no reason for us to be even having that discussion when you're involved with someone else."

His reaction was hilarious, calm as usual. "Gab, they could be anyone's,"

"Oh really Alexander, do all your guests show up with Tampax as an offering?"

At the market, in front of his workers, friends, and the general public, he starts talking loudly about tampons. "Gab, why didn't you say something sooner? I've called you for weeks. Why didn't you mention the damn Tampax!"

"Because if you're seeing someone, I'm happy for you. It's not my business. Friends can be honest with each other, you know?"

"Christ Gab, there probably Gia's or my mother's!"

The mother excuse was a bit of a stretch, but in giving him the benefit of the doubt, they could very well have been his sister's. They've lived together in his previous apartment and are extremely close. I adore her also, but it was no less weird. He then tried to get me to laugh and said he'd get rid of them and use them for tissues at the market.

"They work as nose plugs, too, right?" I could only imagine the faces of those listening in. Hearing their boss argue with his ex-girlfriend over tampons must have been hilarious.

After we hung up, I tried to make sense of our conversation. My mom responded in saying maybe he has a f**k buddy? She was, of course, nearby listening in. What f**k buddy travels with Tampax? No. Scenario two—he does have a serious girlfriend. Still, I'm not totally convinced. He couldn't be so available. Scenario three—the mysterious Tampax woman wants to be serious, so she left the evidence in the bathroom to claim territory. Women are tricky creatures—we often plant reminders of our presence, especially when establishing a point.

Scenario four—knowing him, and most men I've been fortunate enough to be with, the Tampax did belong to a family member, resulting in him now either A: thinking I'm psycho for mentioning it, B: is glad I mentioned it because he now knows I care about the issue, or C: has already put aside our conversation and is diligently working.

    Here we were, broken up a year now and we were still doing this. What does it take to leave the past in the past for possible reference purposes only? Can an ex emerge from ex territory as a new partner, or do they always end up exed?

Chapter Two

FROM MADLY IN LOVE, TO JUST MAD
THE FIRST LIBRA TO CHANGE MY LIFE, BUT NOT THE LAST

Calvin was the talk of the gym—a quiet bachelor on the radar of most females. As not much of a conformist, I didn't deem him future-husband material merely to join in with his admirers. It hit me the day my mother came to visit and struck up conversation between the three of us. He was standing at the register while my mom and I were in conversation, and as he left, my mom said, "I recognize him, who is he?"

My answer came without any thought, "We'll probably get married." After I said it, I wondered, *Where did that come from?* Who knew those words would so haunt me for a while? This single dad had women throwing themselves at him, cooking for him, stalking or admiring him from afar. For many weeks, he'd try to make small talk with me, and I'd go blank to the English language, or any language for that matter. Despite my mute reaction to him, over protein shakes we somehow formed a friendship.

Being a creature of habit, his routine nature helped me build a bond. We became phone buddies—actual late-night talks on the phone, our longest conversation clocking in at six hours. After almost a year of my patiently waiting, dodging any other male interaction, the endless flirting proved hopeless. We entertained the thought of being lovers—he was even just as convinced, but the next step never followed. Not being one to accept defeat, especially in the face of love, I at first sought out the challenge but we remained stagnant. Libras have a funny way of driving me in, and then driving me crazy. He was an exceptional friend but even more the exceptional challenge—leaving me out of words, breath, and brains.

Calvin and the Vortex
Not so Yogi-Like

It's so ironic that last week I was practically skipping to work—I said it was because I love my job. Truth is, I love gawking at my should-be significant other. This week, I wanted to set the fire alarms off and make my exit. Unfortunately, my attempt to do so would probably fail because they are likely broken, just like eighty percent of everything else in this gym. I prayed that one of the kids in the nursery makes a scene so I can call it a day and evacuate. Seven months in the Vortex should qualify me for any job. I could be working in the psych ward and have a better time.

Today, the anonymous naked man sent me over the edge. Not Naked Yoga Man who was, in fact, known amongst other gyms. He used to spread-eagle while meditating along with other poses he'd preform in the men's room mirror. I had two members tell me how deeply disturbed they were, and I calmly said, "Sorry, that exceeds my job expectations."

My boss already takes all my commission, "Gabby, you signed your name at the bottom of the contract with a lowercase 'G.' Sorry, no commission, I'll have to take it." I'll do my regular tasks for minimum wage, but locker room shake downs go beyond my salary. I appreciate members' concern, but what was I supposed to do? Go in there and discuss clothing etiquette with him? Ask him to get out of downward dog so we could chat about common public courtesy?

One of these days, I'm going to type up locker room guidelines for the boys and hang it in there. The biggest problem in the women's locker room is who stole whose boots, and reminding some women certain underwear is not acceptable. I get we're not all Victoria's Secret models. I'm walking evidence of that. I get that menstrual cycles happen, but for those who come in and do an hour of boot camp torture, they should be doing it in underwear that aren't Fruit of the Loom from ten years ago.

Today, I left my ugly, Vortex jacket at home. Seventies retro look is hard to pull off. I was adjusting to sneakers, but I could only stretch myself so far. My boss required me to do regular bathroom checks—this somehow fell into job requirements for minimum wage. I'll refer to my boss as Satan or T, depends on her mood of the day. Sometimes she's wonderfully darling, sometimes she's satanic.

Dates to Remember - Gabrielle Anna

I've learned to give a five or ten minute warning to the boys, but today, my cleaning was interrupted by a phone call, so I put the door stopper down to signal a return. As I was walking back to the bathroom to finish my duties, a member I didn't particularly know or recognize walked in after me. I was friendly and identified myself so there was no confusion.

"Don't worry I'll be done in a few minutes," I said.

His line followed, "Well you and I both know you've seen a naked guy before."

I laugh it off, as usual. *Harmless egoist, sexist flirting,* I thought. *How unattractive.* The feminist side of me screamed, *Why is it that, because I'm a female, I've seen a naked guy before? Ok so I have, but there's a difference between seeing that by choice, and being subjected to it while trying to attend to my duties.* Nudity doesn't bother me necessarily, but his commentary was out of line. I do many things naked myself, but there are social norms—laws even—take it up with Obama, not me.

As I was in there vacuuming, anonymous man decides to change. He doesn't just change—I turned around and he was basking in his nakedness. I cringed, not acknowledging his presence. Another five minutes go by and he was still naked—now five minutes seems like nothing when an alarm clock goes off in the morning. Those five minutes felt equivalent to time in slow motion. I never looked at him or even in his direction, but his blatant nudity was felt.

As I wrapped up my cleaning, I went to wipe down the sinks with bleach—another crazy protocol by the Gym Master. While I was bleaching, the man came into the restroom and actually pisses next to me. He had his choice of three urinals and a bathroom stall, and he peed next to me at the sink. Isn't that a written rule of male etiquette? Never take up space next to the other? I felt ill-equipped, I felt *ill*. I chose to ignore this behavior. However, if I saw him do this to any of the other girls working here, I would push him out of the locker room butt naked and say, "If you enjoy being naked so much, carry on!"

After the incident, I left the locker room, and I wasn't disturbed, upset, or emotionally distraught, just filled with questions—more questions to sit in my head on the dynamics of people. That's what's funny about men and women; if the majority of the men I work with had to clean the locker rooms, they'd likely run into few problems. For one, most women change modestly because we've been warped into taking up little space, being insecure about our bodies and their imperfections, and for the women brave enough to bare it all in such an encounter, most men wouldn't mind. Then those women are subject to be labeled a slut or a catch. It seems in society, women are raised to be innocent and then corrupted.

A word to men; most of you who first corrupt us, break up with us too, so not only are we now no longer innocent, we're bitter from wasting time on your bad boy ass. Must men really wonder at how we've evolved as such mind jetties? It's a social survival skill like men's need to be strong, superior, and violent even. Hell, if guys working here had to clean the women's locker room, it would be immaculate. I can only imagine Alex in here with the Swiffer, vacuum, wipes—he'd be decorating, painting, and even checking the water pressure in the shower.

My biggest disappointment in today's incident was that it ruined my Saturday talk with Calvin. It brought me into a whole other energetic space. For that, I can't be so forgiving, understanding, and rational. If it's not Lulu interrupting me, she even once went to the extent of tackling me on the floor when she saw us in conversation—it's now a naked pervert burned into my brain. Lulu is my coworker who had also deemed Calvin her future spouse. She stated this news before I even knew who he was. After the incident this morning, I couldn't even enjoy how sexy he looked because my turn on button had been turned off for the day. In remission, out of order for at least the following hours. How unfair. He is so unexplainably sexy—Calvin, not the naked man.

The day I noticed Calvin, it was like he stuck a magnet on me. At first, I didn't notice him between the other members, but the day I did, he actually interrupted my functioning and my thinking. At first, whenever he'd talk to me, I couldn't speak. It was sad and discrediting. I would literally be left without words. He'd come over and request a shake and I'd stand there lifeless, sometimes managing a nod. He probably thought something was wrong with me the first two months of trying to make small talk. It was so weird how we finally started talking—he said something about Target, I said I love Target (unsure of where that came from) and that landed me a number followed by his text message.

At the time, it seemed like nothing more than a small victory aiding in my intrigue. Unfortunately, I had to find out Lulu was stalking him, so I had to downplay our progression. Her obsession of survival was somewhat crucial to my safety. I've since then tried to get him to yoga. He didn't budge. He said he would, but, as usual, he was set in his male regimen and orderly life. Oh how I love those older bachelors, but they really require a little preening and one's best behavior for flexibility. Ah ha, more reasons to convince him to willingly take a hot yoga class. Mental and physical flexibility—one more point I can add. Getting to gawk at him dripping sweat on the mat next to me allows me to also be a winner in this scenario. I love the gifts that just keep giving!

Frenemies and Fantasies

Today has me thinking, when do the pieces of life fall into place—into alignment—and what if we find our self in a picture that doesn't quite seem to fit? When the image unfolds, are we the artist or the observer?

I finally realized how much I want out of life, and my desires feel so far away, yet all too close at the same time. It seems life can show up between such idiosyncrasies. In a second, one's life can change, maybe a force or pull in another direction, or maybe just a change in perspective.

Am I doing it right? Is this what I want? For my age, these questions surely bubble up as everything feels transitional. Hey, maybe when I'm in my sixties, I'll be doing whatever it was I was supposed to do at this age, and by then I'll be older, so it will be written off anyway. "Don't mind Grandma sunbathing nude in her garden." "No, darling, it's your turn to do karaoke with Grandma." I can see my future already. Hopefully, my counterpart Rosy will still be in it; we've been soul tied in this lifetime. Together, we are quite the highly evolved beings.

On a serious note, I can't figure out how we're sure of our purpose, and sometimes the uncertainty scares me. Is it about fulfilling roles and obligations so we can live comfortably, or at least appear to be in control? Is it about sucking the life out of each moment with whatever feeling strikes? Is it about shedding every layer of our self, and then dusting off what was there all along? Should I be gossiping with girlfriends right now; because so many of my girlfriends are, or listening to that internal dialogue which I so often dismiss? This stage in life is purely awkward. I am finally making sense of who I am, but I'm subjected to youth and the idiotic behaviors exhibited so freely here. I wonder what age means, a number, and a birth date, an indication to social society that becomes validating or deterring.

Eighteen grants me adulthood, voting rights, and the ability to legally purchase cigarettes—what contrasting rights. Twenty-one and I can drink—helping both the economy and a social life. In my thirties, I'm supposed to suddenly have aches and pains—all thirty-year-olds say this—and the more positive ones claim a better image of who I am. Hopefully, for my own personal values, I won't be living in anyone's basement—family, a boyfriend's, a boyfriend's family's as a worst scenario. In my forties, I'm supposed to have gained maturity—perhaps acquired a little wisdom, and, if I'm correct, as a woman, a better sex life?

How many of these years are simply socially constructed? I seem to be able to have stimulating conversation with a mother of five, yet first I had to prove I wasn't a home wrecker, a bad influence on her children, or the go-to babysitter just because of my age. The practice I get for psycho analysis behind the front desk of the gym is unbelievable. Sometimes people who come in don't even make it past the front desk. Many of the members either exhaust or excite themselves. After venting at the front, they end up just walking out after. For a certain male member, I had to call him out on this behavior, but for the most part, I let them be.

In context to the Vortex, I'd like to talk about my "desirable" who helps me attain a perfect work attendance, extended hours, and one of my coworkers who I am either hugging or fighting with. First I'll get Lulu out of the way; Gym (Vortex) employee, Gemini, friend, and frenemy. She has me so uneasy, half the time I'm not sure if she wants to hug or slap me. She is irrational and impulsive in one moment, and then sweet and forgivable in the next. Sometimes it's too bad we were all raised to be so polite. I wish we would say more often what we're thinking instead of having to read between the lines—our actions say it anyway.

Dates to Remember - Gabrielle Anna

Communication is said to be eighty percent nonverbal. That's what's so beautiful about children and their lack of a filter. Instead, age and experience jade us, shape us, and instead of digging deep into our behaviors and getting to their root, we often develop defense mechanisms and become closet psychos. I try hard to keep my childlike qualities, without feeding my id too much freedom. If I want to dance in the grocery store while browsing, I do. If you ask me if I think your shirt's ugly and I do, I say so. I'm sick of all the miserable people out there blaming someone else for their misery and acting like life owes them something instead of thinking, "What do I owe life?"

The bottom line is Lulu is jealous of me. Due to my being so unfazed, it irks her. She is continuously trying to shake, rattle, and dismantle me. Yes, jealous. Does this label make me conceited or self-absorbed? Reality is, people will sometimes be jealous of you, no matter how good you are to them—it's their own stuff coming up anyway. You just help bring it to the surface. From there, you can either let it hurt you, or just put yourself in their shoes and remember what it feels like to be jealous of someone. I get annoyed because all the energy Lulu puts in trying to figure me out takes away from what she could give to herself. She's twenty-three and from age alone she's granted more "maturity" than me. Instead of playing up her own qualities, she's constantly trying to belittle or exploit me.

Luckily, then there is Calvin at the Vortex. He makes for much better conversation. I dreamt about him two nights in a row; I'd need Freud's help to remember the dreams, but they were likely enjoyable. Isn't it weird how some people actually leave you hungry—engulfed by their presence—and even more by their absence? It sounds wrong to relate to hunger, but it's the best comparison I can think of. If I wasn't so stuck inside my head all of the time and so cautious of other peoples' space, I'd go right up to him and lick him. That's it, just a lick. Then I'd go back to work like nothing happened. Mmm! "Hi Calvin, just thought you looked yummy today and I wanted to lick you—carry on now. Need anything? Water, a towel, my first born?" Or maybe I would say nothing at all-just to let him linger in confusion, just to act like there was nothing odd about the scenario.

This confession could constitute me as a creep—perhaps we're all capable of creep status with certain people. On the other hand, imagine all the people who want to lick you... Eww. The thought doesn't seem so satisfying now. If someone ever came up to me and licked me, I'd probably turn fifty shades of crimson, grab three coffees at the nearest DD so I could evaluate the situation, and then be rambling off a self-diagnoses to my doctor.

What a shame. I can't even enjoy my own dirty thoughts because I'm now wondering who's having dirty thoughts about me. It won't always be dirty thoughts I'm left with, I hope. The day I leave the gym, Calvin can only hope he's not here because I'm not leaving without re-enacting at least one of my fantasies. I'm not sure if it's the idea that I can't have them which intrigues me so much, or if it's simply infatuation.

Most often, our body knows things before our minds do. In circumstances like this, do you put yourself out there, or is it better to be cautious, reserved, and ladylike, and wait for our male suitor? In the wild, a lot of the females do the hunting and mating—what happened to our system here? I realize if we are to date it's not just about him and me. He has a son and I wouldn't want either of them to think I was violating their time together. It would be new territory, but I know how precious that relationship is, so I'm understanding about it.

There needs to be a dating manual, or maybe that's what's so great about dating. The figuring it out, the grey areas, the lines we put ourselves in once we're in the relationship box. I suppose a manual would take away from our personal journey into seeing why we choose who we do, and what relationships bring up or suppress in us. Are relationships fantasies or are they spaces to bring us that much closer to reality?

Monday Night Madness

Another Monday where I contemplated my tactic for finally getting—or, if necessary, taking—my hard-earned kiss. A kiss on the cheek, kiss on the lips, forehead—I was willing to accept and negotiate any or all of the above. How to finally get a kiss from Calvin? With all the self-help books out there, I was nevertheless clueless. I went through this struggle every Monday. It was my Monday madness. Sometimes I was so sure too, my confident self-talk and inner goddess would be beaming with high hopes. *No really, tonight! Tonight is the night. You are sultry. You are a real woman. You've got the power.* I knew I wouldn't be turned down if I made the move, but I just couldn't bear it. My stubborn, unsexy self wants to say, "This time, if you walk me to my car, you'd better make out with me." I needed to be spared this constant role-playing in my head. In these mental scenarios, I'm such a fox, such a fearless female. In reality, I'm flabbergasted and fairly awkward.

Sandi and I rehearsed dance routines for the ladies, and she—like a great girlfriend—pointed out each time he walks by and waves, letting me know he was there. With each smile he sends over, the questions rattle off in my head. *Why did we have to develop such a friendship? Why did I have to become the friend salivating over their significant acquaintance?* I am in absolute mental distress if I have to explain, yet again, why we had made no progress to my circle. I stayed away from dating for months to prove my dedication, and I was no closer to a relationship. The pending sexual tension was going to make me neurotic. After all my nightly phone calls to prove I could listen, prove I could talk, and prove I was a worthy partner, I was left only with the occasional hug. Sexual urges have gone and were now replaced with food. We were on a whole other regimen entirely. I couldn't bear to come home another Monday night and again explain to my mom that our future love life is—pending.

P.P.—A Moment Too Late
December 10, 2011

I've officially aged beyond recovery. The man I once swore I'd marry was finally inviting me for drinks at a bar nearby. I should be showered, prepped, and extraordinary, yet I took the easy way out—cute shoes and a hat—shower nixed.

I was now anxiously waiting on the girlfriend. That makes the situation all the worse—to bring your own friend for a date's friend. Honestly, the safety net of a friend ends up being too much work. If your friend doesn't like your date's friend, or if they do, which is the more desirable outcome? Probably that they do like your date's friend—that's the goal, right? However, things could drastically change if their liking turns into doesn't like anymore. I can't be faulted as matchmaker.

I'm so lame now; I don't drink or like to, and I'm not into bars. Oh good, let's go get drunk so I can then go home and rummage leftovers in my fridge, blow my "mindful" eating, and then fall asleep drunk and unsatisfied.

I get why most people do it. One, many prefer not having to entertain themselves. Two, it's a good update for Facebook photos. I don't have either of these problems.

I find if I'm drinking, it's just disappointing not to have a designated make out partner. Experience has proven to me again and again that drinking wine will make me horny. Red wine, white wine, blush wine—all give me that lovely flush and then I sit there until my happy flush turns to disapproval. After falling in love, I then find I only want to share experiences with the one I love (this is after the perfect Sagittarian—you'll be acquainted soon). Worse scenario is when you're no longer with the one you love. So, I'm then left in my drunken state, pouting, because even to fantasize about the sea of bachelors can't be done. Love leaves me at a mental block.

To further my lameness, I had a notepad I was planning to bring.in my purse. I had a school assignment where I had to observe a setting and write about it—the norms, the un-norms, deviant behavior, etc. A bar was a pretty obvious opportunity. How many young females bring notepads instead of lip gloss to bars? I was certainly limiting my social life here.

I was interested to see how that night was going to go. I knew I needed to join, because the two other times he invited me in almost four years of knowing each other, I couldn't go, and I wasn't going to wait another year or more to be asked out again. We hadn't seen each other for a long time—our lives were different, and this was a great opportunity for some face time. I already played hooky from work that night so I could enjoy the leisure of grocery shopping. I certainly didn't want to be rushed while assessing the Wegmans aisles. This proves where my priorities were.

10:30 p.m. and unless I'm working, I like to only see my eye lids at this hour. Even if I am seen as wifey status and successfully charm him, it seems to backfire. It has never allotted me any dates in the past, just endless compliments and free food when passing by his work.

I hope this progresses me, and earns me at least a snuggling session for the following winter months. I had no problem with a cuddling session from a blast from the past crush, even in my sulking love state.

Dates to Remember - Gabrielle Anna

I miss my ex, Dany, my Sagittarian lover. As said, you'll know him very well later on. I miss him so much that even my once-burning crush for Calvin is now not even a flame. It's clear that Dany's mind is set regardless of what I say, and that he doesn't miss me. I have too much I'm going through right now to keep fighting the karmic battle and win over someone who's written us off.

Was I really so despicable for making my ex and I so uncomfortable? You have to be uncomfortable for any sort of growth. I could've left us in the easy, comfortable, one-sided relationship, living a double life like so many do. Instead, I shook us up every month via email. I should've joined an anonymous group for confused lovers who abuse technology. By technology, I mean in-depth analysis over email. We should've been Skypers instead. It's much harder to break up with someone when you're looking at them. No wonder so many relationships lasted longer in previous years; today, we have so many false ways of getting together and of no longer getting together. Imagine the saved relationships if texting didn't exist, if to break up with someone we could only do in person versus a text or a phone call. God bless those who manage to survive in today's fast paced make-or-break society.

Chapter Three

MR. OCD—OBSERVE. CONCLUDE. DEPART.

After swearing off of men for months, with the hope that my friend Calvin would have a change of heart about us, I met Christian. This gorgeous man was infatuated with me, but his OCD left me insecure. This David Beckham look-alike had a way of making me feel completely comfortable and completely scrutinized simultaneously. His passive-aggressive tone and instigating manner turned me into a compulsive liar.

After a failed relationship, we became booty calls to each other. Exciting and sexy at first, his bossing me around left me horny, pissed, and undecided. I'd dress up for him, meet him for car-side sex, sex in public, and sex in his anal retentive, perfectly ordered apartment. But, ultimately, I needed to move on from our usual protocol.

After cutting him off, he became more enthralled with our physical connection. Months later, as I entered into a new relationship, he instigated, probed, pressured, and grew determined to derail me from my new bachelor. Even offering to become a sex slave, the attempts to reconnect had no limits, but my decision had already been set. Observe, conclude, and depart. This was a man to be worshipped, not dated.

The Effects of Christian
October 30, 2009

By August, I had finally cut all ties with the ex-boyfriend, Saint Alexander, and trust me, that wasn't easy when he was waving vacation tickets in my face or sending me pictures from Vegas, the City of Sin. Those texts were really bombs to drop and be detonated at a later time when you're feeling vulnerable, bored, and hormonal. It was especially not easy to remain broken up when no matter what you do, he was just as loving and as willing to take care of me.

I was on my way to being in phenomenal shape. The recent breakup contributed to my sudden dedication to a workout regimen. I was always motivated after a breakup, curious at what side of me will change. Any partner, whether or not they're worth dating, should introduce us to some new part of our inner self. I should've stayed clear of all men. Regardless of all the people who come to me and complain about their own or their friend's relationships, they continue to insist I get into one. Some say it's like living their fantasy vicariously through me. Others probably just want to know I'm off the market so I couldn't steal their boyfriend or husband. And some are just simply bewildered when you're not coupled. The ones I try to avoid most are the mothers who swear I'd love their son. I'm all for being open-minded, but these situations are a catch-22.

It was a beautiful summer morning—the sky was pink, and I was taking it all in. I was driving to Caroline's 6:00 a.m. spin class, and I had just rediscovered some of Janet Jackson's hits from the nineties and I felt wildly alive. I pushed through the class, no makeup, sweaty, and ready to take on anyone or anything in my path... or so I thought.

When I went by the front desk, I remember wanting to check out the guy next to me, but not caring enough to bother. I think I just allotted myself a glance at his butt and later events confirmed that this was not a butt you could look away from. Through my gawking at his behind, I never actually made it to his face. Still, at the time, I was in full me-mode, and no distraction could veer me off course, not even the ass of Hercules.

The following day, Caroline called and she was going on about how the cute trainer at the front desk asked about me, and she demanded I call him in the best interest of both of us. I rarely go out on dates or out much anymore, and I didn't know if it was the excitement of being on my way to a party, or that I felt compelled to do it for Caroline, but I called him and left a message. Typically, I'm not usually inclined. To my surprise, after my unimpressive voicemail, he called me back while Janet and I were on our way to our luau barbeque. We were going to attempt to teach Zumba at celebrations—entertainment at its best.

What I thought would be a brief conversation—an introduction or hello—turned into an interrogation. After discussion one, I found myself preparing answers for a background check. I hung up slightly bewildered, but intrigued. After our conversation, he texted me later that night to remind me he was still thinking of me. *I'm thinking of you too,* I thought, *trying to think of what you actually look like!* To be fair, I was forward. I said, "I can't remember you, but if you're willing to ask me out after seeing me after a six a.m. spin, I had to at least call you."

For the following week, he called and texted me at least once a day, and we started to get comfortable with each other. At the time, he'd ask, "Well, don't you have any questions for me?" but I really didn't. I don't know if I didn't care enough, no that's not it—I find I'm more lax in that sense. I choose to take people as they are and I felt the first date would determine whether we did or did not have a chance. I knew I'd called for a reason, so rather than weed through his answers as acceptable or not acceptable, I'd go from my gut reaction to our date.

I feel all the time that we burn ourselves with the typical questions of who we are, what defines us, what we do, age, status, previous relationships, etc. But doesn't all that get thrown out the window once infatuation hits anyway? If one likes someone enough, aren't we suddenly compromising or bending some of our "set ideals?" We've become so secure in defining ourselves and others like robots, riding around with our college grad bumper stickers, or continuously updating our Facebook default so people get an accurate perception of who we are, or at least what we want to be perceived as. "Hi I'm Gabrielle, age such-and-such, and I go to school here, and I work here, and I'm a middle child, and here's my Facebook link so you know I have friends." But what does that all really mean? I've learned to at least acknowledge my instincts—although I frequently resist listening to them—and my instincts told me to go on the date. Unfortunately, they also later told me, "You're screwed—fix it or get out of here." Yet, then, I seemed to deny their validity.

Back to the story and its beautiful beginning. This perfectionist continued to try to size me up, and I continued with my laissez faire attitude. Maybe the real reason I wasn't hungry to find out about him was that I was almost convinced I'd already met my future husband. I'm not naïve enough to put my life on hold because of that, and maybe it was more wishful thinking, but I swear sometimes you just know. Something about the interactions between my future husband, aka the friend, always had people buzzing. They seemed to see the something between us that I could feel. I could even see him dating another woman and it wouldn't bother me because I felt secure enough in the fact that we'll be together eventually. I'm sure, on some level, this projection plays on my subconscious. Not quite wanting to invest in dating as I know my future mate is in close proximity. No matter how gaga guys may get me when trying to date, I don't get bent out of shape by them. Maybe things won't work out with Calvin—the Libra love of my life—but, in my head, we've already made it.

Back to Christian. For whatever reason, he had some sort of effect on me. I had developed a classic disorder, unable to get a handle on it. As much as he'd praise me, a part of me felt like I wasn't good enough, like I was being scrutinized. I continuously felt put on the spot—trying to measure up in comparison. I don't know when I finally cracked, but I started lying. No big lies, no deal-breaking lies, no false-identity lies, just little, white lies that would accumulate and leave me guilt-stricken.

I didn't intend to lie—they would just fall out of my mouth. Instantly after one, I'd want to say, "Oh, I just lied," but the confessions made me feel crazy instead of cleared. There really needs to be a manual for dating. Somehow I find myself landing the guys, it's just that, afterward, I don't know what to do with them. Really, what is the appropriate amount of information to share as we first start dating? What does one do when your reaction to someone is being a chronic liar?

Okay, confession number one: I was multitasking on our usual evening phone call routine we'd recently developed. He felt we should talk regularly before our first date—okay. We had quite a few phone dates before actually going out. I was talking to the gas guy, counting my cash, and attempting to sound charming in my conversation with Christian. We were talking about cars; he questioned why I put twenty dollars in my tank and asked me what kind of car I drove. Maybe it was how he asked in such an inquisitive manner, maybe it was because I felt I was continuously being defined before I even had a chance to meet with men. Maybe it was because, until that second, I hadn't really thought about the car I drove, even after once dating a guy with a Bentley.

Hmm... what kind of car do I drive? Seemed like a simple enough question to answer. Until that second, my car was just a car, a means of transportation. It was a little red machine I had come to love after the Explorer died on me, and now, I suddenly resented my little red machine. Is my car now an indicator of status? Prior to this moment, I had never really cared. I thought about Kanye West singing about how he drove a red Escort, pre-celebrity days. I suddenly envisioned myself in a Mercedes, in an Escalade, and then, in the midst of my thoughts, the lie fell out of my mouth.

A Ferrari would've been a stretch. Coming down from my vision, I guess I made a rash decision. Ford Focus. Ford Focus? What the hell? Right after I said it, I thought, *Am I even in a Ford Focus?* Afterward, I was too embarrassed, but later, I decided to confess. The conversation went as such, "Christian I was getting an oil change today and I drive a Ford Escort."

He just laughed and said okay.

"Okay, but I told you I was in a Ford Focus. I'm sorry!"

"Gabby baby, it's okay." This was a true prelude to what our relationship dynamics would be.

Date one was tricky; not only do I dread first dates, but circumstances were trying to drive me to cancel this one, and still I fought the urge. I had to find a way to quiet the part of mind that talks me out of things.

My hair appointment ran late; she cut it a little too short. She waxed off—*off*—my left eyebrow, leaving remnants for my right one. I hadn't chosen an outfit, and due to the uncertainty of our plans for the night, I had no idea what the appropriate outfit would be.

My girlfriends were pressuring me—Rosy because she needed to talk, and Caroline because she was suddenly on a dating hunt to find me a boyfriend. Christian had ignited her matchmaking skills. She has since been leaving me voicemails of possible bachelors. I had a text reminder from her to call Jim the next week—she swore I'd love him, so she went ahead and told him I was interested. I didn't even know who Jim was, but as I tried to collect myself for this date with Christian, I hoped for the best, wondering why dating can feel so torturous. Sitting on the toilet, penciling in a left eyebrow with my LBD on and four inch heels, I stared in the mirror and tried some positive self-talk.

He arrived. *Here it goes*, I thought. At the time, my mother and I were at our closest, so it wasn't a surprise to see her from the corner of my eye, hanging out the window as Christian so politely opened the door for me to get in his car. As we get to the end of my street, he literally stops the car, turns on the light and just stares at me. Staring... at me... It was both unbearably sexy and incredibly uncomfortable. Interior lights are shiny and unflattering.

"I just wanted to look at you for a second."

Reading me, scanning me, taking me in—I was drawn to his confidence, but embarrassed by my sudden lack of it. I later found out he would do this a lot, it was one of his "things." He would literally look at me and into me, and I knew he was taking me in, so I found it to be intimate, but also intimidating. We sat at the end of my street. Boy, was I uncomfortable. Once the staring stopped, he asked for an opinion on our destination.

He knew I wasn't twenty-one, so I felt childish as our options grew more and more limited. He knew I had a fake ID and though he wasn't in support of that, we tried to find neutral ground. I could feel butterflies working their way through my stomach. I thought of how young I felt, trying to memorize my fake ID information, thinking of how I'll drink with dinner without getting drunk.

I don't understand the concept of drinking with meals, drinking and barhopping—I get drunk. The drunk then turns into a sleepy drunk, or a wild drunk, and neither comply with sitting at a bar or making first-date conversation.

On the drive there, he struck himself out once and then almost again. The first strike was when we were talking about kids and he said, "You don't have a kid do you?"

"Uh, no I don't."

He responded with such relief that it was almost questionable as to why. He then went into the pitch about how he couldn't date someone with kids. That was fine, so he wasn't ready for kids, but when you're twenty-eight or twenty-nine and kids are *that* scary to you, a deal-breaker ten minutes into the date is possible. Red flag, one to be noted, but not hung. I was years younger, but already looking forward to kids—a notion that may become conflict if we date. He talked about them like they were a plague. Sure, if he was twenty-one and had this attitude, that would be reasonable, or expected even. He wasn't built for childbearing, just procreating, so I'm perfectly okay with his lack of desire.

However, if we made it five years, would I be okay with that same attitude? These were all possible questions and concerns of mine, as I'm not one to waste my time. I love experience, I love taking life as it comes, but there's a part of me that knows the weight of my decisions.

The second almost-strike was how we hadn't even made it to dinner yet, and he was saying we should go on a vacation together. Had I ever said that on the first date, I would have been labeled a clinger and probably cut off after appetizers. Why does clinginess with males make them cute or romantic and with females it's psycho?

We got to the restaurant and he insisted I have a drink. Even though wine never fails to, at some point, get me horny, tired, or giggly, I ordered it anyway. I decided to take my chances. I tried to order us something that sounds healthy—he's a trainer and I was on my way to this fabulous post-breakup bod.

The dish came out, and Styrofoam looked more appetizing. It was some fishy side dish that even my dog wouldn't eat. Christian then ordered us cheeseburgers and fries—just wonderful! My LBD wasn't made for a burger and fries.

While waiting for our dinner, we moved on to drink number two. LBD and drink number two weren't so compatible either. The meal went well. He was so cute and charming, I wanted to eat him along with it. Apparently my mother agreed, as she texted me all through the meal. I forget what nickname she called him, but let's just say this was not the wine that made this bachelor so attractive. This was a mouthwateringly good-looking man with a stare that could turn your insides out in a minute. He was lucky I wasn't so easily shaken, because if I wasn't so carefree—say we had met a year ago—I would have melted into my seat at the dinner table. With each stare, I would've been a crimson mess.

After dinner, he kept saying how he didn't want to take me, yet he was somehow really into me. I mentioned how I had gone on a kind of blind date with someone from the gym, another one of Caroline's love connections. I could tell he was into me by how he reacted.

"I'm going to call him and tell him we're out right now," he growled.

Possible red flag, or a sign of his passion? This then led into his series of questions which would later become our usual protocol. "What did you two do? Where did he take you? Why did you go out with him, Gab?" Otherwise, the rest of our date went well. I wanted to kiss him when the night ended, but the taste of beer and burgers in my mouth stopped me.

After date one, we talked for about two hours each night, which, to him, was shocking. Our second official date was probably my favorite. We went to a Greek restaurant and it just felt... right. He had this absolutely captivating manner about him. While I usually don't care what people think, I felt like the IT couple. We were the pair that fed each other at dinner and can't stop touching one another. Even in my hot pink, five inch heels and sexy top, we shoveled down lobster, steak, potatoes, salad, and drinks. He was really touchy at first, but comfortable with being affectionate and despite my usual resistance, I didn't mind.

After that, we got in a pattern of hanging out on Wednesday nights. He was living with his parents while things were being finalized on the beautiful condo he just bought, so we'd spoon and watch the news. Again, he'd bombard me with questions, thoughts on politics, what I did from the hour I woke up 'til the moment I horrifically pulled into his driveway. He ended ninety percent of the questions asked with a, "You sure about that, Gab?" which would then send my brain into a frenzy.

"Yes, Christian, I'm sure." Then, in my head, I would be like, *I said I ate oatmeal for breakfast today, but really I ate cheerios.* Then I'd sit in my own, self-induced panic trying to figure out how to mend the lie-that-wasn't-a-lie. Aside from his secret service skills, we got along wonderfully. There may have been a female in the background feeding him information on me, trying to reclaim her place in his heart, but she fell short of redeeming herself.

Dates to Remember - Gabrielle Anna

I knew of a girl we both knew who kept trying to rid me for her own pleasure, but Christian and I were too compatible. I often wondered if his questions came from her plotting. My strengths seemed to outweigh my bad habits. I was always late; this annoyed him, and yet I continued to show up later and later as if trying to unconsciously be difficult. He'd casually comment on my tardiness but then he'd let it go. He was developing cute nicknames for me, and, with our progression, I felt it was only appropriate he be in my MY5 nickname. How precious. That must make us official. We'd hang out, spoon, and he was constantly trying to feed me. I started to notice my workouts were getting shorter and my ass was getting bigger.

I don't remember what date we were on when he finally kissed me, but it took him forever, and he did it at the worst moment. We were about two months in before he actually went for it. So many nights, my inner goddess would yell, "Why hasn't he kissed me?" I'd wait for it, I'd will it, and I'd try to telepathically tell him to do it—nothing. Then, on our typical Wednesday night spooning, he wakes me up from my dozing off, fed me a tuna sandwich, since he had just made one for himself, and then he kissed me. Between my sleep state, carb comma, and far too tight spandex leggings, I felt I failed in being sexy, or making this first kiss significant. Our Wednesday nights became routine—I seem to seek out creatures of habit—and our first sleepover was sufficiently awkward. Making out at two am when tired can be managed, but when the parents are only feet away, I'm not supposed to be sleeping over, and I've got work at the Vortex at 8:00 a.m.—my brain was distracted.

I envisioned a fantasy for us, him being the buff god he was. Yet here we were, getting into pj's, him teaching me how to floss my teeth appropriately. Was this considered foreplay?

"Gabby baby, I like cleanliness. Let me show you how to floss like this, you'll love it."

I shadowed him in the mirror, flossing my teeth, washing our faces together—ah, how refreshing! He was right, cleaner was amazing. I didn't know what type of activity our first sleepover would elicit, but I could get use to this pampering.

The next morning, he did the whole, "Babeeee, don't leave me," as I pried myself from his embrace and covers. It was both a blessing and a curse the way I disconnected from intimacy. At work that day, I felt uneasy and discouraged about entering into a relationship. Am I capable? He was on my brain my whole shift. The thought of us doing it—would I measure up? He seemed to have a protocol for everything, this perfectly organized life—what would our sex be like?

That day, each time I checked my phone to see if he said anything, each text was from my trainer scolding me for missed appointments despite my cancelation notice. Right around my first date with Christian, my trainer had been asking me out also. Today, he was persistent as ever. He was threatening training packages with me.

"Just come with me to a hockey game." So, I finally say I'll go as friends. I had agreed to do so months ago, and with my recent missed sessions, I felt obliged. I came to find out the next day when I was on my way to Boston for the game, Christian finally called me after nothing from the day before. He was finally moving into his house.

Oh the irony. I hadn't even cared to go to the Bruins game, but I had chalked it up for experience. Lie number two or three—Christian kept calling me over and over while I was at the game, "Babe what are you doing? I'll be home from the gym soon, come over! Come see me. Come see my place!"

Shit. "I'm actually in Boston." I was in Boston, I just didn't say who I was with or what I was doing. There I was, with Nick who was constantly reaching for my hand. He'd say, "Do you want us to be on the scantron? Do you want to see if we can talk to some of the guys?" I kept thinking, *If our picture gets on the scantron I'm in trouble.* That night, as Nick went in for the goodnight kiss, I tried to gracefully make my exit. I called Christian on my way home with guilt saturating my voice. I hate to lie. I think it stems from years of my grandfather telling me if I lied, my tongue would be black. At age three, you don't forget that.

The next day, I went to Christian's and it wasn't even twenty minutes before I'd spilled the beans. "What'd you do last night?" he'd asked.

Before I had a chance to respond with confidence, my cheeks were flaming red. The constant beep of my phone didn't help my cause. I confessed to going on the "date." I may have told a mildly softer version of the story, but I confessed. I tried to explain that my trainer was somewhat blackmailing me, but nonetheless I admitted that I had agreed to go—ugh, I just love those Boston bruins.

To make matters worse, he forgave it. I'm kicking myself in the ass because he was so genuinely let down by me.

"I went on a date to last night Gabby," but then he confessed to being in bed by ten because he was exhausted and didn't have my companionship to help him move in. There he was, calling my bluff.

I felt like an absolute idiot. I knew after that, we wouldn't be the same. I wanted to believe otherwise, and we were fine for a while, but then we inevitably went downhill. Once I wrote us off as done, and I was out to dinner with my dear Saint Alexander after months of nothing, Christian calls me over and over again as I walk to the table. God he was incredibly talented. Caught again! I was written off as a compulsive, lying slut.

In our time apart, he got evidence to think I am rekindling old flames. I knew it was over when, the day before our 5k for breast cancer walk, he canceled. The day of! Oh, those passive-aggressives. I wasn't mad at him because I didn't want someone to do something out of obligation, but it did feel lonely. Being stood up for a cancer walk didn't feel good. I blatantly asked him after that if things between us could ever happen again, and he insisted we would be fine and were fine. His apology seemed sincere that I did a small victory dance, thinking we'd make another attempt despite our differences.

Following that, he started to act differently, but he thought I wouldn't notice. He'd try to convince me we were fine as he minimized me. No more nicknames, no more designated Wednesday nights—I had felt his sudden lack of availability as our end. Then, months later, he wanted to reconnect? And right as I was meeting Alexander to catch up.

"What's up?"

"Well I'm out to dinner with my ex… " What happened to my chronic liar syndrome he once brought on? Seems I was back to my awkward self.

Safe Sex and a Singing Sagittarian
November 30, 2009

After work, I decided to go to Christian's despite his annoyance with me yesterday. I was okay knowing that our sex can make up for it. We were now booty calls—we were held to certain obligations. This was going to be a test of the no-strings-attached theory. I was engaging only for research purposes, to then share wisdom and experience with others for the greater good. If the relationship fails, can one remain entangled on these premises only? When a connection is too strong to cut, but the directions are diverse, can we enjoy hanging on in the in-between?

Don't judge me, it happens. He does make me laugh. The laugh-so-hard-tears-were-streaming-down-my-face kind of laugh.

When I first got there, he'd been in the shower, so he answered the door in a purple towel and these slippers that my grandpa has. He had a look of terror on his face. "What'd you do?" I asked.

The answer he gave, I couldn't have made up. While shaving in the shower—hence the purple towel—he clipped just under his penis, right above his balls. The only two balls he is given for life. I looked and determined between the laughter that it was a tiny, almost unnoticeable cut.

"Woooow. It's bad," I said. "I think you may lose both balls." I will admit, it was enough of a nick to bleed, and I don't discredit the scare, but I couldn't help myself. I tried to regain composure as it was clear he hoped for a much more comforting or medical response then what I had given.

He warned me close to twenty times about being easy on his manhood, since he is clearly wounded.

I agree. "Yes, babe. I will be cautious of this horrible injury. You're so brave." This was the best response possible. After sex—apparently the injury didn't affect this—he wanted to cuddle.

Why do guys get so goofy after sex? I wanted to run a marathon, go again, or sleep, and they get goofy. After we did it, he started talking in different accents, singing, and making ridiculous comments. He even started making up tunes. The ridiculous comments reminded me a little of Alexander, and that brought up a feeling I wasn't sure what to do with.

Despite my efforts to help him move on, now that I know he's in Miami with some mystery girl, I was suddenly thinking, *Perhaps I shouldn't have driven him away?* Typical. I tuned back in to the moment.

"Gab, you just moved your hips like Shakira." Actual context. "Go Zumba girl, Zumba, Zumba!" Actual context. This is a step up from after the first time we did it where for fifteen minutes after, he just said "Awwweessommeee babe, awesome. We're awesome." I wanted to match his ridiculous comments, but nothing came to me without laughter.

Was this because, in my heart, I knew I wasn't in love, so I kept a small barrier inside, waiting to have sex with someone I was *in* love with? I guess, until I was ready to give of myself one hundred percent, comments on my part will have to wait. After sex I had no words, nothing—one of the rare times I forgot the English language. I'd like to be more colorful in the bedroom, for talk before, during, after... this was just not me. I talk all the time. Couldn't I be entitled to not having to use an extensive vocabulary in bed? I guess this was better than after Alexander and I would lay there together, he would start calling me vegetable nicknames. I'd have to say, "Alexander, you're not around produce anymore—don't use it in the bedroom." And it was always the "spooning" after. Who can we credit for coming up with this protocol?

Chapter Four
FROM SATAN TO SEXY?

Sherlock and his partner shook up the Vortex with their business-savvy demeanor that later presented itself as devious charm. He liked my blunt nature, and after a little bit of figuring each other out, we became friends. We got along well, like two peas in a pod, each of us really knowing how to be a friend to the other. There was a quiet loyalty between us, and we had a fairly clear perception of one another. We were both very misunderstood individuals who, when it came down to it, knew more then we let on. When gym meetings became strip club lunches, I wondered which one of us truly had control over the situation. From boss, to friend, to that grey area that opposite sexes wade in—a truly special match, and potentially explosive crash, so I felt a need to redirect our path.

New Bosses
January 2010

My life at the Vortex has further shocked me. I was now almost certain I had a crush—we'll call it child crush—on my boss. Possibly on more than one boss. No, I'm not talking about my previous boss, the one ninety percent of her employees refer to as Satan. That would make me both a lesbian, and a masochist. As far as I know, I am neither. I don't mind her, I even like her except for when she's tricking the minds of the masses.

We now had new management. This I never saw coming—both new management and getting all giddy-eyed around my new boss. I couldn't figure it out. *Is it an authority thing?* I ponder to myself for logic or rationale. That can't be the case, because then I'd be attracted to all my bosses, or most of them. Authority and status don't get me in a jumble, in fact, sometimes, they do the opposite. What had me so attracted? Was it just a silly, delusional fantasy I was projecting? Are the stares from my new boss merely hallucinations? Did some sub-personality of me just like the idea of this compared to all the crap I had put up with here? Was I just the optimist for change, so any new boss stepping in would catch my eye? What kind of transference was this?

Dates to Remember - Gabrielle Anna

I now have two male bosses. One looks like a Greek god. He was the kind of man that you had to stop and look at—one of those rugged males who manage to be prettier. This one was undoubtedly attractive, but I had never been interested. As time went on, I met his wife, and I adored her. I felt that we shared the same kind of raunchy humor except she was way wilder. The other boss is not a pretty boy, but something about him oozes sexiness.

Naturally, one would expect me to be infatuated over the Greek god—I thought this same at first. But I found myself gaga over the other one. I had admitted this so far to two people, my mother and best friend. No, wait, a third and fourth party were involved. How do I manage to keep everyone else's secrets except my own? I always out myself! Sources told: Mom, best friend, Janet, my aerobics director, and Ken, a coworker.

Ken can be trusted with the given information. One, because I know some of his dirty secrets and two, he outwardly feels he is a woman stuck inside a man's body that happens to be a sex-crazed lesbian. Strangely, this confession makes perfect sense to me. I respect his sense of awareness and honesty.

My mother seemed entertained by my confession, and encouraged my unreasonable behavior—clearly for her sick amusement. My best friend laughed and went back to talking about herself. Herself, and her boyfriend of the moment. Janet's reaction was half expected and half caught me off guard. She admitted to finding him attractive—it was the effortless look he gave. Multiple people have noticed this look and we couldn't quite identify its draw. That made me feel like less of a creep at least. Janet was also pre-menopausal, so she may not be a reliable source. Ken took the cake on reactions. He so well knew exactly what I was talking about, it was almost scary. When I confessed all of this to him sheepishly, he said he felt the same. His reasoning came down to the fact that that our boss just has the "look" in his eye. Even Ken had seen it. You know the look. If it's coming your way, do not make direct eye contact. You'll be suckered in and strangely confused in a second.

My hopes were that, by writing about such feelings, I could be rid of them, of all the men in the world. I literally passed by male after male each day, unfazed. Now here I was, attracted to my new boss and his boyish looks. Nothing about this scenario was desirable.

We had these great conversations as I get more comfortable around him. I was accepting the fact that odd feelings can surface, so I shouldn't feel guilty. We are half humanized, half primal. If this were the wild, my feelings would be totally acceptable. Still, I found myself in a borderline-awkward predicament.

My emotions are generally written all over my face and in this case it is quite problematic. I wondered if he sensed it or just found me socially awkward. Although I don't judge the multiple affairs going on in the gym, I just didn't want any part of it. He said he was separated, but what were the guidelines of such statement? Separated in your mind? Separated in context? Separated if your new woman comes along? I didn't want to explore this statement regardless of how freely he makes it known. I believe too much in karma. Karma always makes her point and, for myself, she doesn't allow much leeway time.

Possible causes—pheromones? Like the unconscious smell they use to explain attraction? If that's the case, I'm not at fault. Science is to blame. I blame science for a lot of things. Perhaps our pheromones are compatible. Possible cause number two is the authoritative figure theory which in this context is troubling, exciting, and maybe even sexy.

I would never act on these thoughts, so I tried to rid myself of them. Why do you do this to me, bachelor gods? Here's to work tomorrow, another day of avoiding T's—the gym master's—wrath or attempting to have a successful conversation while standing ten feet away from my boss. I avoided the phone each time I saw he was paging me from the office. "OH JUST YELL FROM THE STAIRS, I HEAR YA!" or, "Yes, I'll send T right up, she can relay the message," were both common excuses of mine. I was happy to let her be the Queen Bee of these walls.

Guys at Dolls
March 28, 2010

I was going to write about the weekend's unusual event, but now, of course, as time has unfolded, my perspective has already changed. The weekend went as follows... before my mind has time to change it again. Thank you documentation, otherwise I'd have an entirely different story.

On Friday morning, my wifey, Rose, texted me. She was having an Egg McMuffin with her shuttle driver at school who was apparently married, and in his late fifties. I was in my increasingly morbid death and dying class that I somehow continuously managed to be late for, despite the fact that it was at nine am and I was up at six am.

9:09 a.m. wifey:

<u>I am currently at McDonalds with the shuttle bus driver at school, he's buying me breakfast. I love my life.</u>

9:47 a.m. my response:

<u>You go to breakfast with your bus driver, and I am contemplating going to my bosses' "gentlemen's club" for lunch. Over food, the world makes sense! They said it's a mandatory meeting. Ha. Ha.</u>

These conversations are why despite our separating lives, we will never leave each other's side. Back to Friday—like most of my decisions that I know could end really well or really badly, I was both overly excited and nervous. It's funny because it's hard to get me to agree to something, but when I do, it's always the least rational of choices.

Kareem—coworker, trainer, ex-man-whore—must be scratching his head, totally baffled at how he can invite me out every day with different extravagant plans, even a trip to Florida, and, despite his good looks and boyish charm, I pass it up. The talented man-boy has even serenaded me with Jodeci—great efforts, no reward. He was perhaps the next American Idol and I wasn't interested. Yet there I was Friday afternoon, rushing off campus to go to the strip club for lunch with my bosses. I've never run out of my psych class faster!

Dates to Remember - Gabrielle Anna

After class, I stopped at a new coffee place and fed my only continuous relationship. Like most other relationships, sometimes it picks me up and sometimes it just makes me edgy. Anticipating the day ahead, I didn't know what to do with myself in the hours prior. Sherlock calls me at twelve complaining about how women are always late. I had to say, "Sherlock, as my boss, you can encourage me to show up on time, but for lunch at a strip club, I'm not on the clock, or the gentlemen's clock."

By his tone, I could tell he just didn't get out that much. Time away, time on the clock, time that must be made up later. With healthy space in a marriage, I think couples wouldn't feel so pressured in their free time. I had no concern for happy hour because I rarely drink, and I had no concern for time because I had no companion. Originally, he asked me to ride up with him, but assuming Danielle was coming, I decided it'd be more appropriate if I went with another coworker female. At twelve-thirty when we still hadn't arrived; Greek God called offering to pick me up.

Once Danielle called ready for our outing, it seemed we had very different concerns. I was skeptical about how long I could actually be in a strip club—particularly during the day—and how to factor happy hour into my afternoon. Her concern was that we'd have to look at naked women. Oh yeah, that. True, it was not often I have to look at nipples while eating chicken fingers, but I danced naked in front of my mirror every day, so this in public didn't seem or feel too unusual. As long as I didn't get too caught up in assessing the women's psyche there, I had no reservations.

On the ride there, Danielle and I had a chance to bond. We found the club; it looked questionable, but I suppose all of these places do. However, once we stepped inside, I was impressed. The place was legitimate. I had only been to a strip club once before in my life on my eighteenth birthday. That was the first and last time. On that night, I learned dance clubs were not for dancing, unless you worked there as a dancer—yes, you can fall in love with a stripper, and yes I was just as equally horrified.

This second experience didn't seem so shocking, though looking at the circumstances, it should have been. I was hungry and ordered lunch, even though I questioned the club's cleanliness—as if strippers are in the kitchen making chicken fingers, dancing naked over the food was a stretch, yet, as an outsider, I imagined this. When stepping into the unknown, especially the unknown of that world, one's imagination can flourish. The food was not only edible, but good. We ate and drank, I was feeling the vibes but being with all married beings and in such an atmosphere, I was careful not to feel them too much.

While they were doing shots, I sipped my one glass of wine contently. I knew to drink guardedly or I'd end up either on the pole, or on Danielle's lap. Either way, the outcomes didn't look good. My mom was funny—she kept texting me asking me how my lunch with my coworkers was going. I think, after years of watching me be so sensitive, so submissive, so naïve, she now gets a kick out of my ventures. When she sees me just saying yes to all things that come my way, I feel it reminds her of her free spirit. Not that this is a make-your-mother-proud moment, but it *is* entertaining. I'm sure she also questions if I'll be like her when she was in her twenties, but she was way too devious naturally, mine is situational.

As 1:00 turned into 2:00, and 2:00 into 3:00, 4:00 came on just as quickly. From one vortex of work to another. My first real hang out outing at a strip club, other than when I went with my sister and girlfriends and sat at the stage horrified. The first dancer to approach me broke the ice with a compliment. She could've had me but she went too far overboard. She started playing with my hair, she wanted to wear my hat. Before you know it, she was on my lap trying to lure Greek God and me downstairs.

"Tell your husband you want a dance downstairs," she murmured.

I politely said, "This is not my husband, whatever your name is or isn't. He is a husband. Not mine, but he is my boss and we're having a business meeting." This didn't deter her in any way. She persisted. Then she started to crack—the life story started to bubble up.

Suddenly it came out, darling stripper A was close to achieving her goal weight, taught yoga on the side, will happily show me stretches in or outside of here, and share with me other hobbies. I politely decline. When she finally got the hint, the next one came over and also conveniently ended up in my lap.

Dates to Remember - Gabrielle Anna

Stripper B had a curvy little figure and Shakira hair—we all found her somewhat harsh looking but, attractive. Attractive... until... she opened her mouth—her voice sounded like she ate gravel. "What ethnicity are you?" was her opening line. I get this question all of the time. I should wear a name tag denoting my cultural background. I was picturing her in this little body with Lil Jon's voice and I was far too distracted by its sound to really remember what we were talking about. The conversation snapped into focus though when she made it clear she was into women, and I made clear that I wasn't. Being into women was one thing, but being into women who want my money was not a path I'm willing to take.

The third girl we met at the stage was gorgeous, but the kind of gorgeous that made me sad. She reminded me of a little girl, and it made me uncomfortable. I didn't know if it was because I recognized what was behind her eyes—this innocence that I worried about her loosing. It could've been that we both had similar tattoos, and the relatability made her all too real. She gave us a dance downstairs, a very intellectual one. After our dance, a stripper tried to lure me into a shower, but luckily I grabbed Sherlock and had him whisk me upstairs. Strippers, wet weaves, and my new girlfriend Danielle were also giving dances downstairs, and suddenly I knew I needed to remain seated in the dining area.

As we went upstairs, I met his boss, Dany. I got the business card, and when I took it, I felt a lingering something, but I hadn't deciphered what it was, yet. I agreed I'd be interested in working there, preferably as a fully-clothed server. His readiness caught me off guard. This man could definitely call someone's bluff in a second, "Okay, see you Sunday at four." Sunday at four?

I was interested in showing up and working, but could I bargain with the fact that I require pants while working in public? For all previous jobs, this has never been a concern of mine. While I'll confess to driving naked—once after a spray tan and once for fun—or from getting the mail in my underwear (excused by early hours), booty shorts as an actual uniform was a stretch. Maybe too much of a stretch for me. I was just then starting to look at myself without awkward lenses. By the last hour, I wasn't drunk just on happiness. 12:45 to 6:00 p.m. at the strip club and I had to babysit at 8:00—oops.

I feel the day was ultimately a success. I got home, changed out of my thigh-high boots and slipped into my flats so I could channel nanny mode. When I got to the Furleaves' to babysit, they had even drawn a sign on the driveway that read, "Welcome, Gabby, our favorite babysitter." We ate Chinese food and contently watched Disney movies, easing my life from one role into the next. It was the perfect shift to re-ground me, and kept me from staying out and possibly getting myself into a situation I might not be able to get myself out of.

On Saturday morning, I woke up on a kick. Sherlock called me throughout the day, already wanting to go to the club for round two. Five calls later, I agreed. I got dolled up and then he canceled. This is the problem with going out one night, and having a successful disaster. You're sucked into it before you know it—taken out of your routine, anticipating the next event. Clearly, the adrenaline rush of yesterday hadn't subsided for any of us yet. Now I didn't know what to do with myself. I'd just bronzed my cleavage, picked my shoes, and confessed to my mom that I was going to spend day two at the club.

Suddenly, when I realized our night was called off, I felt bored. Eating lunch in my kitchen was not nearly as stimulating, reading my Deepak Chopra books just felt repetitive, so I walked the kitchen, refusing to take my five inch heels off until I determined my next move. I couldn't put my pajamas back on and go watch Lifetime movies with my mother—my alter ego had already come through. My recently supportive-over-everything, newly-sensitive mother was even encouraging me not to spend my Saturday night at home like I usually do.

The flash went off in my head on what to do—should I call my ex-ex, Saint Alexander in Boston as he's always up for something? Today, my nail lady unexpectedly just gave me these shoes as a gift, and they should be worn and appreciated. No, that's not justification enough.

My mom chimed in, "Why don't you call Dany, the guy who just gave you his card and see if you can meet today to interview instead of tomorrow." No, I can't so easily turn into the strip club junkie after one outing, I'm stronger than that. Her final conclusion was that I call my counterpart, Rosy, or pick up a pizza at Calvin's restaurant. Who was this woman?

      An hour later, when I was putting on my pajamas and we were choosing a Lifetime movie, I kept my heels on for fair compromise. We toasted over tea as I envisioned my next day and potentially other job. Could I give up one vortex and step into another one that was so unfamiliar? Here's to adding experience to my pending "resume" and deciphering the feeling I felt when I held Dany's card. I held it in my hands with such importance, and I didn't yet know why.

Chapter Five

A Perfect Sagittarian
The Not-So-Perfect Situation

P*eople think a soul mate is your perfect fit, and that's what everyone wants. But a true soul mate is a mirror, the person who shows you everything that is holding you back, the person who brings you to your own attention so you can change your life.*

A true soul mate is probably the most important person you'll ever meet, because they tear down your walls and smack you awake. But to live with a soul mate forever? Nah. Too painful. Soul mates, they come into your life just to reveal another layer of yourself to you, and then leave.

A soul mates purpose is to shake you up, tear apart your ego a little bit, show you your obstacles and addictions, break your heart open so new light can get in, make you so desperate and out of control that you have to transform your life, then introduce you to your spiritual master..."

—Elizabeth Gilbert

Dany played a similar role in my life to Rose. Not in friendship, not in body parts or even personality, but in our underlying connection to one another. We related as yin and yang. He was my factual partner who, despite my reservations, became the first, real love of my life. I didn't want love or even look for it, nor did I even think I'd find it in him, but I did.

Early on, I knew something was different, but I had no expectations. A relationship I had determined doomed still managed to blossom despite distractions. The no-bullshit bachelor who once kept women at an arm's length took me back with open arms again and again, despite my monthly break up email. This persistent bachelor saw something in us from the beginning, but as a stubborn Aries, I have to come to my own conclusions. I had us on a rollercoaster relationship, and this can be uncomfortable for the co-pilot.

Once my cold demeanor created too far a distance, we became a pair who couldn't get enough of each other one second, and couldn't get far enough away from each other the next. With our relationship starting on the most unusual of premises, this was the most shockingly normal relationship I'd ever had. So normal in fact, that I had to get us lost without any direction. Instead of holding on to our relationship, I held on to the question, "Can two very different beings still be attached in a constant flux of miscommunication?" When we were finally over, I felt lost. The first man I ever "came" with, the first man to bring out deeply-rooted emotions was The Perfect Sagittarian. I valued so much about him. I knew at one time, if I asked, I could always count on him, and if I asked for the truth, I'd get it.

After the many breakups I issued—many rightfully so in my mind—I could no longer count on him other than to lead me to insanity. Inevitably, my feelings developed for who he is and the respect I had for him. Ultimately, after all our times of intimacy, our final depart would be most pleasant if I get some sort of parting gift—perhaps something phallic. Each time we were intimate, I added another year of attachment to him, leaving me in quite a predicament. In divorce, women get houses, in engagements women get rings—I found my ending request quite equitable. This way, I wouldn't have to date him, my sex life would stay intact, and there would be absolutely no hard feelings between us. It was genius.

May 3, 2010
First Sleepover at Dany's

I hadn't had a call from wifey in three days now. If I don't call for three days, it's generally nothing, however, for some others, it's clear when they're attempting to make a statement. What is a successful relationship or friendship anyway? Is it constant communication that keeps it all going, or is it a lack of actual talking? I love her. I love my family, yet I continuously find myself having to pull away. I get overwhelmed by my *own* wandering thoughts, not to mention anyone else's. In my opinion, a relationship can only truly grow if you're honest, and it seems that my blunt nature has only deemed me a bitch. I sometimes wish my mom would put her old skin back on and be a rock again, yet the new Cindy is all warm and fuzzy so it seems I've taken on the identity of "insensitivity."

Back to wifey—I was supportive of her eHarmony account, and while I found it unnecessary, I drew the line at being supportive of actual Facebook stalking. It's amazing how, as friends, we're so in tune, yet on some levels, we're polar opposites. I don't even have a Facebook page and she's looking for her soul mate on it. On the occasional chance that I can read her status, it's either regarding how fabulous her life is, new successes, masturbating, how busy she is, a thorough copy of her schedule, or something to do with a current lover. Why is it people must post their schedules? Facebook is not a calendar. It's almost as if by proving how busy they are, it gives meaning to their lives, to their stress. You're busy, Martha Stewart's busy, the president is busy, Gandhi was busy—I get it.

I've always felt that, with Wifey, she feels she has to prove something to people. It's like she needs them to love her—to validate her—despite her independence. I loved her before she tried to convince me why I should. If she doesn't call me over tonight for Nurse Jackie, then I'm officially on her shit list.

On Monday, she Facebooked some cute guy she saw on some other anonymous cute guy's page, and they started talking. By Tuesday, she told me they would soon be dating. I didn't fight it—I can appreciate a flavor of the week. On Friday, they had plans to actually meet at a club. Again, I was supportive and excited for her, despite my suspicions of him being Facebook friends, and attending the same college as the asshole who took my virginity (and many other V-cards). When I wasn't being updated Friday night like I regularly would be on a first date, I knew something was up. Saturday morning confirming my suspicions, I learned this new guy slept over her house. I didn't even comment, but apparently, because I wasn't as enthused, she sensed my opinion.

This scenario was unfair to me as it was. If I was upset he slept over, I was either the over-protective, prude friend or the clingy lover. If I lied and said I was "so happy for her," then, when the truth comes out he's not Mr. Right, my judgment will be in question. No word from Rose since. Now she was withholding the generous amount of texts and updates I get from her daily. Where was my storm alert? Or info on why I shouldn't eat this, or all the people who've died that I don't know? For most of our friendship, she's had an infatuation tied with the fear of death. Though it was sometimes morbid, I didn't mind receiving obituaries from her, or trippy news, as I loved to see anything that used her intelligence, as she's multitalented. I missed my Rose. Yet, if she hadn't called me back because I wasn't ready to plan her wedding after a week, then so be it... she knows I'm horribly stubborn.

I can't claim my love life is any better or less complicated. We all have different tolerance levels, or certain deal breakers. This month was new for me, particularly with a new bachelor. We've had a few casual dates thus far.

In my gut, I know this wouldn't (couldn't) become a relationship, but I guess that's why ignorance is bliss. I wasn't ready to pull away altogether either. I got a sensation toward him and I knew he was a good guy—beyond that, we had fun together. I did wonder how different our scenario would be if I'd worked at the club as a waitress instead. My head really wasn't in relationship mode right then, and I suppose I should've reinforced that more before saying yes to future dates. We knew the dilemmas of mixing business and pleasure, but my openness to people typically made boundaries very unclear. On our second "business meeting," when he told me he liked that I distracted him from work, and how new I felt, it was then that it clicked. I was no longer being interviewed as a potential server, I was being interviewed as possible lover. Ooh la la! We started getting together when compatible, and I found him to be quite attentive.

Our date Friday was fun. He was like the Providence version of Alexander. I have to admit, I looked good that night. I can say that proudly after years of insecurity. To match his attire, which was always a suit—not that I mind, because it was very sexy—and to make up for our last date where I literally wore pajamas, I decided on a silk, one-piece, pantsuit. It was funny because when I looked in the mirror, I could literally see myself at age six playing dress up in my mom's clothes. Except this time I had breasts and wasn't tying her bras around my ears or stealing her chicken cutlets.

I met him at his work, giddy with anticipation. I was nervous even just walking into the strip club to meet the savvy bachelor. This date context was certainly a first for me. I don't typically pick up my date from one of those places. Still, I was in awe of the secret life that goes on in there. I couldn't believe I was now meeting a potential date with all that mystery.

He seemed cautious when greeted by my non-hug, but it is rare that I give out hugs freely. For me to initiate a hug feels intimate, whether that's a hindrance or a help, at least when I do give one, it comes from a deeply genuine place. I've lacked in physical affection for years because of my struggle with boundaries. Dany just kind of looked at me with a genuine smile, probably trying to cover his assessment of why I was so guarded.

When asked about dinner, I pronounced salmon or mint chocolate chip ice cream—the green kind only—and this request I found very reasonable. We went to dinner at Bella. I sambaed to our table which felt appropriate as there was an older, Italian gentleman waiting and playing guitar. I wanted to refrain from any alcohol; I don't really drink with meals or even casually for that matter. If I drink then I'm drinking on the dance floor and I'm getting torn up. He ordered me a glass of merlot anyway, and although I don't typically like red wine, it was delicious. I justified the date for experience, and wine for the heart.

Dany was the kind of guy I'd compare to a George Clooney, as I didn't really know why he was single, but it was completely acceptable because of his lifestyle. Since our first, real, one-on-one interaction, I've seen that he has a very dry sense of humor and a monotone voice. Rose thinks his voice is quite sexy. I'd agree, yet it's funny the way the tone in his voice can change my energy. With the both of us being so sarcastic, we found common ground when joking with the waiter. His name was Sergio, and he was horribly nervous. Not the "first time" nervous, the constantly antsy and socially awkward nervous. I pick up energies in other people to the point where it's exhausting.

It all started when Sergio was listing off the specials so articulately, until he had the dreaded brain fart. His blank face scanned his reference sheet and, before he could stumble on any more words, I said, "Sergio, we'll take fries and sloppy joes."

He looked mortified, but ready to accommodate. My sarcasm didn't stop there. While trying so desperately to accommodate me, because Dany and I weren't an "us," I finally put a request with Sergio for boob tape. He had offered to bring me anything I needed.

"Anything? Truthfully, I'm in need of boob tape. Can we do something about that?"

He turned about three shades red and couldn't get away fast enough. The meal was lovely, so lovely in fact, that towards the end of it, I had a small oops. Dany told Sergio that I forgot my credit card, and while Sergio was proposing I work as the guitarist's assistant, with a flail of my arm I knocked over my red wine. It missed my pantsuit, but didn't miss anything else on the table; the white cloth was fast becoming crimson. Before cleaning it up, Sergio was offering me another glass and before I could interject, Dany said I was probably all good with one. He was right. As I would later find out, he often is. I had not planned on dessert, but when Sergio told me the oversized, dark chocolate lava cake was filled with antioxidants (in my favor), and excitable (in Dany's favor), how could I decline? After dinner, Dany and I sat in the car, challenging who could stand the ass warmers the longest. I won.

Before leaving, we caught Sergio doing what resembled martial arts in the parking lot. Earlier in the evening, he had confessed to us he had recently given up cigarettes so I took this sighting as confirmation. I can appreciate embracing other outlets to get us through the dismissing of another attachment. After we had our laugh, Dany asked if I wanted to go for a ride. As we did our scenic drive, he softly asked if I wanted to see his house. "Do you want to come in?"

I took my time in giving a response—it's more entertaining to watch him sweat it out for a minute as I contemplate. As we awkwardly walked toward the door, one part of me was cool as a cucumber, and the other side of my brain was working a mile a minute trying to analyze and rationalize.

We ended up playing Wii for an hour—two adults with the same pondering thought attempting to Wii bowl was a sight I'm sure. Then, I don't even know how it really began, but he reached for my hand and led me to the bedroom. As he so delicately laid me on the bed, he literally just intimately stroked me for what felt like over an hour. Just strokes. Staring at me, counting my freckles, and touching my eye lashes kind of intimate. There was something really comforting in the way he held my head in his hands, or lightly brushed his fingers over my face. I don't do well with intimacy, especially so early on and yet a small piece of me felt trust. He wasn't pushy at all. So well mannered. He asked, "Is this okay?" I wanted to be truly accepting of the moment, so when my brain would stop I'd soak it in. It was hard to really let go because of my outside uncertainty.

The questions in my head stood out like an evil pop-up book. *Should I let this go to the next level? What was he looking for? Did it matter since some lines had already been crossed? Should I have these questions or just go with it because it was... exciting? Was I now technically involved with an almost-boss? Was Dany feeling rejected right now because I wasn't fully giving in? What did I want out of this? How did I not think of this scenario earlier? Was he critiquing me right now in comparison to the strippers he's seen for twenty years? Did it matter that he's been with strippers for twenty years now? Will he write me off for a stretch mark?*

Eyes closed, I cannot look at him. *Should I go back to being celibate? Okay, okay, breathe... I'm single, I'm young,* I repeat to myself. There was calm for a second, then more thoughts. Thoughts about how he oozes manliness, more positive thoughts and then the dreaded reminder that I purposely didn't shave so I'd have a backup plan if I found myself in this predicament. What will I tell Calvin when he asks how my interview went as waitress? Well! We didn't do the *it* that night, and I didn't feel any pressure or dread that I had to, which made it feel so easy.

I wondered if Dany sensed my confusion when he brought me to my car the next morning. I did like him, I just couldn't quite place the feelings, and I'm generally not comfortable going into a situation where my intuition is unclear. I had a pull to him that was gripping, yet I felt mismatched. I felt there was something there between us, but I couldn't tell if my body was signaling me to abort or proceed. Listen to my head, heart, or stomach? I never knew the three could be so divided.

Memorial Day and... Miss... You?
June 8, 2010

I find myself in a predicament—shocking. My latest revelations have led me to a few possible conclusions. One: you speak or think, and the universe will listen—this is one of my more profound conclusions—and two: I should probably send Philip a fruit basket or something, well, fruit may not be sufficient, since he owns a produce company. Maybe a "sorry-I-crushed-your-heart" basket. Don't they make those? And the last realization, what worked for me and moved me into my identity in 2009 and 2010 was now stifling me, but I was having trouble moving on.

Now to this week's dilemmas that seem to keep resurfacing. On Memorial weekend, I went to Dany's. At first, I drove out there in manic mode because I was beyond fashionably late, I was ready to turn around and say "What are we doing? What am I doing?" I suddenly felt too committed, too obligated. I had committed to a double date type day that I knew was going to veer me off my almost-diet, require me to sleep in—which I loathe—and bask in coupled togetherness. We seemed to always be on opposite wavelengths—he was up all night, and I was up all morning. He wanted to spoon, I wanted to sleep. He saw us as a mature couple, I wasn't sure how I saw "us."

Then, it happened. I decided to let go, and the day ended up being fun. I stopped feeling as though I was compromising my weekend, and instead felt a growing... something. I hadn't scheduled this something to come in. We took out the motorcycles with another couple and spent the day outdoors. As the sky turned, we got caught in a rainstorm. All of us were scrambling and soaked, trying to get back to the house after such a beautiful day. It hit me the next morning when I was laying out at the house alone and he had left to do errands, there was a feeling of, *I could get used to this*. It was almost hard for me to leave. That is, until I thought I lost the cat. Anytime I was there, it followed me and stared at me with wide eyes, ready to pounce. Now, the time I was left alone and trusted, the cat was nowhere to be found. As I was ready to lock up, I walked by the island and saw a card from his preteen daughter. It read, "Dear Daddy, I loooveeee you and the cat more than anything in the world." How sweet. Sweet turned to borderline frantic when I thought, *Where is the cat?*

After I searched in the backyard and crawled under the porch—nothing. Could he have escaped? I brought my search back inside—still nothing. No sign. No evidence. No cat. I walked over to his Rottweiler, Moo, thinking I could maybe gain insight, but still nothing. For a second, I thought about calling Dany, but that would be new ground for breaking up. After my contentment yesterday, could I really get dumped as the girlfriend who so irresponsibly lost his family house pet?

It wasn't until I left a trail of whipped cream in the kitchen that the cat came back, and even now I'm baffled as to where he was hiding. Tricky little feline. Cat incidents aside, once I did get home, and I had a far enough ride to really contemplate the situation, I felt sad. I missed my company. Ouch. Was I really missing someone I just spent three days in a row with? I hoped my period would soon follow so I could justify these emotions. It's always easier to blame it on the PMS. Men don't ask questions with that in context, and neither do I. This heavy feeling of sadness led me to determine he and I should have a talk. "Let's talk," the dreaded talk always feels so formal, but how else does one approach it? Isn't it better to go ahead and give the signal? Was this coming up because we were exploring lines of intimacy, and I was experiencing hormonal results? Unfortunately, whenever we do sit down and talk, I usually forget everything I had rehearsed in my head. While sitting at Barnes and Noble, playing scenarios of the talk in my head, Christian—Mr. OCD—started texting me again.

He's been so up my ass lately. It was as if he knew no amount of probing and invitations for sex could make up for the end of our relationship and bring me back. He had broken too many booty call guidelines. He had become an annoyance verses the convenience which is the priority of booty callers. We ended soon after my first date with Dany.

I didn't feel like getting into details. I was already feeling so mushy-gushy. I couldn't now confess my new feelings to an ex-lover. Instead, I responded via text—of course. "Not around. Haven't been around. Won't be around."

He tried, but I just said, "I am busy reading!"

He tried harder. It's probably hard for someone to accept that a novel is more fun than their penis.

"I bet you look sexy at Barnes noble baby." Seriously, Christian?

Later in the week, Dany kept trying to get together and I rejected it. I felt an urge to do my own thing after feeling out of control with our departure recently. From his perspective, I could tell he thought I was just being rude. His way of dealing with it was one word responses to counteract my aloofness. Stage one of Mr. Passive-Aggressive. In my head, I felt my actions were completely reasonable. Did I truly need to submerge myself in togetherness mode at the start of a new relationship? As the female lover, am I on call for his free time? In his words, he said he felt he just reeled me in and now I was falling away again. I was guilty for knowing the truth in that, but how did he know it? Was I justified? I had cut ties with my booty call of a year since Andy and I went on our second date.

I saw Dany on Monday, Wednesday, and Thursday, and I gave up plans to see him again. On Thursday, I got to his house after leaving my plans, and five minutes into the Celtics game, he's snoring. Head on my tummy, snoring. He loves lying on my tummy. I had Rose calling me needing to talk and I was all the way in the woods of Rhode Island, forty minutes off course. It wasn't anything crucial, just another soul mate gone awry. Girlfriends are the go-to for such circumstances. I was expecting this call. I told her this guy shouldn't be given more than a week, but she swore he was worthy of her time.

I saw the first red flag when he continued to reference himself as the "sexiest bartender of the year." That was how he wanted to be acknowledged when introduced. I told her from the get-go she was too fabulous to deal with a male that only answers to Mr. Sexy. I couldn't stand to face waking up Dany with an explanation for my leaving so, instead, Rose and I dealt with her crisis via text. To make matters even worse, Christian started texting me again, interfering with my phone psycho analysis with my girlfriend over text. I felt now was the time to be brutally honest, otherwise he'd keep interjecting. I won't risk my potential something with Dany for sexting with a past, failed relationship.

"Christian, I am casually dating someone. If we decide to be together, I can't be involved with someone else, so you definitely need to stop texting me sexual offers. I told you this when I first went on a date. You and I tried the relationship thing, and then we ended it. I don't see a future for us. We get along great but you had no booty call manners when it was important. Hope you understand and can respect my honesty. Thanks."

His non-response first led me to believe he was going to say nothing. With my mature explanation, I felt satisfied. What could he really say to that? What response would be suitable?

My plan backfired. It had an opposite effect that I hadn't prepared myself for. He then started texting me over and over again, using all kinds of sexual references. I nearly fell off the bed. As if my face didn't give me away enough, it was like the cat was onto me. Dany asleep on my stomach and Zane lying on my left arm wide eyed as if he wanted an explanation. Thank God technology took over and my phone died on its own, because I felt a hot flash coming on. As much as I was so turned off from Christian, anyone who's offered hours of oral sex is going to blush and lose composure. He said he'd do this, do that, again offering himself as my sex slave. Luckily, just as he was sending me a picture, my phone froze and died. Amen.

The next day was the start of the weekend, and I needed my independence. People were trying to crack me and I needed solitude. It was that or a rebellion. A relationship rebellion for being too... comfortable? It was everywhere. The signs and road blocks to make me cut ties with my new bachelor. When I went to work, my boss tried to seduce me—dropping me off lunch, paging me up in the office, sending me on certain tasks as management, reading my books, and asking me questions on spiritual enlightenment. Calvin, the almost-future-husband, had recently started texting me questions about us being together later in life—my dear hippie friend who always commented on my liberation with such envy, he would not accept my new relationship. He said he thought I was far too free to be involved in such things.

The worst one was a gym member who had seen me at the club and caught wind that Dany and I were dating. He knew Danys's partner, so he always acted like he was carrying a lot of information, but my intuition told me he was just looking for some. During every shift, he'd come in and ask for an update. I'd answer "We're casual." and he'd take my remark as a comfortable way for him to say something ridiculous.

"Oh yeah, good thing. He's dated strippers you know. Imagine if you were serious, then everyone would think you were a stripper!"

While he'd chuckle at his commentary on each check in, I'd be having a complex.

Dany's reaction to my withdrawing made me uncomfortable. It created that space between us, and I couldn't decide whether to fill it or let it grow apart. Saturday night, I went out with the girls. I didn't need the space to be devious or hurtful, I just needed to be in a space that felt like it was my own and not someone else's. I couldn't bear another moment of fitting myself into his life. I needed to understand my own ground before trying to stand on someone else's.

Sex Haze
July 21, 2010

"Sex bonds you to others, and in some cases if you are not careful and thoughtful, it can put you in bondage to others."

—Daniel Amen, *The Brain in Love*

I think I have entered the sex phase in this relationship. Sex—whether good or bad—can drive anyone cuckoo. It's amazing how every relationship can teach us something, I think even the greatest disasters are meant to bring us closer in our relationship with ourselves or closer to our relationship with someone else later on.

Looking at my current situation, I can finally, truly recognize and sort out my feelings for Dany. Life is simple, but the lessons are not, especially if we keep denying them. First of all, prior to us meeting, I had really come full circle on my identity, and as I was growing with myself—even if some parts insisted on being stagnant—I wasn't quite ready just yet to grow with someone.

2008 was like an awakening for me, and I knew I had to decide to love myself. All these years I addressed my body as this strange, unsatisfying entity. 2009 was expansion and exploration of my newfound identity. 2010 has shown me that we are all human beings—susceptible to fall and rise—that every person has their own perspective, and as much as we need to give to our self and protect our self, we can't forget the significance of other people and their presence, whether they provide a challenge or a blessing.

When I met Dany, we met on odd circumstances. We met in a strip club—his, to be specific. Not a typical place to find a bachelor. We met through my current boss whose blossoming friendship with me was becoming questionable and, ultimately, we met with my intention of working there. Not as a stripper, but a waitress.

With our first one-on-one interaction for work purposes, I had tunnel vision. Interviewing as a worker and interviewing as a girlfriend are two very different roles. I've never been one to go looking for relationships. As Dany and I started talking, I could feel the shift in our interaction, but his intentions weren't clear to me. He wasn't going to hire me, and I was half disappointed. He said he didn't know if the environment would be totally right for me. He kept in touch, and had a way of listening that made me feel heard. People talked, and originally kept telling me to pursue it—of course all for different reasons.

"Oh then we can be VIP at the dollies." Great, thank you for your input, that was my number one concern.

"He's a great guy!" There was never a dispute about that. Even my mother supported it. I think she just wanted to live through my dating life and this would be new territory to gossip about. The spectrum of encouragement really varied in reasoning.

At the time, I had a crush, but in my heart I knew I couldn't let it go anywhere, so I waited on some sort of epiphany to go off in my brain. I know my instincts and even from the get-go, I had an underlying feeling of us not having a future together. I could already see how great Dany was, but I also saw some sort of discontentment.

Initially, Dany and I talked and laughed a lot. Since there was no pressure in our situation, the communication was very open, clear, and new. As we started to turn toward the dating direction—despite my gut feeling on our incompatibility—I wasn't ready to not allow us any direction either. It couldn't hurt to allow us some room for growth... or so I thought. *What's the harm in doing things together*, I had thought. He took me out of my usual routine, and we'd do things in Rhode Island; it was refreshing to have a place away from home.

The fact that he was a strip club owner didn't bother me. It wasn't the usual nine-to-five, but work is work. At least he wasn't living at home in his mother's basement. The fact that he had a daughter didn't bother me either. In fact, I was amazed by their close relationship. Our age gap made me a little hesitant, but that still couldn't shake me. With my theory, we're all lifetimes old, so being the little guru I am, numbers made no difference. I liked that he'd include me in all kinds of things, and peoples' reactions were shocked,

"Dany dated some girls for a long time and no one ever even knew, he's that private."

"Dany never persists with girls; I'm surprised he's trying this hard with you."

"Doesn't Dany see how you are, especially with guys? You are a guy."

And from my true best friend, Steve, who knows me so well, "You may be the one chick to send Dany into a straitjacket. Be nice, you man-eater."

None of the above had shaken me. It just was what it was and I didn't want to look any more deeply into it. I thought I was on such solid ground it couldn't be shaken, wow was I wrong. Never get too comfortable in your space. Right as I started to feel at ease and consider us as a twosome, I was thrown a major unexpected curve ball. We were going to become a threesome.

His ex was pregnant. Period. Well... no period, apparently. He and I had recently just crossed things over to the physical and my reaction to the news surprised even me. I was heated! My blood was racing, but I downplayed my reaction. My disappointment surprised even me. What stranger was I getting to know? How strange was he, and how did I not sense it? I couldn't get emotional while boxing with the guys at the gym. It had taken me so long not to be viewed as just someone with a vagina. Now, while in the backroom practicing combos with them, Steve so nonchalantly dropped the bomb.

"So are you and Dany still seeing each other?"

"We see each other sometimes." I like my privacy, particularly in a place that breeds gossip. I wasn't ready to be viewed as anyone's girlfriend, however, I had to claim a little territory so I couldn't lie and say no, either.

"Well, what are you two going to do about the baby?"

I felt my cheeks flush. Baby? I knew I wasn't having a baby. I scanned his face, puzzled. I kept my composure so I could get the dirt while acting like I knew all along. Apparently, his off-and-on ex was a couple months pregnant. They stopped seeing each other two months before we got together, and she was now x amount of months into baby making. After I very casually got the information I needed, I threw some punches and then ran out of there like I was racing for a marathon. I could hear the guys yelling for me as I ran out of the gym, but I felt sick deep within my whole body—how did I let this happen?

On the ride home amid tears, amid a call to my mother telling her to pause any Lifetime movie and find me the Fig Newtons, I kept reminding myself, *Well we weren't going to last anyway, we're not supposed to!* And I knew that, right? I cried the whole way home, and I wasn't sure why. I wasn't sure if I cried for being blindsided, out of embarrassment, or because I couldn't accept these sudden emotions.

I got home and told my mom the story, and thank God for her reassurance, because my nerves turned to laughter.

"Gabrielle, just call him. Just call him right now and ask."

I liked that she trusted my judgment enough to offer a solution. We both sat there in suspense as I dialed his number. When I called, he said yes, it was true, and yes, we should have this conversation in person. *Great*, I thought, *I've gone from strip club lunches with coworkers, to strip club dating, and now this.*

I said I needed some time before we met, so we waited a few days. Once we talked, he told me a girl he'd been seeing off and on for two years, who he stopped seeing recently, declared she was pregnant. I had never heard *that* one before with my dating experiences. With a three day window to get pregnant, and the availability of birth control, the amount of baby mamas out there seems to be all too high. He said he was waiting on a blood test to see if the baby was his. How does one adequately prepare for this? We stopped seeing each other at first at my discretion. I didn't want to be the number one Jerry Springer candidate after a few months in my new relationship. The scenario felt too complicated for me.

I went introverted for about two weeks. Outsiders still kept telling me how great a guy Dany was, and poked and probed for information.

"Gab, he really is a good guy and he'd be a great father."

I'd stare at them blankly, waiting for them to realize how absurd that sounded. Then, as time had it, I told myself, *Why not enjoy each other while we can?* This put us in new context, but I decided this scenario could keep us light and casual, which is what I wanted anyway. I wasn't looking for love and romance, I was looking for companionship I could enjoy. This meant we'd have about seven or eight months of dating—I can commit to that. Shouldn't you hold onto the people that you're happy with? He was the first person I felt an underlying trust for and I didn't feel totally engulfed in it, just dumbstruck.

Men often loved me easily, but it made me feel they loved an image or idea of me, or even that they loved me for their own motivations. I never trusted how easily a man could express love to me. Love, to me, was bigger than a moment, or an image, a desire, or even intuition. I swore I'd never tell someone I loved them until I knew I meant it.

After the news, we weren't really the same in the way a normal relationship would progress. I kept myself at a distance. I suppose I had always done that anyway. I did what I wanted and I told him to do what he wanted. He continued to try, and I continued to justify keeping us within guidelines. Little by little his persistence broke down my limits. Since then, the past few months have been kind of surreal. Any growth we had, I dismissed. Any time he tried to move forward, I dismissed it. I told him, "We're not serious." I've led us in circles, back and forth to buy my mind some time, and as the emotional haze has cleared a physical one has now taken its place to cloud me. To keep me in grey area.

We were now having YES YES YES YES YES YES YES sex, or at least I am.

He was the first person I was actually CUMMING with. Hallelujah, I can orgasm. I'd been giving myself orgasms since before I knew what they were. I just thought it was great to hump things. I'd hump my blanket, go check on my Barbies, hump my pillow, then go study my spelling words, ride my bike, hump my bike, etc. And as adolescence evolved, I learned, *Oh that's what masturbating is, but it's only acceptable for teenage boys to be doing it.* So I suppressed my sexuality and struggled with it.

As a woman, I've even faked orgasms, either to lie to myself, because it felt expected, to get things going, or sometimes even to practice my acting skills, but I had never cum. When I would give in to the moment, our sex felt so explosive sometimes, and connected. Afterward, I'd be left with the thought, *How can I ever be with some other?* I literally felt disgusted to even think of having sex with someone else, ever. I'd feel fragile and sensitive. This was perhaps the beginning stages of my love for him.

Now, being the extremist I am, I made sure to cum at least twice and I was hooked. Wide-eyed, high-five-you-when-it's-over hooked. Starts-speaking-in-tongues-during-the-orgasm hooked. Feels-and-looks-like-I'm-high-after-sex hooked. Wanting-to-be-strapped-to-the-bed-swinging-from-a-sex-swing-on-the-ceiling hooked. Irrationally-emotionally-tunnel-vision-on, wants-it-all-the-time hooked.

All of the above left me to reflect on where I've been and where I was now. I knew better than to chase the past, but I as forced to look back on past relationships and see how they've brought me to where I am. Alexander is key; he'll never realize this, but he'll always have a place in my heart. I see now how significant our time was. He showed me that a man can respect and take care of you. He taught me what it's like to be in a healthy relationship with someone, and what it's like for each of you to give to each other. He helped change my perception of relationships beyond my parents. He welcomed me into his life, into his family, into his circle of friends who were all just as loving and adoring.

Calvin was then brought into my life to make me realize the spark you can have with someone. To literally feel in your heart that you're ready to take love on. To realize a person who cares for you will listen with no expectation, and the raw honesty you can have with someone. I didn't filter anything I said to him—we'd have such real, honest conversations and I believed in our friendship. He showed me the importance of being friends with someone first and really getting to know a person. I'd throw myself at him all the time and he wouldn't budge.

Christian taught me a lot about physical attraction, about the importance of chemistry, but that it means nothing if the person doesn't bring out the best in you, or if you two don't share future morals. For whatever reason, I never felt good enough with Christian and it showed. I was trying to mold myself into the image of the girls he dated, even though he found my differences exciting. He felt too perfect. I wear my flaws on my sleeve. The funny thing with Christian and I is we had sex for the first time after our breakup. He also taught me you can be physically compatible with someone, but eventually, your different viewpoints will overshadow it all. We had great communication over the phone, through emails, text, in person and he taught me a lot. There have been other dates in between but nothing truly significant.

And now, all of the above brought me to the heavy lesson with Dany. Our past couple months together have influenced me. Just when I thought I could put a timeline on us emotionally—a this-for-that—I was in this sex fog; we'll call it a sex haze. I was worried about my judgment from here out. I felt so connected through this intimacy that I couldn't separate real emotions from sexual emotions. It crept up on me, but suddenly, despite my laissez faire attitude, I was caving.

How could I compartmentalize us when my body was freaking out? My vagina was literally trying to tell me that it plans on rejecting all penises from here on out. Before, I felt there was no va-va-voom. I felt, *This is it?* Even now, while he may not completely understand me, something fits. I felt consumed by our sex life. Four times this week already and I was antsy for when I'd get to get it next. I felt like his penis was made of chocolate and I was either on a sugar high or a sugar crash. Anything he said that could be related to sex gives me a hot flash. I replayed his dirty talk over in my head quite frequently. That can make a work flow hard when you're dreaming of a spanking and trying to sell a gym membership.

This is a pathetic comparison, but it was like having a backyard. Nothing all that exciting on its own. You go out and play on it—it's fun but sometimes it is what it is, just a backyard. You sometimes want to check out the neighbors, you sometimes want to go exploring, you sometimes don't even want to play at all. Until one day, you're in the backyard and say you discover a treasure chest. This is rousing. Now it's like you can't stop playing with it, you don't care about the neighbors—you may even put up a fence, you just want to hang out with your treasure chest. Now you're even more curious, what will I do with such a reward? And even though you now know you have a treasure chest to keep (my own little hotspot) I can't just say thanks for the gift—even though I had it all along—and walk away. So what to do? I felt needy and out of control. I felt like I needed more, more, more or I'd be insecure. I didn't get it. This relationship sex haze is cloudy. It was interrupting my regular functioning. I was like a kid given candy for the first time. I needed to unfog my gaga goggles. I needed to regain my balance before I became a raging nymphomaniac. When these sex hazes block our vision, do we lead blindly or wait until the fog clears? July 1, 2012

You've Got Mail
Email One to Dany

Okay, I've wanted us to talk for a while now, but then my thoughts feel insignificant or it's bad timing or I just lose the words I meant to say. It's cheesy, but that's why I thought it would be best to write a letter. This way, you can read it and let it settle. When I try to talk, I'm scatter-brained, but if I'm writing it out, there are moments to reflect.

First of all, I think you're a great guy. In the little time we've known each other, we've had some great moments, I've learned from you and respect you very much. But, (don't you love that word?) and maybe you feel differently, I feel as though something has changed. You may or may not feel it. Maybe it's me, maybe you're questioning my age and lifestyle, but I don't want to keep guessing. Something is unbalanced.

I know you're an honest and straightforward person but I'm confused about my feelings. How can you be so sure of what you feel for me? I feel as though, when we first met, we talked so bluntly as friends and now it feels like more of a surface level. I can't do only the surface. I become way too socially awkward around surface-only situations. I've never been in this place before, but I can recognize it in my close relationships.

Last week, my sister had a traumatic experience and you haven't even asked me about it since. I know she's not any of your concern, and trust me, my sister hasn't been involved in my life for a long time, but I do wonder why you didn't ask me about it. I expressed to you I was sad for her. It makes me feel unheard or that you aren't considering what my family goes through. On Tuesday, you asked about my agenda, yet you asked no questions about my gyno appointment. That's a personal thing, you are the person I'm intimate with, and yet no follow up on how or why I went? Isn't that something we should be able to talk about, or did you just expect that I'd take care of it? Rose and I can talk to each other about our vaginas, but don't you have concern for what's going on with mine? She certainly doesn't, she just listens because she's a good girlfriend and we can relate over such things. I'd like you to especially be concerned with the care of my vagina.

  I don't want this letter to seem like I'm nagging or that I need extra attention. You are patient and reliable. Somehow, even with certain things I know about you, I feel a disconnect between us. One second we're moving forward, the next, we're stuck. A part of me feels like it's because we're forcing a relationship that's not meant to be. I feel that, if you're going to be with someone, you should be with someone who promotes and brings out the best in you—maybe that's why I so often prefer to be single. I feel like I'm still doing so much self-work, I don't want someone to feel they're settling with one dimension of me while the others develop and get pruned. I know it's more me than anything. Typical line on those doing the break up. You said it yourself that you felt we were just starting to get somewhere, and now, I've been so introverted lately. This is true. I just don't know how to make sense of certain emotions because they go from one extreme to the next with such intensity. I have these small moments after I leave you where I feel funny being away from you after. I'd find myself missing you, hoping for you—it's like I wouldn't know how to settle into my own space after. I almost don't know how to go back to my own comfort zone and life when I leave you. It feels too distant. This is so new to me. I've never not felt content after leaving someone. When we leave each other, I still feel a tie to you, like some sort of pull reminding me not to go too far. Yet I see you again and I feel like I can't totally embrace you either—there's a wall I'm at. There's some sort of boundary that prevents me from wanting to be completely with you. Then, when I am with you, I feel somewhat reserved and subdued.

Dates to Remember - Gabrielle Anna

The reality is, you talk to me but you don't really talk to me. I think back to our first date, or when we used to talk for hours. Now we're different. You're having a baby and I don't even know how you feel about it. I don't know when it's coming up, I don't know if you want me to ask or leave it alone. You haven't said anything at all about it and it's a big deal. I don't even know how two people can really be together when one is going through such a significant experience without the other. Males and females are different. I can't tell how involved you want me to be. I see you're making efforts. You did pick me up at 3:00 a.m. from the airport this weekend. You did drop me off and pick me up from the airport. You did call me every day I was away. While I was in LA, I was thinking about how my life can go in so many directions, and you have a life without those directions—how will I fit without losing my own? How can you be so confident I do fit? You have your business, a daughter, a baby on the way—issues so different from mine, and in one sense, I love deeply that we have our own lives but in another I feel too apart. It's funny because I think those differences are what some couples lack. I think our independence is key, where some couples give that up. I'm in a middle position because what I value in us, I also resent. Do you feel it's me not trying hard enough or maybe you're worried about offending me so we don't talk about these things? I know you often tell me I have a way of disappearing, everyone says this to me but I need to hermit and recharge a lot. I take a lot of internal time to digest and to regroup. I often struggle with boundaries from people, so when I've gone beyond my limit, I cut myself off from everyone. Are you just attracted to me? Should we be casual?

Are you just dating me as a girlfriend to pass the time with?

Why do you keep trying when I've told you I want to leave us in an open relationship, where we get along and it is just that?

You treat me like you're just sure of us, yet you don't express any thoughts that come up for you. I guess the last situation I want to tell you about is something that happened last month. A friend kissed me the night I went out with Jane. It wasn't a friend kiss. It had been brewing for some time now. I need to get it off my chest. I know we aren't necessarily in a real relationship because of our situation, but if I'm confronting you on your thoughts, I should be up front with mine. I put it aside, but as you've asked me lately how I feel on us, I shouldn't keep that from you. I feel you are special so that's why I'm coming to you on this. *I don't want to work through all this uncertainty alone. I don't want to jeopardize what we could be if we decide. I've not been able to read you since I first realized how attracted to me you were. All in all, if we're going to be better as friends, if our relationship was meant to be some other way and were stretching it too thin—just tell me. I'd rather we kept it as friends, and maybe down the road try again. I'm sorry for ending with such an abrasive statement, but I don't want to ever keep something from someone I care for. I believe I should be up front with you on everything and I hope you can understand.*

Post Breakup Email
July 2, 2010

Yesterday my ego was put in check. I've had glimpses of it all week, but who is ever ready to totally let go of our ego? I feel sorry for the poor bachelors who are scratching their heads in confusion trying to figure out what the hell is going on with me or with women in general.

After a cut-and-dry conversation with Dany, my A-B-C man, and my usual laugh, cry, talk, confessional with Rose, I am brought back to a problem that has been lurking under the surface.

I sent Dany an email this week. Email one for our relationship. Had I known down the road I'd become quite a novelist to him, I'd have never started the trend. I hit send to my two page objection and felt phenomenal. He didn't let me off the hook so easy. Unfortunately, he made me realize, after discussion, the email should have been sent to my own inbox. When he first got my email, I really realized how much he cared for me. He reacted with general concern for my confusion, and he did so quite professionally and lovingly, which is not easy.

At first, when he read it, he was shocked and disgusted (which I assume was because of the last statement). This caught me off guard. He said his stomach hurt, and he could feel his blood rising. I didn't know what to say or how to respond. I felt he was overreacting.

We decided to meet and talk Thursday, and in a typical me fashion, I was an hour late for my own meeting. Now I was the email bitch who couldn't even show up on time. I pulled up to his club and he was standing outside. The walk over to him was slow and uncomfortable.

When we got to his office, there it was—my email. Printed and highlighted. I sat down in a chair that was far too big for me, and for the first time in a while, I really felt small. Highlight by highlight he looked me straight in the face and answered my questions, or at least addressed my thoughts in a professional, direct manner.

"I'm only human, Gabby. I can, for the most part, control my thoughts, but there is a small voice that I can't always shut off. If I don't hear from you for hours, you're changing your mind about plans—you're here, your there, even when you're with me, you're somewhere else—I'm left to wonder what you're doing. I don't want to pressure you, so I try not to ask you too much, even when it's about us. I try to include you and sometimes you're for it, other times I don't know what you're thinking and you won't even give it consideration because you want to do your own thing.

"I feel like when I see you, you don't give me any emotional response. You never give me a hug where you just want to squeeze someone or an excited kiss. I don't feel that from you. You've got some sort of wall up—it's like you're a wounded puppy.

"I know you're in your twenties—you're still young and can do what you want to do. I try to respect your space, so the ball is in your court. It's up to you what you want to do; I'll be waiting

"If you didn't hear from me, or you thought we had plans and I texted you hours later, it's only human nature to feel hurt. How would you feel? And that you didn't feel hurt worries me even more."

This conversation struck a chord with me. I didn't totally understand what it was like to have someone love me. I talked to my faithful sidekick Rose later that night. This is the blessing of friendships and relationships. Rose was a perfect person to talk to as we have similar past experiences, and I can see where they sometimes hold up our future. This incident made me realize how differently each of us has coped with our past experiences and traumas.

We each went to opposite extremes to live functionally. In her position, she craved affection and physical intimacy; she became obsessive and put pressure on her ideal soul mate or partner, labeling every significant other as falling short. She needed people to love her and meet her standards. She'd give and give planning out their future, only to be disappointed or to blame their inadequacies, which drove them away.

If she wasn't being validated, she deemed them the problem and I think her boyfriends sensed her need.

I went the complete other way; I liked to make everything as difficult as possible for myself and those who tried to love me, so it seemed. I knew what I'd give to someone I love, and I challenged those who dared to love me. I wanted to know it was authentic. I saw what my parents were going through and thought, *How can this be love between two people? How can you love someone so much and hurt them so deeply, or enable their bad habits?* I realized how unpredictable and unstable love can be. Love changes; it hurts, it can't be planned, it's sacrificing—that scared me. Their relationship, and ultimately divorce, was consuming and scary. I was finally getting control of myself and environment. Love had no appeal to me—it was too transparent. I saw how many people could only love themselves with a partner. I was too afraid to only feel love through someone else.

Where I am now is also different because of my virginity attachment and my relations since then. I swore and said for years I'd save my virginity until marriage, and I strongly stuck to that. I had wanted to lose my virginity to someone I loved. I wanted to be in love. I tried to convince myself I loved Justy after he did what he did to me, and that tore me apart. He saw me as a body, and used me for that because, at the time, I guess I saw myself as merely a body too. I needed to convince myself I loved him, because to accept the reality of what he took from me was unfathomable. Following that, I experienced waves of grief—typical, transitional adolescence where we all struggle. Growing up, and in 2009 I was truly on the right path to my identity. After a few disappointments, I seemed to fall back on old security—old ways of inadequate coping and defense mechanisms.

While it was important for me to develop a strong exterior, it's no longer progressing me. It's doing just the opposite, yet I hold on with tight fingers. I need to evolve into new growth, new discomfort, and new territory. I have people who do love and support me, so instead of distancing myself, I need to allow love's abundance without being fearful or questioning it so much. Yet instead, I seem to bat it away because it feels too erratic for my newfound grounding.

Dates to Remember - Gabrielle Anna

After this week, I couldn't deny certain signs. I sent Dany the email, and last night, while lying in bed, I thanked him for being upfront and respectful.

He was so nonchalant, "Um okay, what are you thanking me for?"

"Well, I guess, for reading my email so carefully."

"But I knew you needed to talk about it."

"Oh okay... " I didn't know what else to say. Is dating this simple?

Of course, in the midst of all this, Christian had to text me. A previous Sagittarian Lover, aka Mr. OCD.

His texts were a reminder of our incompatibility. "Can you hang out finally this weekend or are you married now?"

"Not married, but can't meet, sorry. We had physical chemistry a while back, and as friends we're fine, but I'm not allowing anything else. It was too inconsistent, and I'm in a different place."

That aside, he knew I'm seeing someone. He bit into the little info I shared about Dany. "Oh god Gab, he has a kid." Yes Christian, people do that. "Oh god Gab, he owns a club." I didn't give him the satisfaction of what type, or which, because with Google today, he'd confirm his own suspicions in a second. Not that the Dollies isn't somewhat of an indication as is. "Well, are you still in school Gabby baby?" I appreciated these questions were all coming from a genuine place of concern. Our back and forth continued, but I can't be shaken once my mind is made. I made sure to leave out there was another baby... on the way... to an ex-dancer—I'm being more careful with my words now, it is a profession like any other!—who continuously Facebook pokes me. What happened to the good old days when your partner's ex didn't have so many outlets to annoy you, trigger you, stalk you, or tempt you to stalk her? For my ex, I felt he didn't deserve all the dirty details. Just confirmation that I am committed to someone else.

Since I was on such a path of clarity, I even texted Calvin. I couldn't have an almost-was husband lingering on my mind. I had such a respect for Dany, I needed to be in the right place to treat him as seriously as I was beginning to see him. This is the Calvin I broke up with Saint Alexander for; surely I couldn't be in a relationship when my future husband was in proximity.

At the time, I'd have never dated again had he given me more hope we'd be anything more than friends. My game plan, at first, was to wait patiently and singularly—until the waiting got ridiculous. I felt that, in order to move on into my new, complicated relationship, I needed to put the past in the past and move forward with as minimal baggage as possible. Dany had enough baggage for both of us to deal with. I couldn't leave the thought of someone dangling—I needed to see if I was, in fact, delusional or intuitive.

I called Calvin, "Did you ever see anything between us?" From here on out, I didn't want this to be a lurking, unanswered question. Calvin confirmed it. He does like me but we were in two different places of life and he felt that asking me for a relationship wouldn't be fair. He said something was different with us, and he knew it. This was hard for me to hear, but I guess I had to look at the situation for what it was and see that he came into my life for a transitional reason. At this point I just wanted him to be happy; I want him to find love at some point beyond his son. As a friend, I hoped for the best for him like I would anyone else. Now, off I am to proclaim my relationship status—taken. Taken, partnered, paired, girlfriend, companion. I wanted no more confusion. I couldn't bear to keep defending and fighting for a relationship I was still trying to figure out. The verdict was in on our stance. Textication

Okay, it's 9:00 a.m. and, despite my attempts, I am too antsy to stay in bed. I'm fueled by my disappointment, so as much as I'd like to go lose myself in a song or drive around and chase the sky, my hangover and these early hours are somewhat inhibiting.

Last night seemed so promising, so planned out, and while everything is for a reason, I would've liked to prolong the inevitable truth at least until the summer ended.

My partner and I were simply not compatible. It was times like last night when I say, "Well, why would I want to be in a relationship to feel like this anyway? No wonder having lovers drives so many people mad." The question still irks me… "What went wrong last night?"

When I was up at 4:00 a.m. eating protein scoops over cheerios in a baking bowl I thought, *Yup, we're over*. I was filled with adrenaline, filled with confusion. Yes, relationships are fulfilling, but when does that fulfillment smother you? No, let me rephrase that, through my tequila tears there was a silver lining of hope, but when I had to take off my far-too-tight lingerie and drunkenly undo a garter belt, I decided now we were really over. What were boyfriends for if I was taking off my own lingerie? Don't they get held to certain obligations? It took me long enough to get into a garter belt and now I couldn't even enjoy the fun of taking it off. So what happened, you ask? He will say it was me and, to an extent, many times it has been, but is that what relationships become? A constant one up over the other?

    My original weekend plans were to go to Vermont with the wifey, I truly wanted to. I'd bugged her about it for a while now. I'd ask, "We're going right? We're still going right?" Originally, I had invited Dany but he already had a family camping trip planned. As the date got closer, I started to outweigh the options and I suddenly wasn't so gung ho about the wilderness idea. After a hectic week, I felt the opportunity to make money and still be at home, see my significant other before another week of trying to schedule each other into our schedules, and then get to spoon and sleep in on a Sunday more was all too fabulous, instead of being three hours away with no signal. I kept thinking of more reasons not to go.

    Rose was mad at me for canceling—that's fair. I knew she would be even though, mid-week, she told me she didn't care if we went. Women always speak in code. The "I don't care if we go or don't go" meant we'd better be going. Ultimately, I needed to worry about my own relationship, not try to play matchmaker in the middle of the woods. That's really why she was disappointed. She knew the ratio of men to women, so the odds looked good.

    I taught my three Zumba classes yesterday. Thank you nutty nutritionist for providing me with a crazy caffeine pill. Afterward, I got coffee with a 60-year-old woman who couldn't stop raving about the way I shook my hips and how if her son wasn't on his second marriage and in Italy, she'd set me up. Nonetheless, "we'll stay in touch just in case." I then worked for T and I found myself trying to get fired as I couldn't bring myself to quit, and I couldn't quite bring myself to stay either. After that, I got ready and prepared myself to be a bartender for Greek God's best friend, Jackson's, black and white party.

Dates to Remember - Gabrielle Anna

It was people watching at its best, however, I sometimes want moments in my life to not be a learning opportunity. Honestly, let me figure some things out down the road, I don't want to know this much this soon. I didn't drink at all; Jackson's wife kept willing me to try the rum punch or a Cosmo, so I lightly sampled them to be socially polite. I know when I'm excited for something or when I really like someone because I kept counting the hours to eleven as if they would lessen by my counting.

Okay—9:00... 9:15... 10:00... 10:15... 11:00... 11:15...

As my departure time neared, I cracked a little. Okay, one glass of sangria... I started to give my warning so I could leave on time. People came over trying to get me to do shots before I left, and Greek God kept willing me to stay. I didn't give in. I had someone I wanted to go home to.

Three text messages sent to Dany to confirm our date and... nothing. Do I stay and work? Do I go home? Do I start driving down to the woods of Rhode Island? Do I have a drink? After much harassment, I agreed to a single, small tequila shot and a little bit of fruit from the sangria bowl. I didn't consider how long the fruit had been soaking for. Next a call to Dany and... nothing.

I was then willed to the dance floor. *Okay, what are a few songs going to hurt?* I tried to remain rational. *I'll kill time while I wait.* Greek God was requesting my favorites as a thank you to me getting everyone drunk all night. He knows I won't walk out on "Poison" and other classics from the 90s. A little BBD, a little Prince... I'd been working since 8:00 a.m., I might as well enjoy myself a little. Jackson had a dance floor next to the pool in his backyard. Somehow, on my way to that dance floor, I lost my shoes. I instead gained Jackson's wife's wildly homosexual father as my dance partner. This was for the best as he was not only the safest bet there, he was a wonderful dancer, twirling me all about. He graciously referred to me as a queen and spun me around effortlessly. After all his drunkenly slurred I love yous to me, we became quite a duo on the dance floor. I then checked my phone. There is not a call but a text message:

<u>I am home now, call please.</u>

Only because I am stubborn, was appropriately buzzed, and probably a little big-headed after my dancing partner blew up my ego, I responded:

I did call. I did text. Now I will head home when I'm ready.

If I've called and texted you multiple times, shouldn't you have just called me back or responded with, "Yes, come on over?" Was I being unreasonable for my aggravation? Despite my many "We've got to talk" attempts, this relationship seemed to continuously dance around our communication. There was either too much of it, or too great a lack thereof. I couldn't be so compliant and abide by this insufficient text. I couldn't be dictated. That was my reasoning.

Shortly after, guilt kicked in. His response was, "Whatever." Of all the words in the English vocabulary, that was the one he chose. Now I was flustered. I was feeling guilty until I read that. I fired off some texts; I even called to keep the fight alive after his non-response. He successfully played the silent treatment. Nothing irks me more. I wanted to fight! I wanted to figure out why I was this upset. I needed more of a reaction. Silence... More silence. Then I decided to call it a night.

People were starting to be pushed into the pool and I could no longer tell who was partnered with whom. Once all the married couples started to skinny dip, I knew that was my signal to leave. Skinny dipping is fun until the single girl jumps in.

I got in my car, suddenly angry at the cannolis sitting in my passenger seat which had been reserved for Dany and me. I cried the whole of the ten minute ride home. Finally nearing home when my eyeballs hurt, I pulled over and left a confusing and unflattering voicemail to Dany. This was a first and hopefully last of its kind. Still, even through my sudden emotions, I knew—I was not this girl. How did I get in this place when this wasn't me? When did I become the woman who leaves awkward messages or tries to text battle?

A cop saw I was pulled over, great. Pulled over and leaving buzzed messages on my now non-boyfriend's phone. Isn't it better to not be in a moving vehicle while doing this?

I looked around the car; I had a box of pizza and cannoli's to offer if necessary. After a short talk with the officer, since he knew me, we settled on cannolis and he then followed me, very slowly, home. I pulled into the driveway and cried more because I remembered my best friend was mad at me for feeling ditched, so she was out at a party I blew off. I currently felt like the psycho girlfriend to the once significant other, and like the absent side kick to my once wifey. Men have it right by traveling in reliable wolf packs, while women either have a girlfriend or a boyfriend.

The sniffles ended at about 3:00 a.m. The late night munchies ended at 4:00 a.m. The feeling of discomfort failed to subside. I couldn't sleep with so much adrenaline. Finally, at 9:00 a.m., was when I decided I was a drama queen. After four hours of sleep, I swore I could sleep no more because I felt better. I could sleep no more because I had damage control to do.

My day went from an adrenaline kick to sulking over the dinner table with my grandparents who couldn't quite understand the situation I was in. My nana thought, by my refusal to eat white potatoes, I must be anorexic, so she just kept pushing Irish food my way. She looked at me with worry when I asked for a sweet potato, or if I refused canned vegetables. At that moment, I didn't need such attention. Rose was over for dinner, and all of them deemed me a brat for sulking. Finally, when I felt their reactions were unsympathetic, I went to my moms.

Following her sickness, she was more loving and so accepting. At least I knew she'd sympathize with my whimpering. She often tells me it's okay that I love Dany, and sometimes I wonder if she was right. She said it again this time, and proposed I confess my feelings. I decided instead to take her secondary advice of showing up looking sexy—the non-talking was more my speed right then.

The standing at the door in a "Hi, I'm so cute, you don't care I'm crazy" outfit is what I decided to go with. I showed up at his doorstep in thigh-high boots, and sexy underwear as if this wasn't unusual.

"Hi, want to let me in?"

He looked at me and laughed. "You left the house like that? Where are your clothes?"

Ugh. He may be honest, but like the intelligent man he is, he let me in. I followed him into his room where he was watching NASCAR, and he explained that he bought a new phone yesterday. He said his daughter was with her mother for the weekend because he thought we'd be together, and that he was irritated with me. I felt somewhat like a little girl explaining herself while being scolded.

There was a time when, to reach someone, we made a phone call—we won't go back to the non-caller ID times, because that was a blessing for everyone, non-debatable. However, now it seems like, with all our ways of communicating, of talking about ourselves, of reaching each other, we seem to be more disconnected than ever.

Significant Sharing
July 31, 2010

I'm quite disappointed when I go to share something with my significant other and they act neither entertained, amused, nor impressed. Give me some sort of reaction! Had he been on the pursuit for me, he would eat up what I shared, or at least pretended to be interested. When someone is pursuing you, you can pretty much tell them anything and, if they like you, they'll be just as invested. Now, in a pod, I feel I've become simply a girlfriend. Doing the girlfriend phone call that must go listened to, but falls short of being truly appreciated. I'm not looking for worship, I cringe with the men that do that. Flattery makes me somewhat uncomfortable. However, I am a funny bitch sometimes—humor me. Now I feel the need to rebel. I feel too vulnerable. One phone call and I'm re-evaluating our relationship status. I keep a lot to myself. I specifically asked, "Are you busy? Do you have time to hear my story?"

I knew from the tone of his voice something was off. He could have honestly said he didn't have time; instead, he listened as if he was doing me a favor. How disappointing. I want to be listened to because of genuine interest, or I want to not be listened to and told so straight up. As a woman I have literally faked whole orgasms before and one can't muster up a laugh?

For the longest time, I was asked to be the more caring, sharing, affectionate, personal partner. I was told it's better to call than to text, that it's okay to hug back when I'm hugged, that I need to be more affectionate, that I need to be more interactive and now my latest attempts go unappreciated. He failed to see my little attempts to bond. By next week, I'll have put us back in the friend box, and right as my brain's restructured, he'll go back to being his lovey-dovey self. I'm not an angel, but this unconventional relationship should grant me a little indecision or insanity. Last night, I emailed a photo from the shoot in LA, no comment. If I don't share, I'm a cold bitch, but when I do share, I'm, what, the overbearing, over-sharing girlfriend? With no response to my picture—nada—and an absent mind to my story today, I can't help but contemplate, *Why do girlfriends try so hard to stay a girlfriend?*

    I should've gone for coffee with all my Zumba ladies this morning. There's nothing more inspiring then my 8:00 a.m. 60-year-old Zumba ladies telling me to shake it up, "faster, faster" and then sitting with them shamelessly for scones after. As I started to question my need for gratification this morning, I thought back to last week when I was at Dany's house.

    Last week, on a walk with Moo, Dany met us back home two and half hours later then when was said. The dog and I had acquired a follower while on our peaceful walk, and I was left to fend for myself with a creepy, Rhode Island woodsmen.

    Poor Moo decided he'd had enough of my George Michaels singing and power walking, so he plopped himself down on the side of the road and wouldn't budge. We sat there for a good ten minutes until this stranger came over and started calling Moo another name.

"Sorry, his name is not Zeus."

"Yes it is, come on Zeus!"

    Just like that, Moo was happily following this strange woodsman. He was doing tricks for him. I had to power walk around the lake just to lose this nut, and then I sat at his home, awaiting Dany. After an hour of waiting, I put on a pair of his shorts, which I later realized said "goo" and went to the packie. Home alone with Moo, "Zeus," trying to ditch the woodsmen, drinking premade sangria, waiting for my undefined lover to come home; What have I become? I went from his admiration in dating, to dog walking companion who waits on their "other" and gets more attention from his dog and creepy neighbor.

Relationship SOS
November 30, 2010

"Re-la-tion-ship. Hmmm. Relation-ship. Is there a correct definition that comes with it?

"For something we are all so caught up in, you'd think we'd have it more figured out. It is the one thing that science, time, and experience still haven't given us much insight on. We can literally land on another planet with the hopes of some sort of discovery, yet we can't decode our own species." If you ask my significant other, we have been dating for almost a year. I was quoting him from the other night. My reaction was something like, "Oooooh god," and not the good oh god, but not the horrible oh god either. I think his perception just caught me off guard. If you were to ask me, I'd calculate our relationship at about six months. Yes, we have technically been "dating" since about April but, as you can see, there are some discrepancies in our cycle. It's amazing how, after being with someone for so long, you know them so well—their reactions, what they'll say, what they won't say, and still oftentimes you wonder, *What the f**k is going on in your head?* Or perhaps, *What the f**k are you doing to my head?* I prefer the latter.

This was my longest relationship. Go figure. The one I never saw going anywhere won't stop going. For my age, there is a little shock value to that statement because it's like a second puberty hits—people are trying to pair you. I feel that, from middle school to the present, how many successful, long-term, meaningful relationships can you really be in? This was also the most off-and-on relationship I'd ever been in. Not off-and-on like we argue and break up—we actually don't argue much or ever even. It was off and on for me—red flag.

One day, I was literally looking at him with gaga eyes and the next, I was putting on glasses just to see him in the right light. It was so odd because I feel each emotion so intensely.

Friday: gaga eyes—I was ready to happily give up my night out and count the hours in bed 'til he'd be home. I'd lay in his bed for hours, excited after performing Zumba routines in his kitchen. After performing ballads in his shower, I was exhausted. On the nights he was working, I was either up and giddy, counting the hours 'til 3:00 a.m., or I was passed out by 11:00.

Dates to Remember - Gabrielle Anna

Saturday, I was still gaga eyes, but they were dim after he came home from work at 3:30 a.m., and my attempts to stay up and be the goddess I was, failed. Instead, I felt him get into bed, lay his head on my tummy, and I mumbled something then went back to sleep.

Upon rising, I felt our schedules too incompatible. My mind told me our schedules were incompatible, therefore we must be, too. That was, until we danced around to my disco mix while he cooked us breakfast. Okay, perhaps I could make an exception for late nights with my lover because he makes up for it in the morning.

Then, he gave me quite a profound lecture on the ride back to my car when I asked for advice. Suddenly, I saw him with such hope and infatuation again. On that ride, I felt so lucky to be with someone so grounded, aware, successful, driven, reliable, smart… the list went on.

Then, that night, there I was again, yelling at myself to break it off. There, again, was the compulsive side of me, *Hi, I'm here again, reminding you to break up. You two don't work. This is not the first-time love you wanted. Your ideal mate should not have a baby on the way and an eighty hour work week.* Once I let my irrational thoughts arise, they'd pour in.

Then there was the rational Gabrielle, *Tomorrow is his birthday—you can't break up with someone on their birthday. You just put together a surprise dinner party. This is bonding time, not be-a-cold-insensitive-bitch time.* By Sunday, I felt relived I'd listened to my rational self, then last night—birthday and all—I was so over us. I listened to Tori Amos on the ride home to mentally prepare myself for a breakup, and as each hour passed today, I got more bitter to the idea of us. My long-awaited period may have influence on the situation—possibly more than I give it credit for—but I actually hoped he'd call and say something to piss me off. That way I have more grounds and guilt and courage to break up.

Today he was probably disappointed that I wasn't at home awaiting him in my birthday suit for his birthday last night. I was disappointed too! I couldn't shake the feeling he gave me. I didn't want to wear a mask with my lover. Those little resentments—those little miscommunications—can keep partners at arm's length. I simply could not be so complying when I felt vastly misunderstood. Continuously when I practically handed him an opportunity to connect with me, score some quick brownie points, he missed the signal.

For the past twenty-four hours, I had been in full girlfriend mode. Not that I need praise, but honestly, a little acknowledgement to see the changes I'd made would have been nice. I blew off my last boyfriend's birthday, and the one before that, I just did what was expected—I went through the birthday motions. Then here I was with my current significant other, I chased around a $35 carrot cake, searched online for a gift that said, "I listen, I get you," planned a surprise birthday party, conspired with his long-time friends to be there, then had to surprise someone who was quite difficult to surprise as he was always so planned out. I pulled it off. I then sat through the dinner party with a smile on my face despite the elephant in the room that there was twenty-something years between us and he's had a whole lifetime without me—a lifetime, kids, and baby mamas.

While they reminisced, I sat looking wide-eyed and clueless. They knew the history of this person who was trying to start a future with me, and I could feel the gap. In trying to ease my discomfort, I ate my carrot cake and his. *Mmmm... It's so yummy I'm going to fill my mouth and stomach with all of it so that I am too stuffed to say anything.*

Then, last night—actual birthday night—I canceled our dinner reservations because he was addicted to work and absolutely couldn't call it off. I decided to drop in with dinner. After being questioned about the location for which I'd brought pizza, I couldn't succumb to scrutiny or be subjected to his perfectionist ways any longer. Maybe he was left with a bitter taste toward pizza after my last delivery gave him food poisoning. He failed to realize the many other times I bring him food—lunch, dinner, snack foods, etc.—on my nanny salary and had never poisoned him. He failed to recognize how often I made sure he was fed while working by driving and delivering food to him on his long shifts.

Then, in our engagement, I grew more and more irritated to see how hard he was to please. Getting him to be entirely satisfied felt impossible. I felt that since he doesn't see certain changes in me, I have to see them all alone. Eek. I sometimes wanted to remind him, "Hi, I'm young and I'm not totally crazy—appreciate me a little." Is that so wrong to want? I don't drive forty-four miles round trip to then be unappreciated. I'd prefer not to spend his birthday in a strip club with pizza on my lap either, but on his day of birth, I tried to accommodate.

Since it was a holiday weekend, I had every ex up my ass with promises of this and that and I had to say, "Go away. I'm picking balloon colors. I'm a committed female. Stop the harassment—I'm sitting knee deep in birthday cards because even this decision is mind boggling." To keep this PG, I won't mention it, but any female knows how competitive males are when they try to wear you down. "Go away, I'm sending my boyfriend gifts while finding out that, in his relations category, is baby mama number two."

Baby Mama 2. For the first time ever, I was tempted to look. She was just a click away. I came across her on Google. Why Google gods, why? They offer too much information. While trying to figure out Rhode Island zip codes, she came up. I suddenly felt a burning pain to get a look at this impregnated mystery woman who wouldn't stop Facebook taunting me. I logged in to Facebook and typed her name. I saw we had thirty friends in common—that, and a lover apparently. I also saw she was Facebook friends with his daughter. The daughter for whom I made a seven pound carrot cake, and *we're* not Facebook friends.

After the seven pound carrot cake sat in the fridge for his distaste in coconut and her distaste in carrot, I pushed down my hurt feelings. I knew to go with chocolate. It's unusual to find someone who dislikes chocolate. When you find yourself suddenly Facebook creeping exes, making cakes for former children you're afraid to run into, and clicking gifts for your other through online shopping, you're committed. Whether I really want to admit it or not, something has happened here.

On this holiday weekend, I was dodging offers from perfectly adequate men, dodging bribery, dodging vacations, and dinners; this was unknown territory. I think I liked myself better when I would go away for a weekend on a whim, or say yes to plans no matter how ridiculous they could turn out, as opposed to finding ways to reach my lover.

And, alas, here I was, wondering yet again how I got so entangled in this relationship. Wondering what was holding me back from ending things for good. Wondering how again, on Christmas of this year, I would end up boyfriendless. Out of all this, I hope men can learn it is not us—the female entity—who's strangely complicated, it's a great percentage of the male species that misses the clues we practically spoon feed them. I can't help nor should be further punished for being born into the body of a woman. I am not looking to be worshipped here or requiring massive amounts of attention, but acknowledgement in my partnership is deserved.

Perhaps couples would be better off with little checking points instead of the denial mechanism or waiting for a boiling point. This is the point in a relationship where women feel justified to withhold sex and men feel shocked by this. I don't want to end up in that circumstance. Houses have maintenance checks, places of service, and so do our bodies—shouldn't there be one for relationships? A simple follow up form would be great to come back to:

"Am I the person you met? Is this answer good or bad?

Are you getting what you want out of this relationship?

Do you want to continue to have sex with me?"

Then it can be dated, signed, and perhaps even a line each partner has to agree to. I'm not sure what men would need to agree to, but I'm willing to sign and say, "Yes, for the next six months, I won't leverage my vagina based on your behavior and I won't hold you at fault for my up and down emotions I feel each time a period comes around. I will instead, accept Mother Nature and go lay myself in grass until I feel grounded again. And I will ground myself in that grass naked. Naked and horny. Perhaps even affectionate if brought chocolate.

Disappointing Departure
I said I... quit?
November 2010

I quit the Vortex today. While I admit I am extremely irrational, indecisive, and anxious around my menstrual cycle, I ignored the fact that this decision may be the result of a mood swing. I have since felt mad, sad, confused, relived, and shocked.

Quit. I hate that word. I don't like to quit anything so we'll leave it as a "permanent leave of absence." The moments we play over and over again in our minds never seem to go how we imagined they would.

If I didn't let go of my ego today, I would've stayed two more years butting heads with T, riding her emotional rollercoaster, just to prove that she wouldn't be my driving reason for quitting. I have internalized such toxicity from that place that my mental health was at stake. I don't know what came over me that morning, but there it was in a moment of clarity. I heard a voice, "Let it go." Let it go? I could have let my coffee addiction go, but I like that vice. I could have let my flustering relationship go, but I'd miss him too much. Then I asked myself, *What else am I really afraid of? What else am I holding onto? Or what's holding me back?*

I didn't expect tears from my departure, I didn't expect a red carpet to see me out, or any of my owed commission to be received, I didn't expect my brain matter to be returned after gym master's lobotomies on her employees, but still, I was partially disappointed.

It was 10:45 p.m. and I was still bitter. By 10:47 p.m. my boyfriend hadn't called to ask how I was doing. I quit my job this afternoon after our departure, and he hadn't said one word about it. I was so hormonal, I wanted to get a reaction somewhere! I wanted to text him just to say, "Perhaps I took a leave of absence in the wrong place!"

This morning there I was, forty-something miles away at his residence, picturing he and I being able to sleep in without my phone going off from work due to crazy dramas, without my having to leave at odd hours because someone failed to show up for their shift and my manager requested I go in. I pictured my new free time to take yoga classes, to maybe even allow myself to spoon with my boyfriend, and here I was—hours later—no snuggles, and pondering if I could actually commit to yoga. The idea of being a yogi sounded so much more lax— the action being of being one just seemed time consuming. I guess the same applies to girlfriend status.

Another crossroad. Here I was, hoping my boyfriend would realize I'd eliminated that toxic place for weakening our relationship, and now I just feel alone. Alone and half jobless. Do I suck it up and go back to the Vortex? Do I walk in next Tuesday for work and pretend like my dramatic exit never happened? Do I go along with this change I created, and try to embrace it even though it's nerve racking and uncomfortable? Do I just appreciate that Dany helped drive me to a decision I didn't quite have the courage to make? The free time I saw as being support for my relationship now just felt empty. How is it that the steps I feel I am taking to keep us together only make me feel farther apart from myself?

Come on, Cupid?
December 7, 2010

Confession...

Despite efforts to brush it off, or moments of feeling the wall between us, today I felt it—like a black hole swallowing me up, it. I hate to refer to Cupid here, but I'd rather someone else take responsibility. I've been shot with the love arrow.

I don't get it and yet I must admit it. I've crossed over to be one of *those* people.

Reasons for confirmation:

If a man named Carlo is making you fabulous drinks naming them in your honor, staring you down with his boyish good looks, and you're smitten but not swayed... that's a love indicator.

Carlo did the classic slip of the number in the hand, ran his fingers through my hair after talking to me about his last gypsy lover, and all I did was smile. Chummy, yes. Curious, yes. But not enough to ignore Cupid on my shoulder, sitting there harmoniously with his arrow, binding me to my lover—it's almost as if he was challenging me to go against his target. I get it, Cupid.

Before I knew it, minutes after that interaction, I'm texting Dany. "Hi!" is what my text says, but my heart is saying, "I'm here! Ask to see me. Please ask to see me!"

He read between the lines. He was at a football game and reminded me of the key outside if I so desired to visit. Soon, I was in his bed, waiting for him to come home from the game. I view that was my victory. As I lay on my side of the bed, ending my night out so I could compress myself in his covers, I realized Cupid had shot me straight in the ass. When I realized later, after I didn't make eye contact with the bartender even when I realized how good looking he was—Cupid sign.

I didn't feel totally stripped of my independence, so I plotted my departure for the morning. I'll just get up and go—my to do list is waiting, of course. I thought about my actions that he'd write off as cold and confusing.

Dates to Remember - Gabrielle Anna

"Why didn't you say goodbye this morning, Gab?"

Then I'd have to say I simply couldn't date someone who thought this, spoke that, and racked up the reasons that we were incompatible. Being his patient self, he'd just look at me with no commentary,-nothing. I couldn't bear it, so, when the morning came, I stayed on my side of the bed. As I looked over at him on his side, something happened. I looked at him and I missed him before I left. I wondered why it was so scary for me to get swept up in this, what I think I'd leave behind if I wasn't abiding by my checklist. Leaving would set a space between us, and suddenly, any gap felt too great. I shut off my pride, I shut up my ego, I acknowledged Cupid's aim, and then I let this feeling settle in me. I let it fill me with its abundance.

I have never stayed in bed with a guy, ever. The all-day spooning has never appealed to me. Usually, I can't get out of bed fast enough, and today, I finally rolled out of bed around 3:00 p.m. only because I had to. I know if I wasn't a working member of society, I probably would have only left the bedroom to go to the bathroom. I was literally tempted to call off all obligations—guilt free—and declare a day of sex, napping, more sex, napping, spooning, eating, and then hopefully more sex. Shouldn't that be a holiday? Think how that would change Americans' lives if all couples were told on a certain date they were beholden to stay in bed with their lover. No work. No work calls. No checklists. Sleeping, sexing, talking, and as a governed holiday, we would kindly oblige like the democratic citizens we are. Let's even make it a paid holiday.

Life's funny like that. Just when you think you've got it figured out, right when you're starting to feel smug, it hits you head on. Love is an especially funny and tender thing, when you let it in, when you're open to all it has to offer—even open to the hurt. Once you accept love, you give it and get it freely without putting conditions on its weight.

This morning, we listened to each other. I know, sometimes I like to think I'm listening and I'm planning a grocery list at the same time. In the moments where I've stopped and listened, stopped and felt, I can feel that "it" between us. All other things fall aside—insecurity, reservation, time apart, making time to be together.

Even if next week I was re-evaluating or causing some great debate on our relationship, I can't say I didn't love. As the bonds got deeper, I kept trying to take detours on this path; I kept stopping in my tracks and I keep waiting for a freakin' asteroid to force me in the other direction. Yet, with each little bump in the road, I somehow managed my way around it. The moral, overall, is this:

1. Admit and accept when you love someone. That statement doesn't need to be a loss of independence, control, or structure.

2. There should be a national holiday declared by my above standards. You're welcome, America. If our society can sell us products that are fake or potentially life threatening, I see no reason for my declaration to be an outreach. We've fallen for much worse.

3. Express yourself when you're in love; if it's real, then it's unconditional. Your value and regard for yourself and partner should be equal.

Swollen—Two Accounts

I am going to reflect on this account as my mother and I decided yesterday it is worth documenting to track it if it happens in the future, and for its humorous purposes. Although, had the injuries continued, it would not be so humorous. So let's make light of the awkward sexual encounters that are bound to happen to any of us.

In 2009, I discovered I may, in fact, be allergic to latex. Surprise! I was with Alexander at the time, and, to be frank, he really couldn't keep his hands off me. My Italian lover was always affectionate. I remember not feeling sexy this particular day. I had recently read from the authors of *Men are From Mars, Women are From Venus*—a good comparison. He said men are like the sun, always hot and ready to go. They wake up to be turned on, while women are like moons; we have cycles. Some of us we want to be cuddled, others want to be handled, sometimes we want to do the handling, and other times we want nothing to do with any of it. So true.

I had gone out to dinner with Alexander's mother and sister, who are both equally fabulous. They were so Boston. They really opened my eyes to the city. We went to an Italian restaurant. Hugs and kisses and wine—they were always so comforting. After dinner, his mom was staying with us at the apartment. Now, we had only been dating a few months at this time, so the relationship was still new. Having a potential in-law downstairs was very new for me. We were upstairs in his North End apartment, and he wanted to get frisky. I was not for it. The mother downstairs and my moon cycle being where it was meant "No, thank you." He persisted. We started and during the sex, my vagina swelled up like a grapefruit. This was a first. To look down and have a flotation device suddenly emerge from your vagina was not a favorable moment. I was horrified and emotional, "But, look at it!" I screamed.

I remember he was like, "Oh, yeah, it's fine. I like it."

Poor Alexander. He would truly do anything for me. Maybe he *was* into it. I can't figure him out, but I was so not into it, and nothing was going near it until the swelling went down. Finally, he got me a face cloth and was sympathetic. He was trying to pat it down as if by smothering it with a face cloth, it would somehow deflate. I locked myself in the bathroom and called my mom. She suggested I take two Benadryl, which I did. While that helped with the pain, I still wanted to come home.

Alexander wanted me to stay, his mother knew nothing about the episode, and I was ready to drive my ass to the ER. I decided on going home despite everyone's resistance.

"Alexander, I have a thirty minute window to get home before this Benadryl kicks in. Your patting on my genitals does not suffice!"

On my way home, I tried to stop at what I thought was a hospital, but no luck. I wasn't thinking clearly due to panic. I was standing outside a fire station while my flotation device made my mind all flustered. Once I made it home, my mom—also horrified—had me pose for phone photos because she couldn't believe the size of my vagina. Great. Yet she fails to take pictures of me when I look normal or in what I would consider appropriate circumstance. Then, the following day, with a visit to the gyno, we found out I should stay away from latex condoms.

Experience Number Two; yes, there is a second one.

This was with my current lover, Dany. I like the sound of "lover," it sounds somewhat risky and romantic all at once. He'd had quite a turn around. We went from "untitled" to "boyfriend" back to "untitled" to "broken up" and now to "lover." Don't ask him what he'd call me right now, because he is currently passive-aggressively mad at me for writing two-page emails to him each time a mood swing of mine bubbles up in our relationship. We didn't seem to do well in the summer months. Every summer, he spent more time with Baby Mama Number Two, and then he wondered why I didn't want to get together on my "scheduled" days.

This incident happened about two weeks ago. I never take antibiotics or medicines, but after trying to beat a sinus infection the "natural" way, I gave in and asked for the drugs. They put me on a high prescription, so high that it gave me a dreaded yeast infection. As a woman with a more complex mind, and an even more complex genitalia, I have to deal with these things.

Now it's possible the incident was yeast related, or even condom related, but regardless, I had Swollen Vagina Number Two. I had hoped my ginormous vagina would be a one-time experience. At least during this episode, I was able to keep calm. He reacted much more positively; both of these men handled themselves with composure, although his reaction was more tactical. He is such a Sagittarian and such a type A personality. The very A = B = C man.

He said, "Gab, girly, the reason your vagina is swollen is because the angle of my penis and the counts of the thrusts..." he continued to explain in his left-brained manner. He always had a theory or procedure for how things worked, apparently even for swollen vaginas. I let him lecture as I was in no mood to debate, even though I blamed the yeast infection and one of the supposedly "non-latex" condoms.

Besides, for the most part, I enjoyed listening to him as he was usually very wise when he opened up. "Girly, I'm coming at you like this. There is friction, there is heat, there is swelling."

I stared at him, waiting to see how long he'd go on with this and what other reasons he'd pull out next. He can explain, but he couldn't reason with a woman whose vagina is growing in close comparison to her head size.

The next day, after tossing and turning all night, I thought I would be relieved to see a non-swollen vagina. Nope, it was still swollen. That being the case, I decided to lay on the porch with a frozen bag of edamame, sunned myself while listening to Diana Ross, and tried to figure out if this whole mess was a "sign" for the end of my relationship with him. An allergy, a sign, a scientific mystery. I do this sometimes—looking for answers in unusual places. What was my vagina trying to tell me? What was my Sagittarian lover not telling me? I knew something was up with us to make me react this way and cause me so much pain. Because of this, I said my goodbyes; goodbye porch, goodbye lake, goodbye mysterious birds. I even went to say goodbye to our cute garden but then I thought, *F**k that.* I wanted to see how the plants turned out, so I canceled out my grapefruit of a vagina being a "sign" and decided to water the garden instead. We were knee high in cow poop to get these plants planted, how could I walk away on my blossoming little beings? While watering... in the nude... with frozen edamame on my genitals, I realized the neighbor who was also gardening... in clothes... could probably see me if I could see him. He now literally knows how I scape my bushes!

These are the two documented accounts of unflattering moments that can surely arise in sex, and the reactions that followed. My boyfriends seem to handle the issues better than I do. However, if their penis, instead of inflating, suddenly shrunk to a little pea after intercourse, would they then be so casual? Could Dany actually agree with me if I told him his penis was the size of a pea now due to the suction of my vagina and the expelling of his penis? I think not.

Lessons of Love
November 17, 2011

Today has given me quite the perspective.

It's amazing how you can teach people how to treat you. Another thing on my mind is how differently people can view the same situation, and how couples can have two entirely different views of love or their relationship.

Steve used to tell me he felt that loving his wife meant providing for and taking care of her, so he worked all the time to support their lifestyle. She ended up cheating on him, and he said the biggest thing he had to accept afterward was that her view of love was in companionship, which he had neglected.

Those lines of miscommunication leave me wondering,

How much of love is just satisfying a deficient need in the other?

How much of love is bringing out a side to them only opened through your interaction? Can there be all kinds of love, or do you only fall in love once? What if our ways to love are too different?

In my life, I've been very fortunate. I've had a few people love me deeply and unconditionally, and these people were all exceptional. They slowly helped me start to give that same remarkable love to myself.

More specifically, I was really feeling the depths of what I did to Dany and how fragile love is. I shouldn't be surprised at where we're at now. I threw up every obstacle in the road to detour us, I stopped at every path, and now I'm left at a crossroads I created. I've known two things all along—two things that have weighed heavily on me—I just didn't know my feelings on each reality:

1. I knew he loved me

2. I knew that, to love him back—to let myself fall in love—meant sacrificing my perception of love.

Both of these didn't entirely make sense to me. Instead I did what I wanted, I acted on impulse—for us and against us.

A part of me would like to go back and see where we would be now without all the chaos. Love has always stirred many questions within me and intrigued my mind instead of my heart. Yet every conclusion I ever come to has never been totally satisfying. I've often had people love me easily and it made me uneasy. I wondered how they could see me, really see me. How much of them truly loved me, or did they just love the idea of what we could be? I sometimes wanted to shout about it stubbornly, "How can you love me when it took me eighteen years to love myself unconditionally and I'm still working on it?" As flattering as it is, I think it's harder to let people love you than it is to love yourself. I've been blessed in that sense, but it can also feel too dense, too permanent.

I think often about doubts I kept feeding myself, but somehow walls fell down and now I'm left standing alone. Today, when I saw him,

I held on to pieces of us that had already fallen apart. I wanted to hug him and tell him I love him because, suddenly, it felt natural.

In love.

Love, lover, loved, loving.

It seems that to love takes courage, but to be loved takes strength.

Which would you rather be? Or is it safe to dangle on the in-betweens?

From Harmony to Hopeless
December 8, 2011

Today, the universe and I weren't in unison. Despite my irritation, I wasn't absorbing the setbacks of today because they were a clear reminder that my life wasn't in balance. It was, it will be, and today it was not.

Last night, I got together with my ex-boyfriend, Dany. It took two days to get him to crack, but I did. Of course, afterward I wondered... why? I've been so stress free since our Thanksgiving breakup, yet I persisted that we get back together.

1. Am I a continuous self-saboteur?

2. Am I horribly stubborn and refuse to go down as the crazy ex-girlfriend?

3. Am I feeling that now I was in better place where I could happily share space and we could make our space together. Hmm, that one sounds nice, doesn't it?

4. Am I finally ready to be responsible in loving someone, and that someone I love is him?

We just love to dangle those exes for a little while so we can entertain either reigniting the relationship, even if were the cause of its defeat or so we don't have to go through dating all over again. I moved around my day a little yesterday for my ex. For boyfriends, this was acceptable. For exes, it was not. I sang all the way to his house, I danced, I felt great, I was feeling alive, I had succeeded, I felt good about where we are at, or at least I thought so. I got to his house and walked in the door... my mojo was already lessening.

Dates to Remember - Gabrielle Anna

When I entered, he had managed to accomplish in twenty-four hours what I keep planning to do in my mind; his house was spotless, immaculate almost. He was remodeling it; candles, new mirrors, beautiful, homey, fresh paint, the vibe and ambiance were all there.

I want to say, "Now?" Should I have taken my recent health turning around, my contentment, and his home makeover as the driving sign that we didn't belong together? I'm gone one week and the house was redone. It's amazing the way it took a final breakup for us both to get our shit done and re-invent. What is it about relationships that make us stop re-inventing? What is it about relationships that puts us so off balance?

I came in, late as usual. He made a comment about if we had more time together, we could have enjoyed a glass of wine before going out. That stopped me a little. What territory did I get myself into? What do we talk about as exes?

I felt different. He appeared different. Yet our motions with each other felt the same. He wanted to eat, I already ate—typical us. Then, as much as it felt we were on polarity, there was some shared tie between us that I couldn't quite grasp. We were both at the same Thai restaurant last night, yet I was with the Spiritual Guru. We had both been browsing paint swatches to convey our mood, yet he did use them and remodeled his house, and I had simply compiled a purse of swatches. We got in the car to go eat. We knew each other's actions—the way the other speaks, moves, what they'll choose—it felt so familiar. During dinner, I could feel the sexual tension arise. They say, when men touch their nose, they're aroused by you. *Cosmo* should have told me that years ago. Over the meal, he stared at me intensely, eyes locked.

After dinner, we got in the car and he asks a question that hung heavily in the air, "Are you staying over?" Men are so blunt.

A part of me knew I would stay over, hoped to even. Another part of me made sure I left clothes at home and took preventive measures so I wouldn't end up staying.

"Not sure yet," I said, and I hoped that, in the following fifteen minute car ride, the answer will be clear to me.

We got back to the house. I knew then that I'd end up staying, and I did. We fell back into the same routine, same motions—I appreciate the familiar and I resent it. He asked me if I wanted a toothbrush.

"Yeah, I'll use your little head."

"Here, pick your own."

I looked at the pink bristled brush as if I was staring at prenuptials. "Okay, I'll pick a toothbrush, but I'm taking it with me, you know."

Men must think women are whacked. For him it's a toothbrush, for me, it took me back to our first sleepover. We got into bed. He was affectionate, but it felt different now. I'd known for a while that he didn't love me anymore, so I couldn't decide how I felt about it. He knew me because he loved me; I had to know him to love him.

We pretended to watch TV for a little while, both entertaining the inevitable. He didn't make a move initially. The silence and non-snuggling killed me. I was wide awake. I thought to myself, *Great, I'm going to lay here and literally count the hours. My head can't rest when we're naked and there's space between us.* Thank God he—as usual—broke the silence and asked me if I was staying on my side of the bed or coming closer. He always asked; I've always liked that about him. He has never pressured or assumed anything of me. I practically jumped out of my skin to get over there.

My thoughts were racing, *Should I start this again?* After a breakup, don't you have to preform like a sex god, no, sex messiah as if to say, "Yeah, you want this ass." *I'm a little tired, can I compete? Then again, if the sex is so great, what if it makes me a little cuckoo?* He is the only man who's made me cum. Clarification: There were past orgasms—never cum—and, after penis deprivation, I could lose my shit. This is the first love of my life. I was afraid to give in, but even more to let go.

We do it. There are a few moments of disconnect, there was a feeling of something missing but, nonetheless, it was splendid. Flashing-in-my-head-today type of splendor. Walk-like-I-did-two-hundred-squats splendid. He got me with the dirty talk. I always swore that, one day, I'd say the dirty things that I think, but it never happened. I can't formulate words when getting it, though I'm honestly impressed with those who can. I can only muster up sounds. Sounds that sound like I'm ready to unleash a gospel—a naughty gospel—but there's a whole 'lotta soul there. I really thought last night I was going to start singing an Etta James song. Nina Simone, Janis, all the classics trying to escape from my mouth. Why couldn't I channel Jenna Jameson in this moment? Instead, I was trying not to belt out the beloved soul sistahs before me.

As the day went on, reality settled in. Thoughts, confusion… You know the aftermath of when you do something a part of you knew you shouldn't? Did I think this would shake me up a little? Yes. In the sheets. This lasting effect? My being grounded… and here I felt it just as shaken.

I got up the next morning. We'd had sex too many times for me to feel like leaving was a walk of shame, but because of our non-communication lately, I wasn't sure how to act. I showered. I didn't want to be reminded of our non-relationship sex all day. I felt a little odd in the bathroom because it was so different now. I reminded myself that the painters were coming, so I left the shades down. I fought my urge to sing in the bathroom, and I cautiously checked out the window to make sure he wasn't there. There was no evidence of him, so I waltzed out of the bathroom, hair in a towel, toothbrush in mouth, butt-naked waltz. I couldn't find the hair gel.

"Dany?" No response. He wasn't in the bedroom. I heard something…

"What are you doing?" I was now facing the painter, naked, toothbrush in mouth, startled. As drool escaped my mouth, and I felt my whole body flush, I half-froze like a deer in the headlights.

The painter and I had quite an introduction. I now wanted to be painted to blend right in with the wall. I was mortified. I'm *never* embarrassed. I could pee my pants in public and keep my composure. I could dress myself in Richard Simmons' closet and not be embarrassed. People could see me naked and I'm not embarrassed. However, this morning, I was embarrassed. Naked, meet-for-sex ex-girlfriend was not my ideal image. No, no, and no! I was too together to be that woman. In the previous months, and our early dating, I wouldn't have minded this image. I had always felt more comfortable in the identity of single woman, and I now cringed at this interaction. Worst of all was that I froze. Staring at them both, naked and perplexed. Neither of them said anything. I left right afterward in a fluster. The rest of the day seemed to spiral out of control with other irritating factors. Breakfast at McDonalds, what nutritious decisions can be made here? Late for first period, and I couldn't enjoy the sex scent because I had to rinse its implications off this morning. A phone call from the ex-boss asking if I was engaged and other suspicious questions. No gas, resulting in AAA and my having to sit on the side of the 495 for twenty-five minutes to listen to the power of now. This led to my missing lunch with Danielle and her hunky boxer who thinks I'd go gaga for him because he's in shape and can take me out for dinner or drinks.

    I don't know when men started thinking that dinner and a drink entitles them to more. I feed myself. The other week, I attended a comedy alone and brought my own filet—I have no time for men with expectations because of a hello. It's a nice gesture, but the way men dangle the food card is somewhat discrediting. At 5:00 p.m. when I was mindlessly eating Tostito chips wondering why I was being punished for wanting to reconnect with my ex, I finally decided not to sit in my own mind. I stop mindlessly feeding my belly, I stop mindlessly feeding my mind, and I moved on to filling my heart.

Fell in Love. Fell out of Love. No One's Ever Stood without Falling.

    December 14, 2011Okay, when did I age myself? When did I become *this* boring? I wanted my femininity back. I think I stopped caring about it because so often people misread that energy. Now, I lived in yoga pants, my hair in a bun, and I failed to tan unless I was at work and it was from a can.

    I was watching old videos of myself, ones that I used to make for Dany, aka the once-was boyfriend. It took me a year to call him that so freely, and now I couldn't even call him that because he was currently rejecting me. Love thyself, and then love others. In those old videos, I was so full of life. His attention felt good, but that was it. Now it was like I advanced too much—my brain went on information overload, and I think I was taking the world too seriously. The energy pills probably contributed significantly to the liveliness in the video, perhaps a consistent shagging did also.

Now here I was—no more energy pills because I deemed them bad for myself even though I was like Wonder Woman on them, boyfriendless because I guess I deemed him bad for myself also. I was currently out of shape and out of touch. I could accept that this was where I was at in my life right then, but I was certainly not going to stay there. I don't know why I make things that much more difficult for myself. I don't change and evolve until I have to. That's what amazes me about life. We can "think" about a year ago and it all feels the same, the motions seem to blend, the routine too. Then, when we truly look back on it, it is then that we realize how much evolves, how much changed that we failed to notice or that we deemed insignificant.

This time last year, I was in Colorado for a medical marijuana convention. What an experience. If I stopped isolating myself and thinking too much in two weeks, I could be in Jamaica with my spiritual guru right now. If I had never let my thoughts get so much energy, I could be being spooned right now by my ex-boyfriend. When you open your eyes and you realize you're running on autopilot, or you realize your rational brain started to take control over your gut—there's a wakeup call. I need to find my clarity again. Anything I've envisioned in my mind has come into my hands, so I need to go with what fits, not what sounds good, looks good, or is most acceptable. Tonight I am vowing, December 14, 2011 that tomorrow will be a fresh day and I am going to take each day just as that. I want to look at it with the same awe that sometimes flashes within me. Just so it's in writing, in a month, I want a happy, flourishing body, an awake and alive being, and to be back with my boyfriend. I don't want this resentful, pessimistic, work obsessed, insensitive boyfriend that I helped to condition and create. No. I want the one who left me funny messages, sang to 101 with me, and lay on my tummy before bed even though my stomach would make ungodly noises.

But Aren't We-Broken Up?
February 18, 2012

It's a Saturday night and I'm alone.

Dates to Remember - Gabrielle Anna

I won't accept pity or sympathy of any degree—I'm alone by choice. Stuck to watch reality TV because my brain is too sluggish for analyzing *Animal House*, and after a romantic comedy made me teary, I'm left to the stimulating and intellectual draw of the *Jersey Shore*. After crying over friends with benefits, and eating half my pumpkin pie, reality TV feels safer. The 60s had the Beatles, the 70s had disco, the 80s had the start of Madonna & other future divas, the 90s speaks for itself and here is our generation with reality TV. What kind of warped reality have we gotten ourselves into when we want to sit at home and watch reality stars get drunk, fight with each other, get drunker, and have sex? These are the representatives for American reality and popularity?

Right now, I could be at *The Addams Family* show with my friend, Caeser. Darling Caeser. Poor Caeser. He was just a minute too late. Sony tablet, games, diamond necklace, champagne occasions, Kindle, comic books, on-call dining-in was just a minute too late. When I really realize all his gestures and efforts, the guilt arises. He's intellectually interesting, he's eccentric, he's genuine, he's comical, he's just too in his head to really do something with it and it's hard for me to watch him neglect his traits.

Right now, I could be with Bradly—schedule manager, share-all, supports and defends me to no end, matcha tea date, and darling friend. I would have liked that. Yet something holds me back from progressing our friendship beyond heart-to-hearts in cafés. We're currently on a lovely schedule of tea dates, however, after the heart-wrenching feelings of this past relationship, I'm scared to ever date again. And it seems anything that even remotely starts to look like dating leaves me frozen.

I could still be sitting at Barnes and Noble pretending to get work done. The lesbian I met with the wifey last weekend now calls me her Saturday Barnes and Noble girlfriend. She makes funny faces at me while wearing her Beats headphones and I get too distracted to do anything useful.

I could be at work. Work? The thought is exhausting. Those late nights disrupt my whole schedule. There is some sort of weird warp that goes on there. On a good night, I can be exhausted but comforted the next day. On a bad night, I sulk about my wasted hours and lost energy there. Any emotion that I feel upon arrival, the place heightens. Nightlife seems to bring to light peoples' darkness, yet they only see the dark as more appealing to cover who's really there.

There was once a point and direction for this piece. I seem to be back in the same space with the ex. In an effort to clear mental space, I'm documenting. Isn't that what made Shakespeare so fabulous? I suppose he and I have that in common. Trying to make sense of the mind in love, of relationships through writing—we just tell our stories a little differently.

I have cut strings left and right, so I'm not quite sure what I'm hanging on to in my own situation. With the scripts in my head for this ex—we've stayed together, we've broken up, we've done the "friend" thing, we've been booty calls, we've been life partners, we've almost procreated—I can never decide which way the story should end. Instead, I leave us back in the awkward territory that I so despise—the undefined. It leaves me divided into two worlds, one where I go and play kind of girlfriend and then go back to my life and search for self-actualization.

In November, we broke up. Truly broke up. Our longest one yet.

By the end of December, we were having sex again. The way non-daters and exes do. It was great at first—easy, comfortable, getting to know each other again with no outside distractions. No expectations. No way to get too entangled. *Why not continue to torture each other without the titles?* we must have thought. The week of New Year's, he accidentally gave me a key. I tried to give it back, but two months later, I still have it. Today, when trying to accidentally give it back, he so coyly picked it up off the counter and nonchalantly asked, "Did you want your key?"

I froze trying to compose my face so I didn't reveal the mental debate that was in my head. Though my head said one thing, my hand said another as, moments later, I was walking away with the key.

After each of our engagements, I was left with a sex tie for the following days, tight and binding. I am not trying to rid anyone of sexual frolicking, getting all hot and bothered, and bringing someone home. If that's where someone is at, then enjoy it until you're ready to ask yourself why you're there and if it's going to keep you satisfied. There does come a point when partnership is more meaningful then experience. The act of sex will feel far too significant to be taken lightly. It makes me wonder when we stopped treating our bodies like the temples they are. We literally let someone into our space through sex and then to write it off as not intimate… that mindset is left for adolescence. I truly believe for myself now, you should only share intimacy with someone you see yourself with in the future, for someone you can be ready to love. For the ex and me, this is posing a problem. Right after my sex bond eases, we're back on our usual day to have sex again and the cycle repeats. Thus, once I rid him off my body, I let him back on and in and on and in. I am back into the grey area with extra tight bondage, and not the exciting type. To text or not to text, to call and converse, to use my key by choice or command, to stop the sex, to make the sex hotter and the talk shorter, to fit myself here then fit myself there, to dedicate myself to our potential relationship. I'm in love; I'm in it, now what? He'll swear I can say I love him, but that I'm not in love with him. He obviously doesn't understand the raging lunatic I've become after accepting Cupid's arrow. Maybe it's too much of a stretch to imagine the perfect situation. I want to do it right. I want to be beside him, not behind or forward where I used to stand. It's clear we both feel that way, still, we're always trying to catch up to one another's footsteps. How do you divide equal power in a relationship when there is such a struggle of balance for our roles?

Last Monday, I told Dany we needed to talk.
February 28, 2012

Talk… it seems we're always talking without ever really saying anything, or what we mean at least. It's ironic too because with such a loud voice in our own head, it's a wonder we're able to listen to anyone else. The way we walk, the people we date, the car we drive—we're always trying to say something about ourselves. Our eyes, our costume, our body, our touch, our resistance, our filled, insignificant lives. We look at the reflection of our external and hope for some type of definition of our self.

Dates to Remember - Gabrielle Anna

I drove to my safe haven of Barnes and Noble and sat in my corner, waiting on an answer, waiting on some inspiration. I felt like crying. I felt swallowed by my feelings. Not one for embarrassment, I sat and cried with my pile of books in front of me, and my café coffee cooling. Danielle suddenly came in and my energy changed. Just like that there was a switch as if my seeing her put me back into the reality that I was crying at my table.

Who was I? Always ready to love and nurture, she came over to assess what was wrong.

"I can't keep breaking up," I told her. "We're not even dating and I'm somehow broken-hearted about us. My heart literally hurts because I love him and I want us to be normal." Within minutes, she had me laughing. God bless girlfriends. Today feels the same. Dany and I didn't see each other the whole rest of the week; we slept next to each other Monday night and then went about our lives. He spent the weekend in New Hampshire with his precious, growing daughter and I spent the weekend isolating myself knowing that would be better than trying to be out, carrying the weight and ache of missing him. I felt like, even all the way in New Hampshire, he had a way of keeping me connected. Ever since I've felt in love with him, when we're apart I don't feel whole. I'm not used to this. If we're okay and on good terms, I feel fine. I could go a week without talking to him and not feel an ounce of separation. If there's turmoil between us, and we're apart, I feel he took a piece of me with him and I feel disoriented

Last night, we tried to give it a go again. With NASCAR on in the background, he asked me what it was I wanted to talk about. Suddenly, I couldn't find the words I'd rehearsed. I said something about living in two worlds, doing the same thing over again with each other and expecting a different outcome. The only line that sunk in with him was when I said it was awkward trying to date other people and only being intimate with him. All he heard was me saying I went to dinner with someone else and that I felt we were in such separate moving lives. We say we're not dating right now, yet he looks at me with disgust knowing I went on a dinner date.

"You went to dinner with someone else, Gab?" His surprise surprises me.

How do you tell someone you will sacrifice the life you planned so they can be in it? How do you tell someone you don't know if the hurt would be greater to stay or to go? Yes, I did go to dinner and am dating, but I was just trying to fill the holes of his absence.

I know that's why I get angry, indecisive, and crazy. Staying with him feels like giving a piece of me up. It feels like missing out on moments that are so important to me. Then, on the other side, it hurts to see myself in those moments with someone else. I meet men, I like them, I see something in them, but they're all just pieces of a picture, never an image that I want to step into. No one else fits when I have to think of a male being with me for my future, yet we can't seem to get past the past. I kissed him and said goodnight after not being able to find the right words for our conversation. The kiss was dead. He came into bed and tried to fit himself in next to me, but my eyes were already heavy. In the morning, he was up busying himself around the house—classic passive-aggressive. We pretended there was nothing to talk about.

The next morning, he took care of the pimple on my forehead, he checked my skin on my back, looking for ways to touch me without really having to. I did the same for him, but couldn't find or touch the right imperfection. Once he felt it was okay to touch me with affection, we were intimate after. It felt awkward; neither of us was sure how to initiate and we were fumbling over each other's bodies even after two years of dating. In my head, I felt I couldn't keep starting over.

After we were done, he sang and was close to me again. Maybe he now felt connected. He has his kids, his career, I have my dreams and my manifestations to keep active, and as we both walk separate directions into separate futures. We seemed to keep at least one finger tied no matter how far the distance between us stretched

Wednesday Lovers

I spent the night at Dany's last night, and a majority of my day as well. As usual, he didn't get to see me spray-tanned, the ultimate femme fatale. He got the mild, vanilla version. While he's made a non-spray tan rule for the household, I'm pretty convinced he'd change his tune if I showed up just wearing that. Bronzer has a way of illusion. Whenever I am looking and feeling like a bombshell, he's so nonchalant. However, whenever I am lacking in hygiene, make up, and manners, we seem to be stuck to each other. I was skeptical to see him. Perhaps I was concerned for both of our psyches. My past, extensive, breakup emails have left him burnt out and bewildered. I couldn't blame him. I went through my outbox last night and he has ample ground for being so removed now, for not wanting to put a label on us. There was literally one sent out every other month, and depending on my mood, they were either direct and rude, "We will not last. I don't get this," or a softer approach, "Let's be casual, friends with benefits, open lovers, best friends…?" Had I been more self-aware, I would have realized most were written two days pre-period. My estrogen was rising and I'd have a freak out. However, once all hormones dropped, I'd say, "Wait, who did that? Not me!" I was also skeptical to see him after the feeling I was left with last Thursday. I felt undersexed and neglected. I left for class still squeamish, but willing to push my time around for another orgasm. Amenable, love-struck Dany would have been willing to accommodate, *this* Dany shut me down not once, but twice, despite my sexual lures. Offering doggy style on his porch in celebration of the seventy degrees was a failure. Offering to drive to him and wait up until his 3:00 a.m. arrival was a failure. I was willing to drink green tea in evening hours and lay there naked like a sex goddess and still, no recognition. Was I stuck in the regimen of one sleepover per week then cut off? I had higher hopes for his penis, and past evidence to prove it. It is not fair to be given one day to get in all the sex you want. One day? What if I feel tired on a Monday?

I had a seminar this Wednesday on sexual health so, as we were taking notes and passing around anal beads, I sent Dany a text. Although a few peers from the seminar wanted to go for drinks from here, the new woman I am looked at them strangely. I awkwardly say, "I'm committed to someone."

They just kind of looked at me, confirming I was as weird as they thought. I felt justified in my mind. I can't be bombarded by sex for two hours and then go for drinks. They try to convince me by calling me lame, but this does nothing for their cause. Instead, I offer to drive a very clingy girl home and text Dany that I want to come over, even though it was not a Monday. I determine these two actions were the safer bet.

While the girl I drove home ended up being a lesbian, I later confessed this. Dany agreed to leave the key on the grill for me so I could let myself in, and he'd walk back over from the neighbors' once I got there. I questioned then if he saw the changes that I recently started to recognize in myself.

Whereas at one time I would never question his whereabouts, encounters and what have you, I now found myself quite inquisitive. "How did you get home so fast?" "Who lives at your neighbors'?" "What did you guys do?" "How often do you go there?" "Did you think of me?" "Are they more fun than me?" I now understand his days of questioning were not to suppress me or analyze me, they can happen like word vomit when committed. So this was what it was like… I wondered how long this phase would continue.

Of all the times I forgot to text, call, and changed plans and direction, I now realized the patient person he was. I now knew how it felt to want to see someone just to see them. We talked and laughed together. I found that, now, I wanted to touch him and hug him and behave in odd ways around him for no apparent reason. This was such an out of character feeling for me, I wasn't sure what to do with it and, apparently, neither was he.

Our greetings and goodbyes continued to be awkward as we didn't know whether to hug, kiss, high five, or carry on in conversation. Sometimes we greeted each other like aliens, sometimes like familiar friends, and other times our hello started with taking our clothes off. That night, we'd go to bed like roommates, a married couple, there was no dirty, hot sex like booty calls, but I stop my brain from wondering and trying to label us. I just accept that we are in bed together and if he didn't want me there, I wouldn't be. We talked about the day, we scratched each other's back, and then we fall asleep in a tangled mess under the sheets. While I still wasn't sure what to make of us, I found myself missing the way we used to cuddle. Of the many times where he'd fall asleep on my stomach, and my stomach would make ungodly noises, convincing me it must be a signal we were incompatible, I now realized my brain got in the way of us.

In the morning, I rolled over and he was gone. I was surprised to find that made me sad. Of all the mornings I left without goodbye and rushed to meet my agenda, now I was left behind. He came back from the gym and we stood in the kitchen, moving about our usual motions. Today we decided to do an obstacle course in the yard. He suggested this when I said I wanted to work out. I could already picture the neighbor on his porch, likely amused by us and our odd behaviors. One week his neighbor will see us out power walking together, the next he'll see us power walking away from each other.

We scanned the yard for props, and he laid down the guidelines. When he had me pushing a full wheelbarrow across the yard directing me to run faster, I realized he was getting too much enjoyment out of this. Note to self—do not let once-was ex-boyfriends put you through an obstacle course. He was possibly trying to wear down my fingers so I'd never be able to write another sporadic email left for decoding. I was later taken to the bedroom, and awarded for my efforts. Ah, Wednesday lovers, so it seemed. This now seemed to be my day of the week for romance. I was actually humping on hump day.

Angel on My Left, Devil on My Right
March 28, 2012

Life is facetious. Guiding us one way, tempting us another. The timing couldn't have been more perfectly planned. After my outburst of the weekend, Dany called me yesterday, we decided we'd talk, and I'd return my key. Before our conversation yesterday, the key felt like a hot potato in my hands. I wanted to get rid of it. My reasoning was that, in the action of giving back the key, I would be sealing our relationship as over. Women tend to do these things; we contemplate scrapbooking it for memorabilia, holding onto it for leverage if we change our minds, or giving it back as the final act to terminate the relationship. Yesterday morning, I had every intention to walk away from us. My birthday had come and gone with no happy birthday from him, nothing. As girlfriend in prior years, I got multiple cards with heartfelt messages and our usual dinner. Now as a friend, there wasn't even get a happy birthday text message. I couldn't even get acknowledgement that I am alive. No acknowledgement to my day of birth. I'm not one for gifts or celebration on myself, but a "thanks for being alive" card would have suckered me in. I thought to myself, *I don't want the house key of someone who can't muster the happy something words to me.* With technology today, one doesn't even have to remember a birthday, we're instantly notified. He doesn't even have to type or speak it. He has Siri for that. There are no excuses. Sitting in Barnes and Noble with my mind set, he called me to talk. Danielle, who's my ally and preaches the single life, was sitting across from me, and the words came out on their own, "Yes. We should talk." Did I just say that? The "we should talk." I'd gone way over my privileges for that. How was it I was ready to seal his key in an envelope marked "No return" and then he calls and I was requesting a departure discussion?

Scene two and I was sitting in his office later, feet barely touching the ground in his partner's oversized chair. We were staring at each other, waiting to see who will speak first. He started by saying I was some sort of evil dictator with puppy dog eyes, stringing us along.

I sat there, scanning him. "Yeah, but I really do love you." I blurted this defensively. Since my profound love realization, I had concluded my relationship book—therefore no longer engaging in other relationships—and then saying it was for novel research, which it was. Since my love realization, I had gone through about twenty shades of girlfriend until I found what fit.

Even the fact that I arrived today in my sweats validates my true love statement. No one goes to a breakup wearing yoga pants, unless you're a true yogi, unless you've already moved on, or if you are in love and you realize a breakup talk is just that—talk.

If I wasn't in love, I would have arrived dressed to the nines. I would have handed back my key with a, "You will never get this," poise and made my exit. Or, I could have played it the other way; nice attire, batty eyelashes, affectionate touch, and warped him in with my female presence. I could have manipulated him with my beauty coyly, and said, "Me? Evil?" Or, if I had followed Danielle's advice, I'd never have had my freak outs with Dany. She claims its better to say nothing at all—ever. She frequently told me to stop exposing myself, and just smile and nod, but that was not me.

Instead, I did the love thing. The awkward, irrational, love thing. There I was, giving my speech on how I was a changed woman who should be taken seriously as a girlfriend. "Yes, I'm here to return your key due to principle, but this is not over! I'm returning it so you'd ask me what's wrong."

He looked at me, "You're not in love, Goob. This situation will always be unfair to you, and you keep acting out because of it. Four months down the road, you'll change your mind again. You'll say this is not what you want."

Where was all of this when he first asked me out? He who said he'd wait for me while I figured us out, and now I'm Cupid's victim and he's suddenly so objective and logical. He told me he had an angel and devil conspiring on his shoulders to determine our outcome. Apparently, saying yes to me was to side with the devil. That was unusual. I wonder if all my resistance for the first year of our relationship was because I was going to love him and I had to act out first, or if we absolutely weren't meant to be together. And the baby, ex-mamas, travel time, and situations in my ever changing life was supposed to veer us off course. Were we both this stubborn, or do we fight for it because, deep down, it's what we've wanted all along? This parallel seems to come up in life. We're left to wonder if all the smoke signals were thrown to make us stronger or warn us for the explosion ahead. After I gave my delivery, Dany very casually kicked me out, "I'll sleep on it." That was his final answer.

"Well I don't want the key of someone who has to sleep on our status. I need more confirmation than that." I meant what I said, the problem was as I said it, he practically had to pry the key from my fingers. As I walked away, I knew I needed yoga to keep myself grounded while I waited for his restful epiphany.

I'd come too far to give us up, so as he stood holding the door for me to leave, I told him he made me feel awful. He didn't even blink. Mr. Passive-Aggressive just stood there, composed as usual. Not one to mind making a scene, nor one to shy from my emotions I shout, "This hurts! You're cruel. I don't like you right now. I'm an angel, not a devil."

He still just looked at me—no commentary. When I got in my car feeling somewhat defeated, I saw I had three voicemails. The first was an overly excited voicemail from one of my ex-boss' (The Greek God's) best friend, Jackson. This is the friend I played bartender and hostess to during his now ex-wife's extravagant bashes. I called him back wondering why he was so set on me returning his call. How'd he even get my number? He pitched the perfect sale: An all-expenses paid trip to Grand Cayman.

I was obligated to agree to four days, but we could stay as long as we wanted if I went. No catch. I could book our itinerary and he'd provide a shopping spree of his card at Nordstrom—I could buy anything I wanted. He had a pet sitter waiting if I had pets, and the absolutely no strings attached was his closing line.

He realized we didn't know each other well, but he felt this trip could be a great way to bridge that. "I just want to be your friend, I just want to do something nice for you" he said, "and I need to take someone!" He then also says Greek God would kill him if he disrespected me, so there were no false intentions.

What a pitch. Damn. I was floored. He has covered all angles and obstacles. He had presented easy, exciting news. I paused, waiting to see what else he was prepared to say. The story was he won an incentive due to his impressive sales and he had to attend a dinner party out there, but didn't want to go alone. This was why he had recently been Facebook stalking me. He remembered me from the nights I hosted and really hoped I'd be spontaneous and go.

Talk about an angel and devil on your shoulder; five minutes ago I was storming out of my exes club with my puppy dog eyes craving attention and now, as I walked away, I was invited on a five star vacation—for free. Oh the test and tribulations of love.

"I'll sleep on it," replays in my head from Dany. Yeah, he'll sleep while I endure these crossroads. I politely declined the vacation to prove my dedication to myself and to the person I love from afar. This savvy bachelor used his sales tactics, and he was a powerful persuader. The angel and devil popped up on my own shoulders now.

"No, I'm sorry. I can't," I said. I reminded myself, *Love always wins. That's the saying, right? Because if it's vacations, sundresses, and my choice of itineraries that win—someone please correct me.*

Last Doll Standing
"I hate that you turn all negatives into a positive"

After much resistance, I have proven myself quite well adjusted. Last night's drinking fueled some not-well-thought-out decisions. Overall, that exception aside, I've reached true maturity. I'm in my twenties—this allows me leeway for the following years, yet each time I fall into that stigma, it's uncomfortable. I'm a couple yoga classes away from being a full-on Yogi, the BS societal norms at this time in my life simply don't fit. I loathe to be boxed by age and gender.

I spent Wednesday and Thursday with Dany, you know, how non-dating exes do. I paid for dinner Wednesday, Thursday, and Friday like the reformed, non-girlfriend I am. That was an attempt to show I wouldn't take advantage of his income, yet he failed to see this. As a struggling college student who worked four jobs, I'd hoped he'd appreciate such effort. The affection he used to have is now sarcasm, yet he swore he wasn't punishing me for our past.

How does one adequately deal with the unknown territory I was handed? I had a pregnant sister, a pregnant ex, and I couldn't even get my own period to come regularly and relieve me of some hormonal distress. Luckily, my jealousy monster had subsided on the touchy subject because everyone had their babies and all was well. I was now experiencing regular menstrual cycles which made me an indecisive, emotional wreck on those three days, but very well adjusted on all others. He told me he'd be doing a bike run this weekend with Jack. This led me to be stand-in sidekick for Jacky. Her man was going out, so following good girlfriend protocol, I would accompany her for her night out—that way, she wouldn't have to think about him on his night out.

We behaved Friday night with chick flicks, but on Saturday, she wanted to go out. After a long day signing documents for my soon-to-be first apartment, and taking the night off, I picked up my pink bubbly and was ready for our night out. We had our usual heart-to-heart on Jack's porch as we finished the champagne between the two of us. All the relationship talk probably planted a bomb to later be triggered by my drinking. I think that was why I sometimes avoided our friendship and drinking.

She told me to hold on for love, hold onto love, she swore she saw the love Dany had for me. She told me there was something different between us, and she had never seen him bring women around like this. I was out of explanations for our failed relationship, and even more failed breakups. I didn't have the heart to tell her I broke that love between us. Instead, I gulped down the pink champagne. We went to a local bar to see a band play, and while I was good at first, I wanted to take my buzz elsewhere. Local bars didn't meet my drunken standards. I was an extremist. After Jacky had vented to me about Jack's other ex being a pain in her ass, she brought me to watch the girl perform. I didn't want to be serenaded by the woman I just listened to you vent about. No, I'd rather we challenge her to a rock off and get this BS out of the way, or go support other local bands where the lead singer wasn't trying to steal someone's boyfriend.

Between female stares, running into family, and one of my ex-bosses handing me drinks literally one lined up after the other despite my polite declination—I knew I couldn't stay in such confinement. I had sporadically quit his family-owned business, and because I wasn't quite sure what to say, the more tequila he handed me, the more I drank. Being the initiator I am, I thought Jacky and I should drop in at the strip club. Dropping in on strip clubs was like a non-spoken code advising women not to do so, but I've never followed societal rules.

Besides that, rule changes when your lover owns one. I'm not a stalking female, I'm too laid back to cause scenes, so I see no reason to be excluded. Couldn't I cash in on nights I was openly invited and didn't go? I never do things orderly. I can respect a guys' night, guys' weekend, whatever, but when I'm left bowlegged after our Wednesday rendezvous and on an emotional period, I was dropping in.

One champagne and sad love talk later, I either wanted to go home or out dancing with a strip club detour on the way. If I got more than once-a-week, designated, evening sex, I wouldn't have to interfere on guys' night. If I had a clear stance on my status, I wouldn't have to interfere on guys' night.

Jacky had expressed to me earlier some insecurities she felt with relationships, and there I was, in the girls bathroom, saying, "We have no reason not to trust them. I trust Dany so much, we can go there." My advice pre-tequila was quite informative, "You have to take Jacky by face value. Believe what he says; don't project your own stuff onto him. He'll feel your behavior change then feed into that negative space. Just know when you two want to see each other, get together and enjoy it— trust that he loves you. I know in my heart he'd never intend to hurt you or make you feel inadequate. Don't worry about his past relationships, they're in the past. Why the hell are we here dancing to one of his exes?"

Later, when the situation was revisited, I was one tequila drink in and my tone turned, "You go get your man if you want to see him. It's a public place and we know the owner. You're the one in the relationship, you can trust Jack. He loooooovessss you. We'll go by the club and say hi. Say hi, make out, then you and I can go out dancing. It's on the way to other clubs, technically we're being polite to stop by rather than drive by." Even now I defended my decision.

We got to the club despite Jacky's reservations, singing along with my Adele CD all the way there—perhaps this was foreshadowing. As we pulled up, I felt a weird sensation—not butterflies but a feeling in my stomach that made me recognize something was about to happen. Parking in the lot, we saw Jack. He was on his way out, which likely had Jacky relived.

"Gabby wants to see Dany. Let's go in," Jacky said. Suddenly she was confident with this decision and I suddenly was not. We walked back inside with Jack and sat in the VIP section with Dany. I instantly felt something was off as I sat down with him, having to readjust. I didn't even say hi. I couldn't mutter the words because my stomach was upset. Typical, confusing me. I crashed the strip club and then didn't acknowledge the ex-significant other I came to see. I suddenly couldn't even form the word hi.

As we went down to the bathroom, I still had a good drunk going. I didn't have time to determine or evaluate if we were making a wrong decision. While sitting with Dany, he was rude and sarcastic. *Sigh.* When men are like that, it's so unattractive. If I was more submissive or more of a manipulator, I would have just made out with him regardless to prove a point—to show that I could crash the strip club successfully. This would not only have silenced his sarcasm, but also would've satisfied my carnal desire—Jacky and I could've been on our way.

Just as I was ready to surrender, the worst thing that could happen, did. A girl came over and sat on Jack's lap. Not good. I could feel Jacky fuming. I thought the girl looked familiar, but I think everyone looks familiar. This woman was looking at me dead on like she wanted to eat my firstborn; still in my aloof state I was unfazed. Looks like that don't shake me. I thought this was just equivalent to dogs sniffing each other's butts or establishing alpha status. I looked back at her and smiled.

I figured that'd let her know she could be alpha for all I cared. I looked back at Jacky, and as the Sicilian side started to fume out of her, I realized what and whom we were dealing with.

Here we were: Baby Mama Number Two, Jack, Jacky, myself, and Dany VIPs at the club. This scenario I hadn't considered. There are many worse ways I could've handled myself. They flashed through my head, but I let them pass. I kept composed. Unsure of why Baba Mama Number Two would taunt me from atop Jacky's hubby's lap, I didn't want a riot to break out.

With my back to Dany, I grabbed Jacky and said, "Let's go. I didn't picture this one!" It was all too Maury status for my liking. I had yoga early the next morning. I couldn't get entangled. Unfortunately, while I was calm, Jacky wasn't. I had to, uncomfortably, accept her reasonable fuming on our long ride out of Rhode Island. Between the depressing Adele music and her scolding herself, me, and the boys all I kept thinking was, *How should I feel?* Buzz still buzzing, Adele and Jacky still screaming, I went into my own mind to reflect.

Today I signed over for my first apartment. I had the choice between a new apartment and no sex life or a sex life and no apartment. Could I ever get it completely right? I loved Jacky too much to argue, and I had broken the golden rule of strip club drop-ins. I didn't have a leg to stand on. I felt terrible for putting someone I so appreciated in a bad position. She and Jack had always had open arms and loving hearts for me. I'd never want to make them uncomfortable, and the situation unsettled me. I tuned her out with visuals of my future as a cat lady. This seemed much better than being a third baby mama. I'm too giddy; I'd never be accepted by the other baby mamas.

As I dove into the images of our non-future, I wasn't totally convinced we were over. I tried to convince myself Dany and I would never speak again, but I didn't believe it. Would I ever date again? Cats kept multiplying in my household instead. Despite my suspicions of them, I knew they'd make for easy company. There were no more excuses to make with my relationship—I'd paid my dues, that was evident. The torture and payback were over. My outrageous nails were gone, I didn't set foot in gyms—even to teach—as those places seemed to breed too much infidelity. My only workouts were with yogis and that was purely for spirituality versus exercise. I checked out more women than men; correction—I checked out only women. I didn't charge my phone to avoid contact from overbearing "we're just friends" males who meant well. I lived in bland stretchy pants ninety percent of the time. I didn't wear makeup anymore. I was like a week in on my prenatals so I could get a consistent period. I was packing on the boyfriend layer without the comfort or protection of a boyfriend—just the comfort of a sweet tooth. What the hell else could I do for this nonunion ship?

A couple months ago when I really believed in us I was even wearing my own engagement ring I bought myself. I wore it proudly. It was delightful. I gave myself a promise ring for our sake, for my dedication. That is until my massage therapist kept it and said, "Gabrielle you're far too independent, and far too good a woman to purchase your own engagement ring. Even if it's in the name of keeping men at bay. Stop punishing yourself because of your ex. Move on!" Blessed Capricorns. I was numb to the situation with Dany, but arguing with Jacky at 1:00 a.m. grew exhausting. This scenario was familiar; all too often, girlfriends will throw away a friendship if it compromises a relationship, while it seems to be just the opposite for males. Maybe that's because males typically have more of a pack mentality. I knew Jacky and I would now never be the same again either.

I dialed Danielle's number, as she always has something good to say, but I got no answer. My final drunk dial around 1:00 a.m. went to my mother. It's so cliché, but moms are supposed to know better. My competitive side was practically willing myself to be shuttled to Rhode Island. My small ego was yelling at me for being so suppressed, "You already look like a crazy girlfriend, you might as well be one. Go over there! Get an explanation. Why is his ex working at the club? Why is she there as a mother?"

On the other hand, my rational self, gave a different argument, "Well, I gave up my key; bombarding or breaking in at two a.m. are not my style."

"Send a bitter text, drunk dial 'til he answers."

"Do you really want to decode drunken texts in the morning? Do you really want the final act to be you acting like a cyber-stalker? Do you really want to drunk dial your ex?"

"But… you can't let Ericka win…"

My little ego knew this one had potential to get a reaction. I contemplated this for a second. My rational self-deleted his number. From spooning Wednesday and Thursday, prancing around in his sweatshirt Friday, to breakup and write off on Saturday. Boy, these non-relationships were wild.

The next day at Sunday dinner, Jack quoted Dany saying that they both agreed Ericka was crazy. "He said she's a crazy ex for acting how she did." Yet, as time stands, Jacky was now friends with her, and the crazy ex spent more time with the three of them than I did. Go figure. I was starting to see a pattern for him. Perhaps the history of crazy exes was no coincidence. This passive-aggressive behavior did something to our poor psyches. Nevertheless, I didn't care that they both agree she's crazy—it didn't explain why she was working there. A night wasted. A restful sleep wasted. I ended up on Google at 2:00 a.m. researching what breeds of cat make the best companions. When I asked my neighbor about it, she told me not to get too many cats because they'll eat me when I die. Unfortunately, I didn't think I could get my landlord to agree to multiple dogs; they were a cat-loving family and I supposed I didn't quite trust them either. Dany said I had a way of turning all negatives into a positive; I'd now have the animals to prove it. So, I didn't get to play my role as Doctor Love, but Dr. Dolittle looks more promising anyway.

Period, Negative Test: The Story of My Not-So-Immaculate Conception
September 25, 2012

Today and yesterday were quite unusual. Between my reactions, my mood swings, and others' reactions, I found myself in a middle state.

In a majority of my relationship with Dany, we relied on the pull-out method for contraception; an OBGYN's nightmare I'm sure. It seemed that, in my adolescence, I thought you could get pregnant even from a high five, then, when I started having sex I seemed to ironically think just the opposite. "Well you can only get pregnant on the window of these three days, and then this has to happen, and then that." For a young adult who gets a period every four months, the pull-out method felt sufficient. I'm not sure how this started. Perhaps I felt excused by my irregular periods at one time, perhaps due to my latex allergy. We somehow found it reliant. Acceptable. Fail proof.

Dates to Remember - Gabrielle Anna

For much of our relationship in the course of two years, I'd constantly get an anxiety-ridden feeling of becoming pregnant. I'd get a period every couple months, and even so, I'd find myself stopping by the Dollar Tree each time it didn't show up. I'd be panicked about the test results, negotiating with God, being absolutely convinced in some moments that it was going to happen. I'd plead, "Oh no, now I'm really pregnant. Shit. Don't pick me Mother Nature, not yet!" I never was. Part of me had the worry, and the other part of me was worried in never getting pregnant. It was a funny line to walk as a woman if, at one point, you wanted to get pregnant. I certainly didn't want to get pregnant, but with all those babies around me, and my non-compliant cycle, I'd sometimes find myself wondering, *Someday... right?* On the rare occasion I'd be concerned in my lack of a cycle, I'd do the test, see the negative, and be done with it. *Yes! All clear!* I'd do a happy dance and slip back into my lifestyle.

In the spring of last year, I started to really advocate my health. I found out from my iridologist that I should check whether or not I was anemic or if I had a thyroid issue. We found out I was anemic, so I started taking an iron supplement and have since had regular periods. It was a gift and a curse. Each time one came around for the month I'd say, "Again?" It was kind of like how I felt about rent each month. Now it felt like it was either here, preparing to be here, or in the small window of leaving. I felt womanly. I felt sensual. I even started sharing a period with one of my girlfriends, Danielle, who I spent a lot of time with. "Oooh, now I have a period girlfriend!" we'd laugh. We related to each other during this, and were a positive support to the other. Despite its sometimes inconvenience, I was starting to like the company. It was relieving. It brought on a new sense of emotions each time it came around. As it has seemed to regulate over the past few months, I've become aware of what specific symptoms to expect.

My last period was August 20th. August 20th to about the 27th. There were the clear indications prior, and then, like clockwork, there it was. I didn't mind them much anymore; it felt cleansing and refreshing. It felt natural. I also started to get used to the idea of it coming and going on its own. I expected this month's period to have a similar arrival time. *Sure, bring it on!* I thought

Dates to Remember - Gabrielle Anna

There was no event or flash moment where I supposed, *I'm pregnant*. Dany and I didn't experience anything to make us apprehensive.

Two weekends ago, I had another level of Reiki training. During the first hour and a half, I cried for no reason. I felt all these emotions for Dany out of nowhere. I just sat there crying about him, visualizing happy moments and sad moments—the whole thing was surreal. It felt good to cry, so I embraced the emotion even though I wasn't sure of its root. Why was I crying over us? Once my instructor laid her hands on me, I felt comforted. It instantly subsided the tears and made me feel grounded again. The only unusual sensation was when she put her hands over me, I got an image of a fetus. A flash of a baby. It was odd, but I wrote it off. I thought I was in a trance-like state, so my subconscious just took a journey and got lost. Really lost. Like, ten years into the future lost.

As the date of the 20th approached, I felt different sensations that I related to a cycle. Irritability? Check. Being an absolute bitch? Check. Odd sleep cycles? Check. Frequent urination? Double check. Cravings—for red wine, for companionship? Check. Fatigue? Check. Drinking caffeine was either like throwing a brick at a brick wall, or like crack in my system. Nothing seemed out of the ordinary. Then, they came at full force. So horny I could freak the f**k out? Check. Amazing orgasm? Check. Isolation and anxiety? Check. Those were the worst symptoms. My body went through its usual motions, and I accepted it all a part of a soon to be flow.

September 20th-24th.

Still no flow, just spotting. Spotting? Red flag number one. I've never had spotting, especially not like this.

I had a high body temperature. So high in fact, I was having a hot flash. Red flag number two. Walking around with a body thermostat of over one hundred was unusual for me. Was I suddenly hot blooded?

Yesterday, when I went by Dany's office to get my key, he asked about my period.

Nothing. No concern, no fear or worry, just nothing.

"Well what are we naming our baby? I'm running out of names"

Go figure that in all the times I wasn't even menstruating and I'd freak myself out over false pregnancies, and now I'd have a flow somewhat consistently and I was cool, calm, and collected on its sudden absence.

Often, in the past, when Dany and I had even joked about this incident, I could see the torment of its reality. Suddenly he was inquisitive about my period being MIA. This time, he wasn't so apprehensive.

"Okay, mama!" The words rolled off him so insouciantly that it startled me a little.

I drove to Jonathan's, my yogi companion, tui na trainer, massage partner and therapist. I drove there as one hot mess. Obsessing, running scenarios in my head, breaking into an even hotter sweat, willing my period, questioning, recollecting—every cell in my body was firing. *He was kidding right? It was sarcasm?* In our years of being together, he had very rarely made a pregnancy joke, especially one with such certainty. *"Ok mama"? I can't be! I'm not ready! He doesn't want a baby. I don't want a baby,* I rationalized. My internal self-dove into conflict, *I'm only four days late. I've been months late before. My period is still regulating.* I tried to come up with any and every possible explanation.

But my irrational side wasn't having any of it, *I'm four days too late. My period has come the past four months. I had a companion cycle...*

My rational side tried again, *I've gotten the typical symptoms; maybe they came a little earlier. Maybe I'll have a light period. We aren't trying. I'm a healthy woman now, my cycle is aligning! We pull out...*

But the irrational side won out, *Oh my god, oh my god, oh my god! I am pregnant! F**k!*

I missed my turn twice. I Googled anything related to pregnancy and periods. I read the posts and blogs related to cycles. Google needs more specifics, every PMS symptom happens to be a symptom of pregnancy also.

I started putting together possible reasons for why I could be pregnant, for why I wasn't, for I could be again. Now I was convinced. As I neared Jonathan's, I pulled myself together and tried to put the thought of being pregnant out of my head. I tried to block out the anxiety. During my session with Jonathan, my mind raced in and out of conscious thoughts. Finally, when I had found peace and calm, he ended the session and I went upstairs. Just as I had reached the conclusion that I wasn't pregnant and that this too would pass, I walked over to Jonathan, beaming in my revelation.

"Gabrielle, I've worked on this and that with your body today, but something was drawing me to your stomach. It was so active and alive today. Almost like what we've talked about with the belly having a second brain, and—especially for you—being a place of energy. I'd love to do my next work focused on your belly."

I tried to write off his commentary. It was coincidence. I felt great. I felt fine. I was fine. Again, I walked on the line of conviction and unacceptance. I was happy right then, would I be that happy if I were pregnant? No, no way.

I hugged Jonathan goodbye and walked out to my car, barefoot. If I were pregnant, I wouldn't feel so serene, so one with the earth. I'd be terrified for such a surprise. I was happy, I felt lively, I felt connected to nature. Suddenly my brain switched; I ran to the nearest CVS to ease my anxiety, to figure out how I'd tell Andy and again I was in a Google panic. I needed answers *now*! With shaky fingers I bought the $23 pregnancy test to be sure, and I ran to the nearest Starbucks thinking, *Decaf coffee if I am pregnant, a bottle of wine if I'm not.*

While I sat in the bathroom—ready to throw up or pass out—I was convinced I was pregnant. This was really it. This was really it. I was going to know for sure if I was pregnant while in a Starbucks bathroom. 1 minute passed. The test proved to be negative. Negative? I didn't know if I was relieved of baffled.

On the ride back, I praised my life. I was happy. I was calm. I was, thankfully, not pregnant. I went to the market to get our typical Monday night groceries for the dinners I made. That night, I decided on a Thai dish to awaken the senses.

That night, Dany came home and I shared with him the story. With all the information I expressed, he was half convinced that I was pregnant. "Well, what if you took the test too early, Gab? We don't use protection." However, he took the news surprisingly well for thinking I was pregnant. First, for most of the night, we joked about it. He picked on me, sarcastically and loving. Still, his being well adjusted made me a little insecure each time I said, "Seriously, I'm not pregnant!"

In the morning I woke up, still period-less. I found myself moving around the house, cautious, as if pregnancy was contagious. There was one side of me that believed there is no f**kin' way I was pregnant, and the other saying, "No, Gab, this time you really are—surprise! You wanted to take your vitamins, you healthy bitch."

Who was that voice? That voice was not my usual subconscious. She is rational; she is the root of me. She would not see a false negative pregnancy test and tell me not to believe it. She's not this irate.

As I made my breakfast and went about my usual motions, Danys reaction was incredibly accepting and something I didn't expect. Before my walk outside he said, "Hon don't wear those headphones, watch out for cars. You don't want to kill two people, you know, if you're pregnant!"

If that wasn't enough, he added, "Girly, you can't eat oatmeal—what are you thinking? It's not on our blood type list!" He had commented on my relationship with oatmeal before, but this time, he kept pressing the issue. "If you're going to follow the blood type diet, you need to follow it one hundred percent, Gab."

It didn't stop there. "Look mama, I've got the dishes. Go eat! You must be hungry" Even in the bathroom, when he did a passing by glance and saw me drinking coffee, he shouted, "Decaf, honey. You know how I feel about caffeine!"

I thought because I was peeing, that would be the last of it. Nope, he felt no shame coming into the bathroom, as we usually carried on whether one of us was on the toilet or not.

"Gabrielle, I think it's time you gave up caffeine for good. Caffeine takes you up, Gab, then it can cause a crash. It exhausts the system. You may not be pregnant, you could just be in a caffeine catabolic state, and that's serious."

Did he know something I didn't? The look he had on his face reminded me of one of the neighbors I knew growing up on the Cape. She would hold a huge magnifying glass and either put salt on slugs or examine all the scary, creepy crawlers under the lens. I would look at these daddy long legs in terror. I now knew how they felt looking up at us. I felt like I was being observed right then, and I could imagine I looked quite peculiar. I prayed that, in that moment, Mother Nature saw my suffering and snapped her fingers to grant me my period. It worked like that, right?

As the day went on, I saw a new side to him. Was he kidding? Was he psychic? Was this ease and support? Was this a Freudian defense mechanism? Was he panicking and trying to ease his own angst?

Watching him walk around and be so accommodating was hard to take. He had always been a nurturer, but I couldn't read his heightened expression. I thought about what pregnancy would mean. I had to think positively in case I was going to get a positive test result. I had not once thought about this in our relationship before, so I looked at it with an open mind and pictured how I'd act:

"Sorry, I can't come to work—I'm pregnant."

"Sorry, I can't go out—I'm pregnant."

"Sorry, I don't feel guilty about eating two dark chocolate bars—I'm pregnant."

"Sorry, I don't have to answer about my relationship status—I'm pregnant."

I started to see the positives with that possibility. That scenario had never occurred to me before. I had never once pictured myself pregnant, especially not together with someone. Sure, growing up I'd get a far off view of me impregnated, but it was a distant fantasy of conception. It was an image of planned motherhood, one that I felt Mother Nature would just drop in on me, like handing me a gift.

Dates to Remember - Gabrielle Anna

I remembered when Rose and I would talk about this growing up. She could always envision herself with a husband—the ideal, wonderful mate—but rarely a child. I always saw myself as a mom very clearly, but rarely with a man. Of course, logically, I knew there would be a father, but I just never could conceive the idea of an ideal mate and what that would look like.

I started to picture a life predetermined for me, one with a set direction to simply love another. I knew that, one day, I'd walk that path, dedicated. Instead of being responsible for myself about which direction to take at every fork in the road, I'd now have a set direction with higher purpose.

Whether it was my instinct as a woman, or the love I always sought from my own mother, I felt a natural inclination to love. Growing up, I'd cherished dolls and Barbies until my parents took them away. Shortly after that happened, I nannied and reared other peoples' children. Would I mind if my future started earlier then I imagined?

I could truly delve into myself for the next nine months. I could finally attend all the yoga classes I wanted; Yogi for me and the baby, it's a must! Maybe Dany would even join as he was generally agreeable. I wouldn't be force-fed food or alcohol to have somewhat of a social life—sorry, pregnant! I wouldn't have to conform to societies ideals for a twenty-three-year-old. I wouldn't have to feel like a hermit with my need to introvert. "She's pregnant. Let her recharge." I could read and write for hours and feel my emotions wildly without anyone's speculation or my own brain telling me to do something productive. I wouldn't have to question the status between me and Dany; there would be interaction for the next eighteen years, whether we were a co-parenting item or not. All the time I wanted to read, study, meditate, evolve, just be, I could have. I wouldn't be hit on in a creepy way—there is an unspoken rule for hitting on a pregnant lady. It's just wrong. Because of this, I could easily identify the males in my life that truly wanted to just be friends and who had no ulterior motives. In regard to women, I could step out of the single female category and into the mamas group. My sister may, for once, accept me as she's changed after motherhood. Were there pregnant women Zumba classes? Perhaps I could start teaching those.

Was I okay with this? I felt the division happening. For the first time in my life, I suddenly looked at someone as the potential father of my child, and it didn't totally freak me the f**k out. It startled me to think I'd share that with someone. I was able to see how much I'd changed; I was the woman who once never wanted to be called someone's girlfriend, who couldn't bear to merge with a male's life. I was the woman who used to sign something—anything—and it felt like too great a commitment. As my perspective changed in the first day of this possibility, I looked at Dany from my body instead of through my mind. It felt nice to see him from my heart. He came back the next night, and my body buzzed around him. I don't know whether it was whacky hormones or a new understanding for him, a new respect that I could potentially even feel him in my cells and be happy with it. I could be vulnerable but okay.

While the next morning, when I woke up nauseous and irritable, one side of me literally blocked out the idea of me being pregnant. I didn't feel well at all, and I wondered what I if this is what I'd up for. *No! Never! I'm not finished with my education. I'm not finished with my writing dream. I have more self-work to do before I can be a selfless mother. I can't become my mother who had all unplanned children. I want to want one and be ready and eager with a partner, not be marked pregnant in the span of a second. I already had my virginity dream taken, I can't let this happen to me without my consent.*

I woke up wearing all my fears on my sleeve—heavy, deeply-rooted fears. I wanted to talk about them, but this was so new, I didn't know how to. I'd also never felt totally comfortable expressing myself vocally. The fears came up slow and painfully: The disappointment my grandparents would have, a sense of a loss of identity for becoming one of *those* women—pregnant and single, the lack of control I felt.

One side of me sparkled with the possible title and hope and maternal instincts. I'd always had a motherly instinct. I mothered my brother. I have countless pictures of us where I'm holding and coddling him like I was his mother. Even now, if someone even asks about him, I go into gaga mode, "He's great. He's a precious being!" I mothered many, many dolls growing up. I'd mothered multiple children as their nanny over the years. I'd been a babysitter from infants to children in middle school without a break, and I'd loved them all as if they were my own. I couldn't deny my desire for children, on whatever terms.

I couldn't deny my deeply embedded hope for one. I couldn't deny my sudden hope either that I would share something like that with Dany, that I, in fact, liked him enough to want to. I knew how deeply he loved his own girls, and I admired their bond. I was happy to know I'd found someone who knew how to love.

Having my own baby belly, being suddenly excused from mainstream society, and having time to bond with my body, time to treat myself like the goddess I am—a creative, lively goddess. No? Yes? Yes? No? Suddenly I was fearful to see either answer, because both would be cause for disappointment.

I called my mother so that I could reflect and digest with someone. I've had all these crazy heightened symptoms—are they some sort of indication? PMS? Pregnancy? Why was I discovering all this information about my body now? Why was I realizing that, at twenty-three, I knew nothing about it? Young women with the capacity to reproduce should know much more about their bodies and their bodies' functions.

My mother took the news well; she always acted well in others' crises. She also seemed relatively nonchalant. While on the phone, I did pregnancy test number two; it was negative. I felt awkward hearing her dissatisfaction, as if she was suddenly bored with me, "Awe, you're not pregnant, Gabrielle."

I never realized how disappointing either result could be as a female. I think, from her experience of having my sister at seventeen, and my sister being pregnant at twenty-one, she must have felt disgruntled when it was a negative. They both shared unplanned pregnancies, and dealt with them on their own, though differently. I suddenly felt cast off and unfit, even though I was relieved to not be pregnant. She probably thought I didn't hear when she said, "You're not Lilly. Go to work, then you'll get your period. Don't get all stressed and make yourself sick. You've always been dramatic." I left unsure if I was reassured or resentful.

As the following morning approached, the volley between desire and relief was there again. I wanted to write my non-period off as a bad mistake. "Where are you, period? I love you! Come back! Please?" I wanted it to come just so I could erase the feelings this situation brought up, just so I could cease my sudden, rising anxiety. I sat in my bathroom and wished for it and wished for it.

As I sat to write and release these thoughts and emotions onto paper, I decided I was going to write it all off as hormonal psychosis. An adjustment into womanhood, adulthood, or maybe even menstruation. Conceivably—no pun intended—my period now wanted to make up for its absence. They say the body adjusts every x amount of years. Maybe now mine was telling me it was getting ready to endure a baby. That, in the next few years, it will be fertile and willing. Maybe my physical body felt one way, and, as usual, my practical mind can't quite keep up with its sudden desires.

Another unexpected turn for the Sagittarian and me. While I won't share out loud all the things that this situation has caused to bubble up, I will note them for my own understanding and appreciation. As for my current reality, I wouldn't think of sex until my period had come and gone. Negative test results were only comforting when you're not burning up in a hot flash. Whether it was actual body heat or anxiety, until I was in a flow, I wouldn't be content. The irrational side of me was convinced I conceived on Labor Day and we'd be having a Gemini baby. I was officially back to being horrified. Mother Nature, please... not now.

Chapter Six

Final Chapter — New Year's Eve

Well this wasn't how I envisioned waking up. Wrapped in the arms of my lover, perhaps. Sleeping soundly on the unmoving Tempur-Pedic, perhaps. Even when I didn't see Dany and me making omelets together before my two hour mindful meditation and yoga with Jonathan, I still didn't foresee this.

The reality was that, on New Year's Day, I didn't wake up with a lover, or alone with this fabulous awakening. I woke up with a period. I woke up in a tangle with my heated blanket at one hundred degrees, smoky eye makeup still intact. Eventually I would laugh at last night. As of this morning, I had slipped into the bliss of masturbating until that bliss turned to tears when I thought of my loss. I accomplished a whole to do list in my head while masturbating, practiced my tantric breathing while masturbating, watched my brain play around with yesterday's events while I was still masturbating, and then, before carpel tunnel could take hold, I got up. I refused to slip back into my dream that was more fragments from yesterday. Why couldn't the whole thing have been a dream? Couldn't I write off yesterday and a three year relationship with denial?

Prior to the past couple days, I hadn't given much thought to New Year's this year. Last New Year's Eve, I was flying out of Jamaica and made it back just in time to be with my family for the ball drop—quite a perfect ending.

I spent the following day at Jack and Jacky's with Dany, and so the year went. As the night was approaching for 2013, I started to really value it. I never get overly excited or worked up over my birthdays, Valentine's, anniversaries, and other holidays. I wanted this day to be different. I wanted to welcome and embrace the new year and say goodbye to the past.

Days before the holiday, I had somewhat formulated how I'd want to bring in the New Year. I didn't want to party, I didn't want to be in the city, I didn't want to be with a large group of friends or masses of people—I wanted to be with my type A counterpart. I envisioned for us a prosperous New Year's Eve and then I envisioned myself as a yogi and spiritual comrade for my mindful meditation the next day. So what happened?

Two days before New Year's Eve, I woke up at Dany's. After a long and somewhat miserable Friday night at work, I wanted to snuggle and sleep in next to someone I cared for. When we got up together in the morning, he was moseying around as usual, and I wanted to allow my body and mind more hours of nothingness. He came in firing on all pistons; the electricians were across the street, he had to do this, he had to do that, he now needed security cameras because one of his manager's houses had been broken into. I understood. Most of the time I understood his behavior, but it seemed we worked as opposites. He was often rushing around. Nothing was ever good enough, and I simply couldn't keep up. My reaction to the situation was love and assurance that the world was a safe place. I offered positive affirmations about his manager. His was tactful safety planning and buying another gun. Our oppositions either fit nicely with one another, or left us like strangers.

Once he wasn't so riled up, he sang and danced around the kitchen proposing I stay and make breakfast while he showered so we would have more time together. I thought about it, but I wanted to be home in my own space. The cuddling need from last night had been filled. I knew if I stayed longer, I'd feel I compromised. The words were already flashing in my head after recent events, "I don't want this relationship."

My view of my needs and desires in a relationship was starting to rapidly change and exceed my feelings for him. Especially after our hardships in the fall, I didn't have the passionate, overwhelming love for him anymore. I went through such a hard experience in October and it made me realize I needed to direct some of that passion, love, and attention inward.

Like any awful experience, once we emerge from it, typically new thoughts are left to assimilate. I felt I wanted a lover where I could sleep in as late as I wanted, and then we could go get breakfast together and bunker before the snow storm. This was certainly not my relationship with Dany. I had chosen a lover with two baby mamas, a thirty mile drive away, and the work ethic of a mad scientist. Rather than try to communicate my mixed up feelings, I felt healthy space would be appropriate, so I departed.

Dates to Remember - Gabrielle Anna

That day, I successfully made it to yoga, made it home just before the snow storm got heavy, and treated myself to take-out and *Sex and the City* DVDs. I cut myself off after season three, and brought myself to bed loving my independence, loving my femininity. Thank you, girls!

The day before New Year's Eve, I woke up feeling fabulous. Wanting to take my time rather than rush to yoga or church, I had a mellow morning and spent time in a café nearby. After my spiritual guru shook up my life last year in pushing me to be comfortable in free time, I filled my days with it now. I was supposed to stop by a family party, but to be around so many energies felt exhausting.

As the night approached, I did my New Year's Eve shopping (suddenly I was so in the spirit!) and Rose and I planned to meet. With fun presents for Dany, and some toys ready to go for role playing, I felt accomplished. I believe that, for most individuals, you meet someone who is your exception. Dany is mine. I often got shy in trying to initiate sex or in wearing something sexy, but this was 2013 approaching. I wanted to share role playing with him, I wanted to share the reserved part of myself with him.

I took a small step on Christmas Eve, but it didn't work out. I had a very sexy, red lingerie outfit, but Dany had drunk too much at his annual Christmas party and fell asleep on me. Though disappointing, I swore the next time would be different.

As time was nearing to meet Rose, I anticipated how things would be between us. Ex-wifey and I hadn't talked since the summer. I wasn't nervous or anxious, but there was an underlying feeling of dread. We had a disagreement and with neither of us spoke again until I recently broke the silence. She and I met for dinner that night, and while in the beginning I felt somewhat removed, a shift happened. Suddenly, I was looking at her with such care, with such affection, with such hope. We sat in her car and talked for hours—a highly emotionally charged conversation and reunion. It was hard to get out of her car and leave her, because neither of us knew where we'd be from here. We shared such a deep and emotional conversation, I was overwhelmed. I wanted to make plans for New Year's Eve as she said she would be home alone, but I remembered my commitment to Dany.

As I drove off, our conversation set in as adrenaline. We talked about so much, and so deeply, I couldn't sleep. I texted my beloved little brother to see if he'd sleep over and although he so politely accepted, I could hear his friends chiming in the background for him to stay. Trying not to be selfish, I told him we'd take a rain check.

To ease my mind and all its workings, I told myself Dany and I could talk about what went on at dinner the following night. I knew I couldn't make preset expectations for him, so I determined I'd talk to him about sex and I to get it off my chest without looking for any answers.

At 2:00 a.m. when my brain and body were still on such an energy rush they could have hiked the Himalayas, I texted Calvin. Someone had to be up, and I remembered our late night conversations from years ago. A minute later, there he was, and as our debriefing put me at ease, I fell asleep, excited for my New Year's Eve date and the day ahead.

The day of New Year's Eve, I was a hot mess. I'd had about four hours of sleep and I had to be at the women's shelter. I wouldn't let inertia or tardiness bring me down. I would conquer and celebrate my last day of 2012!

Despite my lack of organization, I managed. I made it to work only a few minutes late, and one of the new girls was there for coverage. Giddy with my day ahead, and silly from my lack of sleep, I talked excitedly with my coworker about my finds during my insomniac-state the night before.

The night before, I had been determined to find a cool, new restaurant to try and a new drink to try—I wanted to do something new and out of my comfort zone. Procrastination and all, I found an event in providence that allowed you to buy a ticket which granted you access to twelve different venues and they had hypnotists, comedians, bands, a masquerade, bars, and an art gallery. Perfect! I pictured myself with one of my fedoras in a jazz bar. I saw myself in the art gallery with a glass of wine and beauty around me. I saw myself volunteering for the comedians or the hypnotist. I saw myself at dinner, dancing. *Everything looks good*, I predicted.

I agreed to meet my coworker for a drink later as she knew so many places to go and she was somewhat adorable after confessing her breakup. She had a quirky sense of humor, "I wanted to go to New York for New Year's. He said he didn't want to go. Now he's going to New York for New Year's, and I'm here."

"Well, what happened?"

"He had just gotten back from Germany, and while he was there, he didn't talk to me much, so when he came home, I said, 'If you aren't going to talk to me, then don't!' He said ok and dumped me. Before, he was all, 'I don't want to do New York for New Year's,' now he's going with the two other couples I made plans with." She seemed to take it well and I liked that she was somewhat awkward. It made her feel really real and relatable.

As we printed maps of the venues we'd walk and the food we'd try, I texted Dany for confirmation. As I started color-coding our plans for the evening, he called and I could hear a grouchy tone. I pretended not to notice, "Are you sure you want to do this? I'll get us the tickets on my break if that's okay." Compliance. Initially he had told me he'd leave work by four, and then six, then we settled on a 7:00 meet up. He was the one who asked me about New Year's after all, now he seemed quite unenthusiastic. "Okay. I'm going to the hypnotist at six. You just call me then we'll go to dinner and make it to the comedians by nine."

My nana and grandpa called shortly after to confirm 5:00 p.m. dinner plans. I broke the news to them softly; what twenty-three-year-old at 2:00 p.m. on New Year's Eve can agree to a 5:00 p.m. dinner with family? With eleven family members? A part of me wanted to be with them, but I was excited for my night ahead. I had plans. I made a commitment.

Throughout the day there were party invites from friends from work, people going clubbing, Sandi's family party—nothing fazed or swayed me. Gabe had been inviting me all week to Miami for New Year's and, being his fabulous self, he had gotten a table at South Beach and wanted to fly me down. I envied his independence and direction. I appreciated all the years of our friendship. We'd always had such an easy relationship, but still, I was set on my plans and intentions. I liked to envision how fun that trip could have been, but I'd only allow it a moment to sit in my mind.

The day went on and I continued to beam. Despite my anti-socialness to the scenes or the parties, despite the breakup story from my quirky coworker, despite my germophobic fear after my other coworker showed up flu-stricken—tissues everywhere, runny nose, and cough—nothing could take me down from my beaming. I would dodge all sickness! I would dodge the weather today and wear a fabulous dress and my new lace shoes! I would dodge time and manage to be out of here early! So it went. Everything in unison.

I purchased my yoga tickets for New Year's Day. I made it out of work an hour early, and decided to take my new free time to go freshen up at home. Would I wear fiery red? Would I wear black and be sophisticated? Would I do gold for the New Year? White for cleansing and purity? These were the thoughts that paraded around my head on my ride home between the cranberries and my 90s grunge music sing-along.

Dany called me apparently just as cranky as the day before, and I felt his dissatisfaction during the phone call. I tried to make him laugh, but there was no pleasing him. Did work bring this up? I felt there had to be more feelings brewing. I offered different places for dinner reservations, but with an uncertain timeframe and my unsatisfied lover, we left it in the air. Any optimistic comment I made, he shut it right down. I could've said I'd ordered us a rocket ship to pick us up and we had plans to go to Mars, and he'd simply brush that off too.

When I got home, my fumes and happy buzz started to subside. Exhaustion was kicking in. Even the title of unhappy girlfriend was kicking in! Reality became clear—my relationship was no different. I was still trying to perform for a perfectionist and was falling short. That was how it typically felt. Work was never good enough, so he'd say. I was never good enough, so he'd sometimes say. It wasn't even 5:00 p.m. and I could feel my eyes growing heavy and my mind growing irritable.

In previous years, as a crazy Zumba instructor, I'd pop an energy pill now and be buzzing right through the New Year, but I didn't do that anymore. Oh, I miss those days. I tried to keep my sexy vibe up, so I played some chill, wave music, I made a snack, hoped the carbs would keep me silly, and I decided which hat would assist my character that night.

The hat would be a prelude to my role play. I wanted to start this so when school ended, I could still express my imagination. Besides, after our rocky sex life in past months where I was confused about a pregnancy, I wanted to shake things up. I'd started my collection: a nurse's outfit, a school teacher, a suit, and one of his ties. The thought of trying something new uplifted me a little.

I made a call to Rose; after our emotional evening the night before, I hoped she'd want to get together. I really wanted to be with her, but I got no answer. I sent her a text, but still, no answer. There was a tinge of hurt in her lack of a response, but I tried to brush it off.

I sent Dany a text and he called me back to discuss plans. In our conversation, he sounded just as miserable as before; he had managed to carry the same miserable tone that he had at 9:00 a.m. and it was now 6:00 p.m. Ugh.

MJ was calling me on the other line, and when he and I talk, my remarkable Pisces is on the same page as me. He wanted to get together and be neutral, but he only wanted to stay in town. No! I wanted to be in a totally new setting. I wanted to be listening to jazz, drinking a drink I've never drunk. I wanted to eat an exotic dish; I wanted to dance barefoot to the drums. He was so sweet offering to just kick it together and discuss worldly topics with me as we usually would. He even said that he didn't mind being the backup plan. I loved how cool he was, but for tonight, his energy felt too laid back, too laissez faire.

My coworker at the shelter kept firing off texts to me, but she was all over the place—picking up cousins, at an ice skating rink, wanted to meet here, wanted to meet there. I called Dany and he offered to meet me at nine for the comedy show, and we'd just skip dinner. No! My patience had ended. On all other dinner dates, my typical response was, "I don't care." In the past four or five months, I'd had dinner ready every Monday night, regardless of how my Monday went. I didn't like the feeling of being that rigid, but today I was decisive. I was feeling needy and I wouldn't compromise it. As my image of the evening felt completely contorted, I realized it was too late for me to go to my family dinner, too late for me to be in Miami, too early for me to be at the party in Peabody, and I felt completely let down. I needed to nap and regroup.

I texted Dany so he wouldn't call me and think I was ignoring him. I told him I'd be staying in for the night as I was exhausted and over the holiday already. No response. I knew he read it, but I was too disappointed to reach out for discussion.

I brought myself to as close to a sleep state as possible and, an hour later as I arose, I felt like the queen of England. My fabulous hippie friend invited me over for homemade rum and asked me to give him a reading. It sounded tempting, but with my hopes still set on a romantic dinner and wine with electric music in the background, I decided to take myself out. I'd be my own date.

I knew that most places would require reservations, so I settled on a place nearby that Dany introduced me to a couple of years ago. Their menu was boring, but I liked the name Vintage, and as my memory recalled on a previous day, they made good drinks. It was now 8:30 p.m. so I knew I couldn't be picky.

I invited my mom out for drinks, but she was already drunk and I couldn't blame her for it, I invited Mike Jones, but he wanted me to chauffer him, and I was already en route. As I thought about calling another girlfriend, I saw my Deepak book in the backseat and determine I'd rather bring in the new year with him for a gentleman. Enlightenment by Deepak and Pinot sound like the most satisfying option all day!

I called Dany and told him I was taking myself out for dinner and a drink, and we'd touch base afterward. At the time, that felt like the best fit for me. The day had brought up questions for me, and I didn't want to push them down just because it was a holiday. I thought, *Can I date someone who lets work bother him to such extremes but continues to be consumed by it?*

I walked into the restaurant alone, and the maître d' walked by me numerous times despite my efforts to get her attention. Finally, while she blatantly ignored me, I asked her, "Do I need reservations here? I thought I didn't, so can I sit down?"

"Oh, I thought you were waiting for a party..."

"No. I am my party."

"Okay. Is a seat at the bar okay?"

"Do I have to sit at the bar because I'm alone? I plan on eating; I'd like a table."

She looked me up and down and then walked me over to a corner spot. I pulled out my Deepak book and hoped to fall into the chapter, or at least be distracted. As I tried to catch eyes with waitresses walking by, no one came over. The restaurant was fairly quiet and yet no one came over to wait on me. Menu-less, man-less...Would someone please make eye contact?

I finally got the bartender's attention, "Wine, please!"

She came over, "Is it just you?"

"Yes, just me. Can I get a glass of Pinot and a menu?" She came back with wine—ah, finally—but still no menu. Instead, she read off the New Year's specials: For $35, I get a five course meal; for $50, I get a six course meal. "No, I don't need all that food. Thank you, though."

"For the thirty-five dollar special, you get four glasses of wine—"

"Four glasses?" I laugh. "I drove here. I don't need four glasses of wine. I'm good at two."

"If you do thirty-five dollar special, I won't count the glass you already have. And, for the fifty dollar special, you'll get a whole bottle."

"Really I'm good; please bring me a regular menu."

She let up, and suddenly I realized the stigmas of being alone on New Year's. The ideas society perpetuates are just plain ridiculous. Imagine how at ease all of us would feel if we didn't feel we had to meet societal standards. I felt for the people who were alone tonight who didn't want to go through that type of judgment by being their own date.

I drank my wine happily and I felt okay. I felt fortunate for being able to take myself out, for being okay in my own company. I felt truly blessed to be so secure in myself now. Growing up and even years ago, I'd worry about how others saw me, and remembering that feeling allowed me recognition and gratitude in how I've changed.

As the bartender came back over, I was ready to order, "Can I do scallops over the goat cheese salad?"

"Well if you do scallops we have to charge you for the scallop meal."

"Umm okay, what can I put on a salad for an extra charge? I don't want the scallop meal. I want a salad. I want scallops on it."

"You can do chicken, shrimp, steak, or salmon."

"I can do all of the above, but not scallops?"

"No, not scallops."

"Okay, shrimp and another glass of wine, please." When she left, another bartender came over.

"Where's Dany?" She looked eager and enthusiastic. Part of me wanted to spare her from my truth, but it was heavy in my mouth and body. I was quiet. I paused. As my mouth opened, the wine assisted my speech. I could hear myself giving her too much information, but I couldn't even stop it from bubbling up. I wanted to talk to someone! I wanted to know if I'm being ridiculous or rational!

She listened so sweetly and even invited me out. I felt bad about just blabbering about myself, so I hoped she'd talk about herself a little. She revealed she was twenty-two, married, had worked all day, and was going to meet her husband and brother-in-law for a party when she got out.

"You're twenty-two and married?" I looked at her wide eyed. It sounded familiar and foreign at once, and left me feeling somewhat befuddled.

My meal came shortly afterward. There were two shrimps on the salad. Really? I brushed off my dissatisfaction—after all, it was New Year's—and I slowly finished my second glass of wine.

With Dany still on my mind, I planned on stopping by his work to say hello and talk about how today got so off course for the both of us. He asked me to bring him something to eat, so I sat and read while I waited for his dish to come out, and then I met him at the club baring sushi. Not quite how I thought we'd meet on New Year's Eve. Did the title of the day alone have me so attached to an idea, or was it other lurking emotions?

We sat at the bar, both of us quiet as he ate. I could feel the tension so I didn't bother to explain myself, I just made small talk. He felt awkward and cold next to me, and my insides screamed, "Hey, I'm disappointed too!"

After an unsatisfying and even uncomfortable time together, I was ready to leave—what else was there to say? I had no idea how, in the span of a day, we'd grown so far apart. I felt buzzed. I felt mismatched. When we went to say goodbye, he called the day just a "bad one for me.

Things happened. Work needed to be done. Today was the only day I could do it," but I couldn't write it off so easily.

My breakup words came up like vomit. I was suddenly pissed off at him. Doesn't the girl who waits all day, eats alone, and still brings her man sushi at the bar have a right to be? One after the other, I softly said words I certainly didn't expect to say. I thought I felt he wanted the same, and his reaction caught me off guard. He completely changed personas. The coldness I thought I felt now turned to ice. This person who felt like home to me—this person who was a safe haven—I suddenly couldn't recognize.

I scanned his eyes and face for something familiar. He expressed such anger and withdrawal from me. He asked me to leave, told me we had no reason to talk again, and that if it was over, it was really over. I hated that we had to be so final. His love for me was confusing. I knew I loved him so much I could let him go if that's what he wanted, if he met someone else, if we grew apart—it hurt to not get that back. It hurt to watch him cut our tie right in front of my eyes. I didn't want to move. I didn't want to walk away, and I felt raw. I stood there and cried. Crying for me, for him, for the us that wasn't.

As tears streamed down my face, I was surprised I even had any tears left for us. I didn't know the breakup talk would be so dangerous. I didn't realize he had reached his last limit with me. I stood in the doorway choked up. "No, I won't leave! No, I won't!" It was confusing to have such a great buzz and be so emotionally flustered at once. It was even more confusing to be so attracted to makeup sex.

F**k! Wine and absence are sure an aphrodisiac. I couldn't expose my insanity. A softer side of me wanted to reach out and hug him, to be what he needed, to offer the physical affection he ridicules me for denying him. The softer part of me knew that, if I took his hand and put aside my own frustration of the day, we could get through this. The angry side of me, however, felt like kicking his door or throwing myself on the floor in a tantrum. Worst of all, the horny part of myself wanted to do it so both of us could think and talk in a calm state. Why is makeup sex so good? So hot and heavy? So emotionally charged? I was turned on. I was vulnerable. I was pissed off, confused, each one coursing through me in waves. My quiet sex goddess was surrendering inside me, *Please just f**k me!*

As I tried to ignore the conflicting emotions within me, tried to ignore what it would feel like to have his hands on me, I stood there half crying. I couldn't bear the thought of being this intimate and this exposed with someone else. I couldn't picture anyone else ever bringing me to be this alive and numb at once. How had I forgotten what it felt like each time I asked for a breakup? We'd latched on to each other too deeply. I truly believed that, if we could part on good terms, I'd feel okay. I'd be able to put us in our place and be grateful for what we shared, but to see how fast and bitterly he'd push me away—I couldn't shake that.

How was it that last Monday he was asking me about marriage, and this Monday we were over? Both felt so extreme and definite. When I finally left after stubbornly protesting, after arguing, I couldn't believe how ugly the situation got between us. I couldn't believe we could bring out these sides of one another. I couldn't imagine fixing it. We'd never had an argument, and this one turned us both ugly. When I got home I felt emotionally exhausted.

The next morning, after a miserable sleep, I woke up with a period. Each time I let him go, there it was, like clockwork. We'd reached our final chapter. I'd always left us space for chapters to fill, but knew all beginnings have an ending. Even as the author, I'd kept writing us new beginnings. I guess sometimes an end is exactly that.

Memorial Day Memories or Monogamy?
2013

The rush of Monday had subsided. The sun was no longer shining a bright, fiery energy. There is a dullness today, probably tempting my inner female to crawl back to my familiar lover but I won't do it.

This writing is dedicated to all the parts of me I continued to meet, and promise to embrace:

It's dedicated to Sonya and her unconditional friendship that day—

It's dedicated to, as Sonya would put it "the three year mark of an era,"

and it's dedicated to freeing the layers of our personality that unravel.

Whether they unravel by experience, time, or, to put it simply, if certain situations release our inner crazy.

To backtrack as honestly as I can remember, let's just say the Sagittarian and I had not quite ended after New Year's. Our space apart came and went. I even bought a dog to replace him—an impulse buy.

I drove to Connecticut to find the same street name as Dany and a puppy with the same birthday. This little being melted my heart, but I knew I was just filling a sudden void.

The first day I brought the puppy home, I had an inner flash of reason, "Shit, what did I just do?" Then, after a few days together, each time I had to leave him, I felt this overwhelming emotional response. My landlord's disapproval I could ignore—or deny all together in my justifications—but I did start to feel selfish with my work hours and my lifestyle. So, after I found the puppy another, more appropriate home, I also found myself back at the home of a certain lover.

Love? Lust? I've stopped naming the "it." By now, Dany and I don't call each other anything, we just continue to call each other. When I refer to him, no verbiage seems right. I couldn't call him an ex because he'd been there and back too many times. Partner gives us too much credit. Partner is how I would answer if you asked me what my ideal counter would be. "We're partners." That has such power. We've called each other many names, but I'll save "partner" for when I know someone's got my back and is my equal.

In the fall, he had been calling me mama until he saw me unravel at the absence of a period. In the winter, he referred to me as wifey until I broke up with him on New Year's. That was fueled by the onset of a period. After our final chapter turned out to be not-so-final, we decided not to call each other anything.

Over the past few months, we continued to stay intertwined. Right when I feel we'd mastered our ability to just float along, I was taken aback. Each time I think I'd caught up to a feeling he'd felt and I was ready to move forward with it, he was too jaded to realize.

Dates to Remember - Gabrielle Anna

The week before Memorial Day, we'd made plans to see *The Hangover* on its premier night. The old me would've woken up that day and decided then to make or break plans while the new me was much more rational.

The day before *The Hangover* premiered, I had a feeling we weren't going together. When I texted him for confirmation, and he said he'd be working, I had nothing more to say. I wasn't disappointed or mad or jealous, more so just dumbfounded. Was he going to tell me?

The next day, he called to talk at one point, leaving me a message while I was at work, and I wasn't impressed. I knew if I answered there would be potential to get together, and I had nothing to say. I sent him a text so he'd realize I wasn't ignoring him.

As the day went on, I got no response. When I questioned this hours later, he forwarded my text from the morning. Was that some kind of jab? I seriously loathed when he underestimated my intelligence as a person, as a practicing spiritual guru, as a soon-to-be-psychologist, and especially as a female.

After telling him this behavior was childish and I wasn't going to play games, he called me like it's nothing. He literally called me to talk about the weather, and then critiqued my lack of conversation. Neither of us reached out to the other over the weekend.

When Sunday approached, I broke the ice and he called me, "All is fine between us, Gab, see you tomorrow."

"Are you sure? It's Memorial Day—what if you have the girls or want to do something else?"

He says it's Monday we usually make plans for Monday, and I was half convinced.

On Monday I woke up angry at him, and it was manifesting in my body. I wasn't totally sure what I was angry about, so I brought myself out to nature, and tried to rid these feelings into the earth. I didn't want to be angry, but I recognized many things I actually as angry for, all the wounds that went unaddressed. I started making my list. Did he just stick me with any hurts he felt I gave him? Are we constantly going to be stabbing each other with little arrows because neither of us ever feels quite appreciated enough? After I allowed myself to feel the span of my emotions wholeheartedly, I let them go.

My Monday went along and still, I got no word from him. I got the lurking sense that something was up. I meditated that night and felt rejuvenated afterward, calm. When I was finally ready to call him, I got no response. So, I did what any pushed-to-her-limits, suspicious female had the ability to do in 2013—I reactivated my Facebook and started creeping. While I was in the forest trying to heal us—or myself—while I was in meditation, while I was writing novels, he certainly was not.

One of his bartenders had tagged him all afternoon in posts of their bike run and binge drinking. By her eighth selfie of the day, and drunk commentary, I was back to being pissed. No nature walk for me now, I had morphed into full ram. I called Rose; she was unavailable. I called Mom; she was unavailable, too. I texted Danielle because she'd tell me the smart, manipulative thing to do. Then I texted Sonya. I was about one call away from my darling brother, so I was relieved she answered. "Sonya, will you go with me to Dany's house? I want to get my bag of clothes."

"I've been waiting for this day. Be there in ten! Screw *Sex and the City*."

After she hung up, I felt a jumble of things: amused, loved, bewildered? I'd let us get so dysfunctional that this was how friends reacted at my mention of departure. And just like that, Sonya, who was never on time and, quite frankly, often lazy showed up fifteen minutes later. No detours. No makeup. No ditching me at the last minute with some ridiculous excuse. She pulled up at full speed and ready to go.

We drove to his house—aka the middle of nowhere—and I filled her in. I felt so lucky to have her as a girlfriend. I felt this deep sensation to give back to her next time she needed emotional support. We drove along, reminiscing, laughing, and catching up.

As we get closer, she told me her IBS may act up. Now? I started to feel my own nerves too. To calm myself, I admitted out loud why I must do this regardless of the end result, "I am always the bad person in this relationship. I always feel a sense of responsibility for being inadequate. Now I want him to see he doesn't treat me lovingly. This doesn't make me feel loved. He isn't even honest with me. I can't bear another breakup where I get accused of being the cause; no, I deserve to point out his bullshit. I deserve to have a reason like this to leave him.

Otherwise, I'll keep us hanging. I want to catch him on a bike with girls from work so my eyes can catch up to my heart."

Like a good girlfriend, Sonya agreed. On this car ride, she was heavily insightful, empowering, and loving. I remembered the importance of solid friends. I pictured my future, true partner having my back like this.

As we got closer, I almost chickened out. I questioned if this costume was too unfitting. I wasn't this girl. We were houses away and Sonya's pep-talking me while I inched my way to his house. Suddenly, my fuel had emptied, and I just wanted to go home and read. Sonya wouldn't let me turn around so easily.

When we pulled into the driveway, we saw his truck and his car. The house was dark. Due to my impulsive nature, we had no plan B. We didn't even exactly have a plan A—just the drive and my poetic justifications to follow through with it.

We sat in the car, and at the other end of his yard, I saw a fire. "Maybe that's them!" We got out of the car and headed past his volleyball court. As we approached, I noticed that now would be a time for my night glasses; I couldn't clearly identify anyone. As we neared, there was no clear path. Sonya looked at me for confirmation. "I'll lead the way," I replied, not quite thinking clearly. I trudged us through the bushes. I trudged us so forcefully that, after we pricked our poor legs and I laughed so hard I was crying, I trudged us right into the neighbor's yard.

Once we approached, it was three, innocent girls—perhaps women, I couldn't totally see without my glasses. Nevertheless, it was certainly not the women we were looking for, and like smart little ladies, there were no men.

"You can take the driveway," one of them muttered as I directed Sonya and I back to our grounds. It was a slight fail, but worth it. We were both laughing so hard, all nerves had subsided. Now what? We were somewhat ill-equipped for a stakeout. While sitting in the driveway, we bonded. Sonya, who was fairly jaded and unimpressed at this point by love, I consoled. Funny how life has such a give and take. As our stake out wound down, we committed a small breaking and entering. No, this was a more minor crime. We entered, using the key beyond its intentions. However, we needed a bathroom…

After about two hours, we decided to call it a night. Sonya, so supportive, had offered to stake it out as long as possible. "We could even spend the night!" I appreciated her enthusiasm and the kick ass friendship moment, but I was over it.

I sent him a text saying, "Clearly we are over after you blow me off today, when I see you every Monday. This time I just want you to realize, it has nothing to do with my behavior." We headed back to my apartment and deemed the trip ultimately a success. Once we got back, we were still fueled with adrenaline, so we reminisced some more in bed about our Martha's Vineyard getaway for the fourth—about love, about novels.

At 2:00 a.m. Dany called. I didn't respond. He hung up and called again, four more times. I finally answered only because of Sonya's encouragement. At this point I'd had hours; I was as cool as a cucumber. Nothing could rattle me.

"I'm sorry I didn't call you. I had a crazy day—a long day. I was here. I was in Connecticut. I'm at work now. Are you home?" he asked. The once-trusting Sagittarian was pulling the passive lying trick. I recognized it because I'd used it before. This was a time when you didn't lie, especially to your lover—you just didn't tell them the truth either.

You say, "I was here. I was there," leaving out the key information of why you were where you were and who you were with. It's true, I still couldn't call him a liar, but I could spot this tactic for saving face when I heard it.

"Wow, yeah. That sounds like a long day," I responded. "I'm home. I wasn't in so many places today."

"Can I come over?"

"Right now? Why? Dany you've slept at my house a total of five times."

"I want to. I'm fifteen minutes away."

"Have you been drinking?"

"… No."

I decided that in person was the better way to have this talk. We hung up, and I heard his motorcycle pull up within minutes. Sonya left.

When he came in, he acted guilty—overly talkative, overly affectionate. He was suddenly concerned with my eight hundred page novel on my bed. He commented on it multiple times as if it was the most interesting thing he'd come across lately. I doubted my research on women's lives was that intriguing to him. Due to my recent Facebook skills, I knew this was not the case. We went to bed. I wanted to give him the opportunity that night to say something to me—anything.

I asked, "Don't you want to tell me anything before we sleep?" Nada. In the morning when I couldn't lay there any longer, he insisted on sleeping in.

"Okay, well, you need to move your bike, so you can just go. Okay, I have work. Okay, would you like breakfast? Okay, don't you sleep more comfortably at home? Okay, construction workers are here; they can't work around your motorcycle, so you'll have to move it… and drive away on it" He ignored my comments. I gave in when he pulled me down from standing over him and started stroking me. With his fingers trailing down my face, my breasts, and landing on my stomach I forgot what I had just been negotiating. *What is one last hoorah?* I thought.

I could think and be more loving after an orgasm. I let him use his fingers and because my body was so familiar with them, I came with complete ease. Two orgasms later, I felt great. I sprang out of bed and let all of the hormones wash over me.

"Dany, what you did yesterday was rude. You blew me off. You intentionally hurt my feelings. I'm not doing this anymore. I'm not waiting around for you on Mondays. I'm too special to be someone's Monday-night bitch. That's it. I can excuse behavior because of things I've done, but that's it. I'm not responsible for this one."

He just sat there looking at me. He'd heard from me that it was over before, so I was sure it was just background noise to him by then. His apology held no depth, so I felt absolutely no connection between us. I offered him a banana in the kitchen; refusing his own, he takes half of mine. This was very unflattering after having just cut the cord. The child in me wanted to say, "Take your own banana! Eat off of your own spoon!" I resisted. I felt too great from my orgasms. I felt no other emotion than sheer sexuality.

He persisted for a kiss, and I realized he was still there. "Why Dany? For what?" I couldn't figure out these moments where he totally didn't acknowledge my state. I watched him leave and I didn't feel sad, attached, or guilty.

The whole day I was happy as a clam. I felt proud of myself for all the areas I'd grown and developed. I felt different. I buzzed into work right on time; though, my morning had been significantly delayed. Our new nail tech even offered me a fabulous, shellac manicure before any appointments. Thank you, Universe. Thank you, new job. Thank you. I loved my work. I loved the new me. I loved that I had all that I'd worked for without pulling on people, or pushing others to get there.

Memories or monogamy? Memories or monogamy? When did we stop believing wholly that we could have both?

He knew what my body craved.

That can be a funny thing between us.

My words never quite make their way out to him.

Everything in my head that finds we don't work, the underlying knowing that we don't fit and really never did.

All the ways where I feel disconnected.

But when he slid into bed last night, he got me.

Fitting himself between the layers of my within.

That's what I'm afraid to miss.

It reminds me he's merely my reflection.

Of when I want to be loved, of when I don't.

Of all the pieces that fell away for him.

This week I've been yearning for that type of familiarity.

We didn't say anything to each other, and as much as I crave communication.

I've always liked our silence.

He traced over my skin, my skin that has trusted him.

Dates to Remember - Gabrielle Anna

He feels the black lace between his fingers and knows he's invited.

We don't talk or kiss or miss, but there's a rhythm to our breath.

The heat of us together penetrates my skin.

As he works his hands, any thought is quieted.

I'll really miss our type of silence.

He holds the weight of me, drawing out the depth of my moans.

And here I have no disconnect; here he feels like home.

I want to cry; I want to cum; I want to yell; I want to sigh.

There is no mind.

There is no time.

Between this quiet, I give all of me to him.

All the layers, and he slips his way in.

All the dimensions, and he fits.

A part of my home resides in his skin.

Dates to Remember - Gabrielle Anna

Chapter Seven

A GEMINI STORY

Vince was the son of a successful family. Each child was attractive and unique. His split personality went back and forth between intelligent entrepreneur who could talk circles around many, to vodka-induced, wild depressive; though, he never lost his charm. Comical and bright-smiled, he was smitten with me and reformed some of his "bad boy" behaviors. Together, we laughed so hard that I always referred to him as my abs partner because the laughter was the only way my stomach got a workout. His animations and impressions could bring anyone to tears from amusement.

Another proposed Miami ending with an Italian. Wanting to leave behind the seasons and his mood swings, he offered a vacation to Miami, but what male and female can travel together—to Miami especially—and remain just friends? He also supportively suggested I'd do great as a dancer there while he pursued his creative ideas. It seemed we were setting out after different dreams. I envied his opportunity, but had my own light to follow.

April 12, 2011

I'd been single for a full weekend, and already, people were trying to match me up again. No thanks. The whole time I was dating, they were trying to get me single. Now, I was single and they didn't approve of that status either.

It's funny because guys always think there must be another guy when you break up. That's certainly not the case. I plan on dating myself only until I need kids; then, I'll make the exception. Charming right? These days, I can even bypass that option.

It's not that there aren't eligible bachelors out there or that I'm this fabulous girlfriend—my recent exes will probably tell you I drove them mad, but I drive myself loco too.

I've been blessed enough to meet and be blessed with wonderful men. I said goodbye to boys years ago. I'll take a man-boy any second, but right now, it's clear I need to take on myself and myself only.

I will, however—for entertainment purposes—recap on the single life this weekend. Brace yourself. One weekend of being single already seems one too many.

Saturday morning started off wonderfully. I made it through a boot camp class, which I never would have gotten up for had I not been single. It's like my mojo kicks in hard gear when I'm solo. You'd think it'd be the opposite. That night, there were plans to go to one of my old boss' official grand openings. I now know why I kept turning down the offer of going out on previous weekends—the drama, the gossip, the hangovers. Need I say more on why I'd rather read self-help and spiritual masters books at home?

I felt good about going even though I was already annoyed on the car ride in. Upon arrival, the first person I saw when we walked in was my previous, female boss, Lil T. I honestly like her, but she's like a mass-manipulator and I was in no mood to be mind-f**ked. I'd done enough to my little brain lately. So we made polite in the ladies room, and then most of us avoided her.

I came with Danielle, Chelsea, and her brother Vince in the Infiniti—aka the bat mobile. Danielle could easily have been cast on *Desperate Housewives* and Chelsea and Vince as the Italian Kardashians.

When we went in, Joey ordered all of us shots. I decided on the sugar mixes with a splash of booze instead, please. Danielle and I went with our usual Saint Germaine cocktail. We took photos; one of my old bosses (the Greek God) told me I looked sexy while posing in a picture with his wife—my expression showed in the picture. Really, now? Red flag number one on why "single female" is a risky label. Couples at the flash of a thought may loathe you, cast you off, try to swing you, befriend you for entertainment, etc.

I looked around and it suddenly seemed like so many people were coupled. Chelsea texted her new man and argued all night. Great, with technology today, we can now even fight with our significant others when they're not there. Danielle was followed by her boy toy with his sweet compliments in her ear all night. He was adorable, and I wondered why the heck I had to send an email to my ex-lover stating we had no future together just a few days prior. People I didn't even know somehow knew me and knew me as a "pod." No, "Hi Gabrielle, how are you?" I was now "Dany's girlfriend" aka no name. I didn't correct some people, others' commentary I ignored, and at one point, I got a little aggressive on poor Jim.

He came over to me and called me Dany's girlfriend.

Not wanting to small talk I blurted, "Next time, find out peoples' relationship status first, and why don't you say hi to Chelsea instead of just taking eyeshots of her ass?" We should leave a window of a few days for solitude after a breakup, so others don't have to be subjected to bitterness.

Doing the Cupid shuffle, I made my way into the ladies room, composed myself, and made the elite decision to call Dany. Yes, now, while I was out at the grand opening—drunk dialing from a toilet—that was appropriate. I called him, did the whole I-miss-you-do-you-miss-me slur, literally made a sad face at myself in the mirror, and then made my way out of the bathroom. This resulted in more than two cocktails. I no longer wanted to cause trouble when I was out; I instead wanted to just trouble my lover with my version of a check-in.

The night progressed, and, oddly, I didn't know what I did for all those hours. I knew I didn't engage in much conversation. I spent time at the DJ station, though I didn't do much dancing either. I had one stalker of the night; he wouldn't lay up. He caught wind of my name and thought that by saying it repeatedly, I'd think we knew each other. It's not going to entice into flocking to you just because you overhear my name and then keep repeating it.

I just looked at him and said, "Okay, 'stache!" He had the most obnoxious mustache. One cannot expect to pick up females with an overgrown, downward 'stache. He was very persistent, so avoiding him and previous bosses had me somewhat occupied.

As the night went on, I sensed Vince would probably flirt with me, after I saw him flirt with most of the females around. He was naturally charming and an extrovert. Chelsea was suddenly trying to play love connection, but I just dodged it.

I didn't want to enter another relationship where people said to me, "He usually goes for the stripper type but you're like the stripper who isn't really a stripper!"

I knew everyone meant well when they told me that, but I'd become a little cynical to it, "Yeah, you're right, I'm not a stripper because I'm trying to do the whole nine-to-five thing and it sucks. I live in stretchy pants and sketchers because of it." The rest of the night had its usual, drunken, mini-disasters, one of which was when two of the most attractive males there had a wrestling match on the stairs with two parking attendants. I knew there would be far too much testosterone in the place; you simply couldn't have that many egos butting heads, especially with booze involved.

When I was finally ready to end the night, I sat and people-watched. I love to do that anyway, but I was too drunk myself to really enjoy it. I felt my eyes burning. It's funny because whenever people are naughty, they insist you get just as naughty with they are. The guilty love company. This's probably why, ninety-five percent of the time, I chose to be the sober one.

As we made our way to the car, all I envisioned was my bed. Awe, no penises; not my past lover's penis, literally just a down comforter and some carbs. Vince had other thoughts when he jumped in my car, said he was drunk, and that he needed a ride home from the gym.

I didn't think much of it. I think I just said, "Shut up; Tony Tone wild thing is on." He did crack me up though—must be part of his game. I laughed so hard for a second, I thought I might pee myself. He was picking on me for the fact that my car resembles a closet; there was even a prom dress in the back seat. He asked me something about being homeless, and then offered to give me one of their apartments.

He later offered I move down to Florida with him; he swore I'd be successful as a striper in Miami. We got back to his house, still laughing. He wanted to show me the apartment he was moving out of, you know, in case I want to move into it, so he said.

I really didn't see any action coming so I willingly went in after trying to figure out how to shut off my car. "Gab, turn the key."

I think I said something like, "Listen, this isn't an Escalade, it's my jimmy; I know what to do."

We went inside. He tried to offer me booze, but he'd moved it. He then tried to offer me a tanning shot from the fridge; I should've taken him up on that. Bronzing and bonding were a decent offer.

We decided to watch TV. This was what started his confession to me about how Charlie Sheen was, in fact, a great man and an idol. I debated that for a while, but he insisted he's a brilliant man. You don't tell a girl, ahem, woman that Charlie Sheen is your idol and think she will agree.

I fell asleep but kept waking up to the sound of my own sleep chatter. He was entertaining, but I couldn't even keep my eyes open. I was asleep on the couch in less than ten minutes. Once I started to wake from my sleep state, he brought me in on the Egyptian cotton sheets. I was ready for zzzzzs and zzzzs only; he was ready for a heart-to-heart. At any other time, I could've given advice and listened, but at 4:00 a.m., my social skills were limited. I was so tired I hadn't quite figured out where I was as I felt a large comforter over me.

The following day, I got to attend a baby shower. Everyone had babies, I had a hangover. Oh to be young. The funny thing is, I am the baby-crazy one, just baby-less. It was for the best, I'm sure. I still needed time to take care of my single self.

Four days as my single self, and already my ex-boss had called me three out of the four days, I wound up in a man-boy's bed offering half-asleep guidance on parents—let's hope I gave good advice. Fifty percent of me was loving the *vida loca,* while the other fifty percent was ready to chase down my ex and reason with him about why he had to take me back.

He liked clear-cut things. I could have a poster board drawn up tomorrow for presentation if it meant saving me another single weekend. Or I'd just go my style and let whatever comes into my head come out of my mouth, "Please don't subject me to this!"

Looked like we'd be going from breakup emails, to take back emails.

Chapter Eight

SPIRITUAL GURU: HOLISTIC HELP WANTED. HEALING WANTED. HONEY? NOT WANTED!

I met brilliant liberal Dominque on a full moon in November. It was the eleventh. I was at a desperate time in my life. Physically, I had a benign cyst that surgeons wanted to remove, and emotionally, I knew I was not nearly as healthy or happy as I could be. My life had turned around dramatically since 2008, but certain things were still in transition.

Dominique became my spiritual guru—enlightening, thought-provoking, creative, intelligent, refreshing, but mostly overwhelming. His motto of "let go" wasn't focused on my health—it was in letting go with him. He offered me a protocol for health, and in that trust, tried to mold me into his minion. Not only was I seeking a healthier lifestyle, I was coping with the depth of my feelings for Dany and re-identifying our relationship as over.

Dany ended things with me, and while I didn't believe it was the end for us, I was coming to terms with this adjustment. Romance was far out of my mind. Dominque's pressure for "sharing time" did anything but put me at ease. It did just the opposite. As cool as he was—as flattered as I was—I lost respect for him. I wanted to keep him as spiritual guide, a consulting confidant, but the pressure to conform to his standards was far too high. I was inspired by him, but as much as he was able to see who I was and wanted to be, I felt him constantly pruning my reflection.

I lost it. I couldn't deal with all the ways he'd "suggested" I change—or else. I ended up telling him to leave me alone and stop trying to manipulate me. I enjoyed his company and it exasperated me that I couldn't simply just do that. I learned a lot from him, but his lines of mentor and mate were too entangled. He wanted me as a walking mascot for the center and as a lover. He wanted me to mirror how he thought I should be. I am not that compliant.

Jamaica, Scene One
Spiritual Guru and Student or Bonnie and Clyde?
December 28, 2011

I felt split in two, literally. It made me feel bad for f**kin' Gemini's. How is it our minds and bodies can feel so disconnected? How is it that my and my mind can feel like two separate entities?

I leave for Jamaica tomorrow and I'm completely divided about it. One side of me can already see myself on the island in complete bliss, and the other side of me doesn't even know if I'll make it to the plane. A part of me knows the trip will be such a wonderful experience, and another part of me is already aching to come home.

For starters, I shouldn't have seen Dany last night. He agreed to get together. Certain habits that used to work for me are no longer working, and I'm having such a hard time breaking from them and staying in balance with what does work for me. Previously, I had no desire for intimacy, I didn't want to give any part of myself to someone else, but now that I have, I don't know how to move on from here.

Regardless of the fact that we were no longer dating, having shared a bed with Dany last night, and leaving for Jamaica tomorrow knowing the person I'm going with wanted to sleep with me, had left me completely unsettled. Even though nothing had happened between us, just knowing that he wanted to sleep with me felt so invasive. It was hard because, as a writer, as seeing what one individual or one open experience can lead to, I want to be open to all of it. But, as a woman, they all want to love you.

That's always bothered me because I felt that they loved an image of me, and I was completely blindsided by what they saw. So many people want to be loved, and I've been fortunate to be loved by fabulous people, but it never totally fit right. It always made me feel like I lost a piece of myself to them, or that they wanted more of me than I was capable of giving. Was that what it felt like predominantly as a woman, or just in my own stubborn head? Was I afraid of vulnerability to someone, of attachment? Not to the Guru, but to Dany. To anybody?

When it came down to it, I realized that was what always made me push people away. That feeling of knowing that I'd disappoint them. Anyone who'd ever loved me, I threw curve ball after curve ball at them, anticipating their exhaustion. I'd always felt that they were more in love with that perception of me, or their own ideas of who I was.

Dany loved me so comfortably; I felt that and it bothered me. He trusted me and saw me in his own interpretation, but I wasn't ready for that, so I acted out and lashed out and test his love.

Alexander was so ready to love me, ready to share a life with me in Boston. And while a piece of me fit in Boston, I didn't see all of me there. I didn't see moving my life forward with him because I knew I had to make decisions independently, without the influence of someone else.

Now there was Domique who I leave with tomorrow for Jamaica in a quest for healing. I had tried to make my relationship with him clear and keep him at a distance, but he was so incredibly cool, and he'd opened my eyes in such a way that my gut told me not to back off altogether. We'd had multiple signs that act almost like checkpoints telling us we were in balance, at least for the time being.

I went to his holistic center looking for inspiration and I found it. Unfortunately, I wished I could find this inspiration from a woman. It'd be such a relief to meet a strong feminine figure I could learn from without having to feel there were underlying motives.

Here I am tonight, dreading a week away together. I knew he was going to expect something of me, and it bothered me that any interest or interaction had to have obligation.

I said, "I want to be friends. Health is my concern, and I do want you to help me," but those words didn't seem to register.

Especially after sharing myself with Dany last night, I couldn't even think of someone looking at me in a sexual way. I used to feed off that. I think it must have been when I was fragile. I felt like this exterior view of me was such a contorted view of what really is. I want relations with Dominique, but not all the attachment. Healing is intimate but why did I have to share intimacy? What happened to the opposite sexes being friends without underlying intention? Why was it that, so often, males are either manipulating the interaction or giving us ultimatums?

I'm never one to go back or to live with regret, but I continuously found myself wondering how I let the lines get so interchanged. Why did I let the boundaries become so muddled? I always made it clear I didn't want involvement, and yet I danced along the lines hoping we could find a compatible space.

I suppose it was partially because I'm not a prude, and I'd like to think there can be sexual energy without sex. It's this hard toss up because when you're viewed as the object of desire, you're let in.

Dominique welcomed me with open arms into all of his space and that was comforting. I wanted to sit in it, take it in, and absorb that feeling of having someone be so open to you, so inviting, so trusting—but their expectation leaves me guarded. I start to feel this need from them, their desire for my conformity and camaraderie. Then they accuse me of being unemotional, uptight, and any other female-degrading verbs. I act out because I start to feel stuck in that space, as if I have to be an object in it—to fit into their world—when I have such big visions for mine on its own.

That's what gets me annoyed—when people do nice things for me. Because I feel like there's always that hidden reason for their extension of kindness. That's the one thing I never do to people: when I call them, it's because I want to hear their voice; when I want to get together, or even when I don't, I'm honest; if I say I love you, if I say I need space, it's with honesty. But other people seem like they act on this underlying drive. A drive to obtain you, a drive to get things from you by all the giving. I want someone who does things for me because they genuinely want to, without all the baggage.

I think it's because, in any situation, I feel compromised. To be with someone, you have to calm a side of you and keep that part measured. Tonight, I don't want to be here at all, but because I agreed to be here, because we leave for Jamaica tomorrow, it felt irrational to say no. I then had to explain and excuse my behavior, discuss it—all the efforts that go into that end up exhausting. I didn't want Chinese, I didn't want company, I wanted to be alone. There was this beautiful rain storm and it had me in a zone, there's a familiar feeling I felt last night of companionship between two people—Dany and me—and that had me in a zone, too. I felt a shift within me and it was perhaps related to a period where true and deep emotions became heightened.

I'd be most content at home, willingly alone with my laptop and Bob Marley as background noise. I had Caeser calling me five times now, and he begged me to hang out—that was someone I'd make an exception for.

He was absolutely nuts, outrageous, and somehow had deemed me his shrink, yet I knew underneath it all, he was wonderful. He was genuine and understanding. He'd burned me musicals on CD, offered any takeout in Boston, and after I'd called five different places looking for The Labyrinth DVD with no luck—he got it for me today. It was such a small gesture, but the fact that he tuned in and was that attentive was flattering. I wanted to watch it, simple as that.

I was in my team shirt that he gave me and feetie socks, and I wanted to watch musicals and The Labyrinth together. Even though he's sporadic in his behavior, I was oddly intrigued by him. He was so bright and contagious, just sometimes his energy was too expansive. When I can get him grounded, we have such intense conversations, both learning from one another. I wanted to give him a great hug and both of us fit into our spaces on his L shaped couch and debate over movies.

Yet, since the beginning of our friendship, he'd been flighty and kind of dominating in personality. I was intrigued by him because, from his name alone, many hold a view of him; from his credit card, from his connections, people see him one way. I didn't grow up with that experience, and I was unaware of it until hearing his perspective.

I'd known him a little over two weeks and I had gotten to see a person behind the image he felt held to. He told me today how he missed his mother; it was such a sincere moment. I so appreciate that type of honesty and trust in me.

But, I'm off to Jamaica tomorrow, despite my inclination to be home watching The Labyrinth with my new friend. Passport destination as an adult, number one.

Escape from Jamaica, Scene Two
December 31, 2011

The sun hadn't even risen yet in Jamaica and I'd been lying awake for two hours. It was official. Before I talked myself out of it, before I made excuses, before I justified my staying for "novel" purposes, I had to get out of there.

I'd really outdone myself on this one. I tried to leave a party early, and there were awkward goodbyes, but it was manageable. I talked myself out of dates, which was irritating, but manageable. I flew out of a f**kin' third world country with no service, that was going to take some persistence.

I honestly couldn't stay another day. The trip was meant to be for learning and healing purposes and while that lesson was learned, I was on the wrong lesson plan. All I've done is eat; out to breakfast, out to lunch, and out to dinner. Eat and sleep. That sounds fabulous until you realize that's all you'll be doing. It was thirty degrees at home; I'd sleep just as easily there with my down comforter and Prince serenading me to slumber.

I could deal with no Starbucks in sight, I could absolutely deal with no technology, but what I couldn't deal with was Fantasy Island with my non-lover. If I was more submissive, I could've appreciated this, but I'm not. If I had the fantasy or the lover part, I could appreciate this. Alas, I did not.

This vacation was way too lovey-dovey for me. Ick. Having to spend time with someone, okay. Having to cohabitate with someone takes compromise. Having to travel with someone was chancy. A honeymoon with my spiritual guru was not intended here.

Three days was enough "togetherness" for me. I was no honeymooner, I'm a realist.

I must be overly infatuated by the other, anticipating sex, or having it to spend this type of intimate time together. We are literally in a hut together, and in the twenty-four hours of each day, I can't even pee alone. We were in Jamaica, it wasn't like I'd go venture a walk by myself. I knew two weeks would be a lot, but I thought eleven days would be a compromise.

I couldn't take away from what he taught me over the past month, but it more so served as a checkpoint for me, a reminder of the necessary clean up I needed to do. His advice, his way of living, was genuine and impressive, but he'd had years to master it. I was twenty-two and my guru was over sixty. While I could share and agree to a lot of his knowledge, I believe it's an individual's birthright to find his or her own path to that knowledge.

The worst was each time he'd ask about my ex-boyfriend for the sake of conversation. He'd ask, "What did you two do together?"

"A lot."

"What's 'a lot'? Did you take a vacation together? Did you go skiing? Did you do this, did you do that? Was he even conscious, Gab? Was he awake?"

"Yes."

"Doesn't sound like it, Gab. Seriously babe, what are you doing with your life?"

He was always scrutinizing my life, as if it didn't exist until he came into it.

I seem to have a talent for putting myself in the most awkward situations and scenarios possible, then reckoning how to get out of them. My rational brain and my free-willed self are in constant conflict. My guru is all about power over the mind, what fits, and balance. Okay, so right now, the "now" wasn't fitting. Love you, Eckhart Tolle, and I'm in the moment, but I was freaking the f**k out.

My guru said we were "sharing time."

I said I was "counting time," at least until I was out of there. I thought we could share time, just not all of my time. Having Yoda trying to eye-f**k me didn't put me at ease. Jamaica fits. Helping people fits. Being stuck to my guru round the clock fit too tightly.

This was way too much companionship for me! I had never gone on a vacation with a boyfriend, yet I left with my guru one month into my apprenticeship. My wonderful impression was that we'd be here, seeing another side of the world, gaining knowledge, and preforming the light and sound therapy. Instead it was just lecture after lecture from him.

"Gab, seriously, when are you going to stop your bullshit and start teaching yoga? Stop hanging out with energy vampires. You will stay sick if you do, and you don't have the energy or the constitution for it."

Dates to Remember - Gabrielle Anna

Eleven more days, twelve hours a day, sixty minutes an hour more of that.

Money rules the world, obviously. Money and peoples' need for love. If I had money, I'd be on a private jet home already. It was a four hour flight, but if I could bicycle that without losing luggage, getting lost, and making it in those four hours, I would. I would channel Lance Armstrong and cart my ass home, stopping to gather coconuts, mangos and Jamaican coffee for my ride back. If I had thought of an escape plan prior to leaving, that would surely do. I'd even have a phenomenal ass with my return home after all that biking and squatting. I knew this trip could be too long. I mean, it was eleven days! With the money I was going to lose, trying to get myself out of there, I should've just gone to Vegas. That's a little more where I'm at right now. I want to be dancing wildly in a night club, not hiding out in huts on my non-honeymoon.

I could already see the look on his face when I tell him about my departure in the morning. He said people hadn't been able to handle this trip before, and they'd left notes the next day with a goodbye.

I could already hear his speech, "Oh, you must be prejudiced. Oh, you're not as spontaneous and alive as I thought you were. Oh, you're tormented by your mind and can't deal with the quiet. Oh, go home to your ex-boyfriend and your issues." The point is I know who I am, and I needed to be reminded I need a little spontaneity in my life, just not this much. I needed to stop making myself suffer so much each time I needed to hit a realization. This must be why they call them breakthroughs. Practicing little ways of self-control, discipline, regimen, and release will be good for me. A four hour plane ride, an uncertain amount of money spent to get on that plane, and flying home New Year's Eve will definitely give me plenty of time to converse with my mind and get things in alignment.

It is now 6:00 a.m. I've eaten my breakfast, stared out the window, willing the sun to come up, checked on my period, which seems to still be in flow. Mother Nature is, for once, helping and not hindering me. Thank god that's an outward excuse to keep him away from my vagina. I kept asking him to find me tampons in Jamaica just to keep him reminded each time he even tried to glance at me with sexy eyes.

I worked discreetly with the hotel manager today, using their landline so I could get a flight out of there. I made a call to the darling grandparents and told them to please be on standby for pickup. Caeser emailed me, but I couldn't get enough Wi-Fi to respond back. Perhaps I'd try to send him a smoke signal from the beach so he could send over the jet. I believe his family was going or coming back from the Bahamas; pit stop please?

Chapter Nine

OH SO "CLEVER"

Caeser, who I'd had a great friendship with initially, tried to lure and dazzle me with his extravagant and privileged life that he often rebelled against. He was generous to many, but was somewhat baffled by my indifference to the social light. We'd had an instant friendly connection that fizzled fast due to his beyond-eccentric behaviors and his battle for dominance. He was a loving, creative character whose vast intelligence could sometimes immobilize him.

In one minute, he could say something so intelligent or heartfelt, and in the next he'd say something completely crazy. He'd given me many firsts whether it was our times at the Arena led by his golden key or our trip to Broadway where we turned down after-parties to get sandwiches at the best New York Deli instead.

He was a down to earth and passionate person who had a great imagination. By wanting to extend beyond his loving Dad's lifestyle, he forgot what outlets were right in front of him. He didn't seem to see or feel at all those who loved him, it seemed he instead felt resentful to their shadow. I liked spending time with him, but his destructive ways kept me at a distance. We were very much companions in friendship, and he kept me on my toes with his fun facts, Freudian facts, and freak flag.

Coffee Shop Connection
December 24, 2011

Today was an interesting day. It seems I was too much in observer mode lately to be fully present. This point of my life feels like I'm a sponge. I feel I'm having all these experiences and I'm watching them and myself in them. I'm not sure if I should soak up the experience, or just let it wash through me.

Some people would have freaked out to have had the day I had today, yet there I was at 1:00 a.m. trying to quiet my brain from the surreal images of what had happened and what was to come.

Exactly a week ago I met Caeser; that name means a lot if you're from this area. Last week, I was at work and Jamie pulled me aside and said there was someone who wanted to talk to me.

When I saw him, I thought he was someone else, so I kept talking to him about a coffee shop, "Oh Caeser, I used to be an avid coffee drinker. I love cafés. Do you enjoy your coffee shop?"

The barback so generously updated me. "Do you know who you're talking with? Does the name mean anything to you?" No it didn't.

When Caeser came back, I didn't acknowledge what I found out. It seemed irrelevant; we clicked. However, he couldn't resist it. He started an inquisition with me so I would have to ask who he was. He then invited me, nonchalantly, to an island in their family jet, and to a game.

Women have our breasts and voices for leverage, men have their toys. We're both funny creatures, really. I agreed to the game. The family vacation felt like more of a commitment. He was waiting for some sort of overwhelmed joyous reaction from me, but I didn't have much to say.

At the time, another bartender gave Caeser's card to some Korean guy on accident, and as our boss offered to cover Caeser any money he needed, I realized his pull. I saw the way people reacted to someone with his type of connections, with status. I guess it was nice to see loyalty still existed. Although not so much in marriages or relationships today, but in our faithful sports teams. If only the players had as much loyalty to the team as the fans do.

The next day, he left for vacation and he called me multiple times each day from the island. We talked once, a very long phone call where I found a couple of red flags, but they seemed insignificant. He seemed charismatic. His scattered thoughts were refreshing. There was something really honest about him that I liked. I wear my mind on my sleeve, and he seemed to also. With all his word vomit, I didn't even have a chance to regurgitate mine. He had no problem telling me blatantly that he planned on stalking my Facebook. The way he spoke about his therapist was like how some people speak about their pets. His belief in group therapy, his love for the arts, it was all very honest.

Ultimately, I found out he was family-oriented, well rounded and he had an odd fascination with me. I told him his insanity didn't bother me, and we could be friends. He was comfortable with my unconventional expression, so he accepted me as well. Both of us didn't fit our common perceptions, so we shared in a lack of conformity. We left it at he'd be home in a few days, he would contact me Friday night, and we could plan for the weekend game.

At about noon, he came into my work. One of the floor hosts practically signaled to me with enthusiasm; he couldn't get me over fast enough. It was as if my keeping Caeser waiting would ruin their connection to the season, as if I was going to come back with season passes or a golden ticket. When I got upstairs, he was behind the counter by himself. He got to choose his VIP seating. He could have been swinging from the ceiling and no one would've cared. He could have been running the upstairs bar and I don't think they'd blink an eye. There was talk about the game for the next day and how we'd meet up. As the night ended, he asked for a ride and I agreed. Surely he'd have no problem getting a taxi, but I didn't mind a few more moments to figure him out.

When we arrived at his place, he begged and begged me to come in and hang out for just an hour. After I felt a little boring, I decided to say, "What the hell, I'll come in." I wasn't sure how to say no to someone's persistence. It was clear "no" was merely a challenge to him.

His apartment was rather large. It felt and looked like a mad scientist lived there. He showed me musicals which brought him a lot of delight. I appreciated the laxness in us watching YouTube videos from his TV.

When I decided it was time for me to go, he started pulling strings. "You can sleep over and sleep in my bed. I'll take the couch."

I wasn't sold.

Attempt two, "I'll take you shopping in the morning before the game so you have fresh clothes and something to wear."

I still wasn't sold.

No response.

"I don't want you to drive this late, especially after you said how tired you were."

There it was, throwing out the safety card. I accepted. I was weird about certain things. I guess I knew to trust my feeling over my thoughts. My thoughts often mislead me but my feelings felt secure. I felt he did like me enough in friendship to not be a creep, and my eyes had fallen weary anyway.

It was funny to because, as I lay on his couch, I thought about how I had a small shift inside me. I knew the second I agreed to sleep over that he was going to do something that would irritate me and I would feel I'd given a little of my power in not going home. If he tried too hard, he'd hit that nerve and make me not want to go to the game the next day. I let it be; I felt it coming on where we would not be compatible, and that his freak flag would be apparent sooner then I first expected. I didn't mind because to know sooner allowed me more leverage about how to handle this situation. We watched videos on the TV and musicals he knew word-for-word. I saw him getting up and doing something in the other room, but I didn't pay attention. I said I' was tired and ready for bed, and that's when the surprise came before the non-surprise.

We walked upstairs and he so proudly made me a bubble bath. I had no desire to get in it, but he was so pleased with himself, I almost felt bad to have said no. He even talked to me outside the door so I could get in first.

It was lukewarm—yuck. I like my water so hot my skin burns. So hot that you actually have to go in toe first, to ankle, to knee, and slowly work your way before getting in the tub.

Our bathroom chat was where he got all cuckoo. He was standing in the door way, facing the other way, rambling on about particular conversations he'd had.

Any time I thought I was ready to get out, I'd say, "Okay, I'm good," he'd hit the jet dial.

Dates to Remember - Gabrielle Anna

"Caeser, I'm starting to prune, can we talk in the morning?" Jet dial.

The button was conveniently by the door and easily in his reach as he happily carried on our conversation. The bubbles were so high that you could only see my eyeballs. While on his kick, he even brought out his smoke machine. I was now in a bathtub with a smoke machine sitting in front of me and Caeser playing Benny Benassi from his iPod.

He talked about exes, he talked about family, lots of personal, personal shit. I was truly surprised how much he revealed to me. It was like he was so open in my hands, and I thought about all the people who would take advantage because he made himself so vulnerable. Ivy League grad, successful family, privileged background, family entrepreneurs—here I was watching him spill his emotion to me erratically. Here I was submerged in a tub looking for a life raft.

After that, I left my spray tan residue and climbed into bed. It was now 5:00 a.m. and I knew I wouldn't sleep. He tucked me in, got in his cashmere jumpsuit, and then headed for the couch with his beloved iPad.

As I weighed the pros and cons of going to the game and not going to the game that day, I fell in and out of sleep. Three hours later, I got out of bed, too uncomfortable and restless. He hadn't slept at all. He was literally pacing the kitchen like a mad man in a tracksuit, iPad in one hand and cell phone in the other. My Facebook was up on his phone, and a picture of me on his iPad. I knew from here on out, it would be ugly. I tried to talk myself out of the game in my most polite way, but after a couple failed attempts, I thought, Oh f**k it, this is an experience.

I said it'd be best we take separate cars as I had to leave early, and he admitted he wanted to ride together so he could talk to me about my thoughts on death. Like I was going to say no after that.

Our car ride was interesting. He talked a lot. He asked me question after question about my previous relationships, trying to outshine my exes.

"Have you ever been to a game? Those sound like good seats, how'd he get those good seats? Do you think our seats are better than his passes? Should we take a picture for Facebook so people know where you are? What'd your family say? Let's get them souvenirs. You're not really impressed with today, but to some, it's a pretty big deal, like they would kill for this."

I saw him as someone with all this money and he was desperate for recognition. I realized how empty he felt despite all his possessions. What was even sadder was that I could see how transparent he was despite how so many people looked at him. He was a reflection of what they thought of him or wanted him to be. I think he just wanted to be seen and heard for who he was, and I knew he had a lot to offer.

We got to the game and it was cool getting a behind-the-scenes look. He bought me team gear—"Anything you want in the store"—his guarded eyes watching any time I even browsed men's apparel, he got his friends club seats, bought them a few souvenirs, and then we headed back toward the stadium. The friends of his we'd run into seemed to pay no mind. We sat in the box and it was beautiful. I felt almost out of place being around that kind of money. Money just feels so false, so misleading, so translucent. Here I was, struggling to pay bills on my own, and yet I felt indifferent to it regardless. I saw how it' was never enough. His dad was polite, warm even. He hugged Caeser, and in the hug, I saw the connection he had for him. It was really beautiful, though Caeser didn't recognize it or I guess felt he'd outgrew it. I wished I could take a snapshot of that moment. I wished he could see what I saw. When you're the one in a relationship and you experience all the turbulence, defenses can keep you from seeing the love underneath. He was constantly on the defensive. I wished he could see the love I knew was there. All too often we just don't receive love completely by how we see fit, and I understood that's how he felt.

I left early.

This made sense to him and he'd snap out of his delusion for a second. Not quite how I imagined such an experience, but an image is never as it seems. It seems even when we're holding a golden key, that doesn't mean we'll choose the right doors.

Dating Cautionary
January 22, 2012

I was kicking myself in the butt. I seemed to only catch on after the fact. Let me emphasize here:

Realization number one—

Dates to Remember - Gabrielle Anna

Be careful whom you date. Dating always ends, and often not with the best results, otherwise it wouldn't end. That's simple enough. I first say this because dating can taint us and make it that much harder for our future significant others. Also, be constantly conscious of your karma—it matters. After my naughty behavior, karma sought its vengeance on me. I hope today is the final piece as I am now back to my conscious, mindful, holy, little self. I had to finally say, "I got the memo." But, karma aside, my cautions for dating...

On to previous bachelors and the impressions which followed. Alexander, for a good while, tainted the overall city of Boston for me. He was my first relationship—my Boston boyfriend. First, showing me to the city before I was twenty-one, taking me to fabulous restaurants, introducing me to fabulous people—many of those being the North End Italians. He made the balance of life, fun, and love seem so effortless. Dany, my Rhode Island lover, tainted one of my now favorite radio stations. It accompanied me on my many Rhode Island drives and we've have had multiple sing-alongs to that station. After each of our breakups, I couldn't bear to listen to some of my absolutely favorite songs. That is just cruel! He ruined practically the whole 70s era for me. Thank god we didn't listen to Prince together because Erotic City is too good to give up. As sexy as his music is, I will never make love to a Prince CD for such reasons.

Christian ruined pretty boys for me, at least for a while. He was one of the most pretty man-boys I had ever met, but he was far too high maintenance for me. I couldn't even lay my hair on his white couch without a hoodie. He and his foreign furniture—such beautiful objects.

And now for the kicker. I had to do it. I had to be pursued by the owner of the Zebras' son.

This basically meant that my no interest in sports was now interest in sports, but I walked a fine line there. If I didn't date, I risked missing out on things that suddenly appealed to me now.

Dates to Remember - Gabrielle Anna

Our unofficial dates were not only refreshing, they were substantial book material. As a writer, I approached many experiences that way. What was worse, however, was if we did date. I was a borderline dating assassin, so we would later break up and I didn't want to be jaded to an entire sports team. I didn't want to hear the word Zebras and cringe. It was already beginning...

We went to our first game together. I looked forward to going because I was flattered he asked me. Me being me I said, "Oh, I'll go, but I'm leaving early." I had plans and I wasn't going to adjust them in the name of lures. The root of me was not swayed by material things or social status, so I was often removed or unfazed. This made him work that much harder.

"You're so deep," he'd always say. This wasn't his response on my remark to a skanky musical I wasn't leaving to attend, but it was a theme for most of our conversations.

Game One—My private tour, gifts from their company which just felt like more dating lure. Men have their toys for leverage, women have their breasts. I left early that day and went on my way to a musical with one of my friends.

Game Two—He asked me nonchalantly, but this time, I felt more excitement. I suddenly had a growing interest in sports. I went with him and one of his friends who wasn't very well liked, so we all kept a low profile.

Game Three—we went just the two of us and it was fun, but I felt a little disconnected. I thought he was trying to impress me with this lifestyle, and I liked him just as he was. The fact that he couldn't see that was baffling to me. He sometimes seemed uncomfortable by his failed efforts to impress me. I felt like he was trying to keep me up with distractions and it only left me feeling exhausted.

Game Four—He asked me at 4:00 a.m. if I would go with him; that left little time for preparation. He had called me all night at every hour even though I didn't answer; that made for uneasy sleep. I then ran off of three hours of sleep, which was not so flattering no matter how much bronzer or caffeine you are prepared with.

He overslept, so we were late. Then, at the game, despite my royal treatment, his attention was so scattered it only left me feeling awkward. I was sitting by myself with the whole family in their beautiful golden box. There were multiple, well-known socialites at my side, and I was texting my mom and ex-boyfriend. My mom felt distant to me, and my ex was home with the flu, so I missed the comfort of certain familiar people. I felt I was sitting in this beautiful, ideal image, and I only felt a desire to get out of it.

After feeling a little down and consuming way too much at the sushi bar, I couldn't bear to sit there and wait on Caesers return. I was inches away from a senator who I certainly had political questions for, and a rock star. I kept myself composed as to not be rude, but it took a lot of will power to not bust out one of his songs. I initially ventured off to meet a girlfriend, VIP pass and Caeser's ID in hand, but it was far too cold for me to be outside when scanning to find her in lines. Exhibit A: the jaded effect was beginning. How could I go from riding in a golden elevator, personal chefs, and attentive assistance, to now standing outside in negative degree weather, confused, and trying to identify someone in a sea of fans wearing similar outfits?

I decided to walk around and was then hit on in an elevator of drunken fans. I couldn't be bothered by such attention. My need to be a hermit was now extremely deep. Finally, while Caeser was making his rounds, meeting people, and generally being all over the place, I headed for my car. I had a seat behind an incredible artist in the Zebras' elite section, and here I was, sitting in my Kia. After all those years of singing to him in the shower, and here I was in my Kia listening to the Power of Now. I had truly tried to make an exit after all the mixed signals from Caeser and the confusing thoughts that filled my head, but I got caught. The security guy actually wouldn't let me leave the lot, and I am so horribly stubborn, nonconformist, and baffling even to myself, that I decided to sit there and sort out my thoughts instead of going back in.

"We can page Caeser and find him, but you can't just go."

"No, thanks," I said and pouted in my car with my cell phone whose battery was dying. If this was the type of monitoring I was under as friends, I couldn't possibly imagine if we dated. Besides, I thought of him like a crazy sibling. When we'd get together, we'd often order take-out and watch classic films. I'd had too much psycho-analysis going on of myself and of my surroundings. I stubbornly sat in my car and read Deepak while listening to the Power of Now. On the ride home, poor Caeser was trying to assess my odd female behavior so I should have assessed then that this episode would not allot me privilege points for the following games.

At the time it didn't faze me. Today, while I am in my fleece PJ's, refusing to watch the game, I am fazed. The very few of my family members who I discuss personal matters with are now accustomed to my traveling for games and have sent me texts saying, "Ooooh! Ahhhh! Have fun!" whenever I do so. The one game in the past month I was not at, not only did multiple performers go whom I admire, but also this was the game that determined all games, and suddenly that means something to me. I was actually interested in whether we win. Suddenly, the switch happened. I found myself actually discussing sports—properly even. I learned the rules of the game from a reliable source. I found myself parading in my team attire to show my loyalty in style. I found myself suddenly exposed to sports everywhere. I saw the swarm of followers I should have been. I should have been there too, cheering on my newfound love of the Zebras. I'm naturally supportive of those people in my life, and if I'm loyal to them I'll parade anything around.

I refused to watch the game. I actually boycotted it. I was supportive until the national anthem did me in and my mind was left to envision all the fun I was missing out on. You know things are always better when you don't have them, of course. I'm also so neurotic that while listening to the unfortunate calls against the team, I found myself saying, "Yup, I was lucky, and now I'm not there, so they've lost their good luck charm." That was how I justified my absence from the game. I didn't even know if I wanted them to win or lose.

The moral of all of this is: Be careful whom you date. If you genuinely enjoy walks in the park, take a puppy, not your boyfriend. Your puppy may pee on your floor, eat your favorite shoes, and whine at your lack of attention, but he will love you unconditionally. And if you don't have an icy heart, you will love it back unconditionally, too.

If you genuinely enjoy Starbucks, don't date someone who works there—despite the lure, despite the savings. In my case, I should say don't date the owner of Starbucks whom, as my dating record shows, I will break up with. After which, I will not only have to give up my romance but also my matcha teas. On second thought—maybe I *should* date the owner of a Starbucks.

I'd already dodged that curse before. I met someone at my Starbucks spot years ago; he came over to my corner where I am often furiously working on a novel or procrastinating school work. We went on one date and after I stopped responding, he'd casually show up there or try to intimidate me from the economy aisle at the bookstore. This didn't faze me. Avoiding bad dates in public is no problem. Avoiding stalkers who know how predictable you are is no problem. Leaving jobs for coworkers who work a little too closely to you is uncomfortable, but it's no problem. To avoid a whole sports team, though—that can be difficult…

Valentine's Day 2012

When I looked back on last year's video montage of Valentine's Day, I saw that I'd been giddy and bright eyed. Perhaps it had been the Redline pumping through me, or it could have been the effect from my new Vickie's purchase, or maybe it was the "boyfriend" factor…

While my feelings for Dany had gone from one extreme to the next, I seemed absolutely content in that moment. Are real partners the ones that can make you gaga-eyed one day and cross-eyed the next? Was it so complicated because he'd brought out my own reflection?

On this year's Valentine's Day, I was not as enthused. Should I have woken up overflowing with love? Should I have been purchasing Hallmark cards that expressed my devotional feelings as this was my only day where it was appropriate to announce them wildly? I was trying to talk myself out of a stomach bug, I didn't want to wear anything related to love, and I had no desire for a Valentine's Day humping.

My mother was the first Valentine's text I got; I hoped that wasn't a foreshadowing of my indecisive future. Her text was something along the lines of, "I love you, a kiss, Happy Valentine's, and P.S. I need a breast exam (aka you're the only one who will do it.)" Great, what a successful start to Valentine's Day when it wasn't even 8:00 a.m. and you already have a date to feel up your mother's breasts.

Following was an ex-girlfriend Valentine's Day text, a girlfriend-who-I-go-through-phases-of-love with, then there was my father who probably presumed his happy Valentine's Day text would alleviate him of his lack of fathering. Then there was the ex-boyfriend who I either needed to keep in ex land or we needed to determine our status, the random guy who thought he was relevant when he wasn't—they usually just want to remind you of their company that they think you're missing.

That was followed by girlfriend Jacky who invited me to dinner that night with her children while she was with her fabulous boyfriend, Jack. She finally stopped saying how in love I was with the Sagittarian so, instead, she waited for our schedules to all align for double dates. However, as loving as she was, and as much as she loved Dany and me together, dinner on Valentine's with her sixteen-year-old son was not exactly how I envisioned the holiday. I adored their family, but the only sixteen-year-olds I planned on spending Valentine's Day with were hopefully my future children.

Caeser had booked time with me two weeks prior to this, so I received a confirmation text from him.

Darling Bradley, who was then my schedule manager and recently caffeinated companion, said hello. I was delighted to hear from this true soul.

And Calvin, of course, sent me a simple, "Happy Valentine's, Gabrielle." Well, thank you once-was future-husband.

Valentine's Day was nothing out of the ordinary. While my life was always out of the ordinary, the holiday alone did not put me in a lovey-dovey zone. I wish I had booked my gay friend in advance. I walked with him to class that day and he was just so fabulous. He pulled off feminine sensuality better than I did. His Nordstrom attire was perfectly festive for the day. We should've gone on a non-date together, ordered fruity drinks, and helped him find a lover. His current fling was gorgeous, but not the right fit—his words, not mine. Though I can confirm the lover was gorgeous. He was one of those gay men who made women question their femininity, and men, their sexuality.

As the day progressed, I had mixed feelings about my Valentine's night ahead. My feelings had totally changed with Caeser, although we had a good talk on the phone—I liked how he called for phone conversations, which was such a rarity.

When it was initially taking off, I fell victim to the texting phenomenon, but now texting just felt too invasive and impersonal. People shouldn't be that available all the time; it starts to take away from our own boundaries and changes communication. With all the means of being in touch, we seem to be a society somewhat out of touch with ourselves and actually communicate less and less despite the resources. Having to compartmentalize everything with all the surrounding stimuli can make it hard to be in the present.

As Caeser and I talked, I hoped he saw my standpoint and kept things casual between us, as I valued our friendship. We came from opposite worlds, but laugh a lot together, and where we were different, we respected one another enough to challenge each other without being condescending. That was my kind of unconventional relationship!

Maybe I'm indignant to Valentine's today because I hadn't grounded myself from my weekend with the ex. Yes, as exes we still managed to wind up somewhere in each other's radius, if not together. I still felt quite airy. We spent the weekend together—me, he, and little G—moving around like housemates in our undistinguished territory.

I seemed to find myself in different roles; one holiday day later and suddenly, after committing to two weeks prior to hang out tonight, I was curious as to what Caeser's perception was of Valentine's Day. I had the impression we were getting together to endure this holiday together as single people.

I took my vitamins. I meditated. I was far too calm to exercise beyond yoga. I almost needed someone to piss me off so I could be motivated to hit the gym again. I'd been faithful to yoga since December, but that just mellowed me out more. I watched my inspiration, Ellen Degeneres, which led to a dance party in my kitchen.

Dates to Remember - Gabrielle Anna

As the night approached, I had plenty of time to get ready, but I was still late, as per usual. I should've seen that as a sign, as a defense mechanism, as something! I am only late and disorderly when in avoidance or unacceptance-of-reality mode. Other than that, I feel I have all the time I need. Even in moments that I know will be good for me, I'll sometimes avoid and resist, as if my ego knows it will have to subside.

I had no intention of staying the night. I left the bag at home to provide myself with an adamant reason to leave. On the drive there, I missed my exit twice. I couldn't get my head grounded and in the right direction. Having known this, but also having known I was committed to plans, and the fact that I cared for Caeser, I carried on.

I got there and he was gone, but he'd left the door open. I was reading comics on the couch when he came back with a few bags in his hand. In my head I thought, *Okay... he must be giving me something. Okay... he did it minutes before I arrived?* I was wrong. Like a good Valentine's date, he followed the protocol almost to a T. He went into his room and pulled out a bag, meaning it had already been there.

It was beautiful, red, French, lace lingerie. So beautiful, only a type of foreign model could get away with wearing it. I didn't have the figure or confidence to wear this piece. Then, as a "sorry I pissed you off" gift, and "this is because you didn't come to the best game" gift—he literally said that line—he gave me a gorgeous necklace.

Here I was thinking I'd cleverly and festively picked out for him three comic books—three comic books after an hour of indecisive reading on the floor in Newbury Comics. The manager there seemed thrilled to have a girl in stilettos with a pile of comics in the corner so adamantly reading. I'd come close to browsing every piece on the shelf before making a decision. He'd come over every now and then to check on my progress.

I thought I'd give Caeser his little gift and we'd do dinner—men always want to feed your tummy. Feed your tummy or get you drunk. Once guys figured out I'm not one to drink, they're practically spoon-feeding me any possible calories they can buy or cook. It must be some biological way to fatten us up and prepare us for child-bearing or something. I'll have to look into the reasoning for this madness. Comfort, adoration, subconscious, a trap? Perhaps as simple as they like to eat and we should too. Thank you, God, for blessing me with this metabolism.

We had intelligent conversation as usual; he is very smart, and I valued that about him. Sometimes he was so smart that I'd feel dumb. He had so much knowledge—worldly and other types of knowledge I wasn't even aware of prior to his sharing it. Typical Ivy League grad—precocious family, smart but with an edge, and eccentric.

We laughed, although not as much as we used to; I don't think I appreciated him as much after some disappointments on his end. He made honest efforts to improve, though. He let me order when we'd dine in—he knew I loved that. He didn't engage in excessive phone calls while I was there—there's a fine line between appropriate and rude. He had his cleaning lady come twice a week so I wasn't lounging in his disheveled mess, and because he was a smart man, I felt that he thought Valentine's guaranteed him some loving, finally.

The night went on. I was full, but I ate my oversized, apple, pure sugar dessert. I got sleepy. It was liquid sugar in a bowl, basically. Men simply don't get that, while their full bellies provoke more sexual activity, a woman's full belly does not.

"Oh good, you ate your entire dessert. How about some tiramisu, too?"

"No way, Caeser. You keep the chocolate away from me!"

"Oh, good, that's okay. How about your red lingerie I bought you?"

I was skeptical about how I thought I'd look in that lingerie before our dining extravaganza, and to hear that in the same sentence as tiramisu was just mean. More dessert it is.

In the past hour, I'd gone into a food coma on the couch and he was now flirting with me?

I politely said, "No, Caeser. Let's watch a movie before I go."

We settled on a movie and a sleepover. We do those sometimes like two peas in a pod on his large, L-shaped couch. Though I never know what I'll find in or on the couch, I'm comfortable.

I set my alarm for 6:30 a.m. and we put on a movie. On prior sleepovers, he was either out cold before me and snoring loudly like a banshee or he didn't sleep at all. While we were sitting there together with some movie classic, he tried. Just went for it. Expecting-some-

Valentine's-Day-love tried. I didn't blame him. He felt he followed the Valentine's Day protocol and I was veering us too off course.

I literally said, "Sorry, it's still not going to happen. No. I thought we were just mocking this holiday together."

I'd never seen someone's eyes get so big. He even tried to call me evil in a non-insulting manner. He actually said the word evil, very carefully, very sweetly. By the look on his face, the sheer shock, disappointment, confusion, more lust—he seemed to be driven by rejection—him weighing of what to do from there, I'd say he handled himself fairly well.

He pulled out the appropriate cards first, "Do friends give their friends jewelry on valentine's day? I thought with all I do for you—not that I don't want to, not that it means you have to do anything for me, not that I expect more of you because of it—but wouldn't you think, especially on Valentine's Day, that I like you?"

That was valid.

"I'm kind of turned on more. I feel like I should have just gone with passion and not stopped."

Not so valid.

"I've tried to respect you, and that's why we've hung out as friends. I didn't want you to think I was just after you sexually. Gabrielle, that's why we've hung out like buddies."

Extra valid—I appreciated the honesty.

"Don't tell anyone about this—after all, I can't even get it on Valentine's Day—this is embarrassing. Do you think I'm gay? Did you think I was gay? I'm obviously not gay; I'm attracted to you. This is because we became too much of friends, isn't it? We watched too many movies together, huh? I have an erection right now; my balls are going to explode. I think I'm going to have a seizure."

Not so valid.

"You know, I was going to take you to Disney World."

Comically half-valid.

"I don't just take anyone to Disney world; I was thinking we'd have some intimacy."

Comically valid. What was it with men, vacations, and expectations? With Disney of all places, you are going to manipulate a happy girl toward sex by "the wonder of it all."

I held my ground. He tucked me into bed on the couch and I fell into a light sleep shortly afterward.

In the morning, he practically ran out to make sure I was still sleeping after his alarm went off obnoxiously for early hours.

"Sorry! Sorry! I hate that alarm! Stay asleep honey; it was for me, not you." Oh, that was seriously precious.

When I got up, I saw he was back in his bed. I felt guilty leaving without talking, but I had some mental organizing to do, so I let him sleep and left a note. Happy Valentine's Day, 2012.

Last Valentine's, I had made a video montage. I said something along the lines of, "Men, this is the one day you're guaranteed sex if you follow the protocol." I actually said that. Shame on me! What's that other saying again, "Nothing in life is guaranteed"?

Alice in Wonderland

A Day with the Mad Hatter: Hand cramp and all, I decided to document. The following excerpt is going to be way too much information, unflattering, a little raunchy, and yet, ultimately, relatable. Lastly, this is for the good of society. I am coming down from my intense high and I'm questioning how safe my new present really is.

Yesterday, I taught Zumba and agreed to visit Caeser after my weeks of absence. The night before, he had come by my work and bought a bottle of Dom to keep me company, so I at least wanted to stop by on my outings. Between reading my new romance novel, building the Great Wall around my vagina, and Wednesday's rejection from Dany, my main goal of the day was to take on the sex shop. I had a mission—re-identify and explore my personal sexuality, determine what novelty or outfit expressed my alter ego, and if all of the above failed, at least get my boyfriend back and blame it on my newfound accessories if he absolutely refused. What intelligent male can turn down sex in the name of research? I know, I know, there are people out there changing the world, waiting to escape from their nine-to-five, and my priority of the day was what I could find in one of *those* places.

I worked last night, I still taught today despite a lack of sleep, I aced my test Thursday, and I'm a fairly productive member of society through smiles and abiding by the law. We seem to find justification in exempting ourselves from many of our odd behaviors. I was going to let myself slide on that one. I'd earned the right to a new vibrator and a sexy costume. I wanted it even if I only paraded in it at home while I was watching Ellen, as a boyfriend treat to be used when my ex was not avoiding me—or better—when he is. Instead of catching up on my sleep, I wanted to be productive in *something*.

At the very least, it would make for a fun trip, and at the most, it could either help me to get my boyfriend back, keep me away from boyfriends, or perhaps turn me away from all sexuality until the horror wore off. I was sold.

I got to Caeser's and he made me laugh instantly. When we see each other, I often show up in yoga pants, so he looks at me in such awe whenever I show up actually dressed and presentable. People always seem so amazed when I leave my yoga pants at home, and decide to do that thing people call getting dressed. I told him my mission of the day; we could talk to each other very freely. I loved how honest we were with one another; it was playful, candid, and heavy at times, but nothing is refined or limited. He was very open about himself and receptive of others. Being the good friend he was, we decided to take on the sex store together. God bless friendship. I respected his taste in magazines, he respected my search in sex.

"She's looking for a Madame Curie-like costume, no, a Star Trek one."

He kept trying to get me to blush at the store, but I wasn't so easily embarrassed. My rebuttal was not that I wanted to be costumed, but that I wanted to explore my alter egos. That was much more fun than being in Freud's office.

We browsed, both in awe of what lined the walls—curious, confused, intrigued. Even in here he managed to be a little impulsive with an arm full of goodies, "Ooooh, what's this? What do you think of that?"

We explored as nonchalantly as if we were grocery shopping. The most I'd gathered so far was a pair of red stockings; they were nothing extraordinary, but for $5 they're the perfect addition to my little red corvette dancing.

So far, he had glow-in-the-dark condoms because he thought they'd look really cool, a hustler magazine that he swore wasn't nearly as good as they used to be, and objects that he found amusing. Amusing and sexy, he wasn't sure.

As we walked by the register, we came across *the* object. It was apparently worthy of a case. It was purple—a soft purple which made it more warm and inviting—and neither of us understood what one would do with this thing.

I asked the guy working behind the counter.

"You want to know about the intensity?" he said ever so coyly. His eyes lit up with an underlying deviance. Both men behind the counter began to equally rave about the toy in all its glory. They referred to it as if it were some sort of elite object made for athletes or porn stars only. Had they gone on any longer, I would have thought one required a physical just to purchase it.

When I saw the price tag, I was appalled. $250! I would not subject myself to such an object. As we advance in technology, the prices advance also. Oh new iPad, that's an extra $400. Oh, the new iPod, that's an extra $150. Oh, a new vibrator, apparently the extra cost also applied.

I don't know if Caeser felt sorry for me, felt like challenging me as a woman—this is no ordinary vibrator—wanted to find a way to contribute to my sex life, needed a way to exert his impulsions, the list was endless, but nevertheless, he bought it for me as an upcoming birthday present.

I was resistant at first; I couldn't accept that. I saw how he ever so casually added it to his armful, smiling like the Cheshire cat—I couldn't decline. My horror and awe weren't enough to hold me back.

After we finished our shopping spree, we flagged down a cab, goodies in hand, black bagged and all. We got back to his house, ordered our sushi, and were ready to pop in the Kardashian porn for evaluation and research. I bet that it was leaked and directed intentionally, he felt otherwise. I won.

The next morning while at home, I debated working out or working on my new project. I had time to kill, and it was a gift—I felt I should at least read the instructions. It would be impolite to not give my birthday gift a fair chance. Besides, the instruction manual was provided in over ten languages. How supportive. If I found myself too fearful to give it a go, I could at least practice foreign languages until I was ready. At least I could justify this impulse buy by their nondiscrimination, worldwide reach, and if the orgasms were as good as they promised, perhaps even world peace.

Once I got over my awe of the object, it wasn't so bad. I experimented for a few minutes then passed out for the following hours. Later that night, I thought I should give it a better shot—okay, round two.

Round two was far more effective. I loved it. Worth the $250, though if I had any request, I would say it needed a clock attached to remind one of time. It should have an automatic off switch where, after an hour of use, you're timed out for the next five hours. I've now referred three of my girlfriends to the new tool and have been YouTube browsing for a consensus on this piece of equipment.

Dear Caeser, thank for encouraging and enabling my odd behavior and my hermitting for the weekend.

The next day he referred to himself as his own cockblock, and his house being like wonderland. He said that after he invited me over, and I said I was busy.

"Honey, are you already choosing that thing over social interaction?"

I couldn't lie to him; he was right. It was only day two and I'd written off the outside world. Kids play with new toys intensely at first.

It was my birthday week, I was inclined to do so. $250 for a vibrator, I was inclined. When two sex shop gurus propose it as a literal challenge and are beaming at your buy, I was inclined.

There was no dispute. I'd call Caeser "Cheshire" from now on, or "Mad Hatter." He called me Alice. I could appreciate this because, for many years, I wanted to be a blonde—this was likely the closest I'd get to that fantasy.

Each time I visited Wonderland—aka "Mad Hatters'"—apartment, we either indulged in complete gluttony—he has a sweet tooth and loves excessive behaviors—or entered into the weird realm of our psychology. I could only anticipate what trip followed. We were quite a trip together!

Chapter Ten

LIQUOR, LEGALITIES, AND THE LEO

This defense attorney completely baffled me. Yes, defense. Somewhat counter intuitive, one may say, to my profession. I'm never one to be conventional.

The moment I met him, I knew we'd be involved somehow, and the thought left me uncomfortable. Us... really? How? When? He had a weird effect on me that made me almost edgy. I met not only my match in the challenging sense, but my horoscope match as an ideal mate. This was somewhat of a conflict.

This Leo took me by surprise with our first, late lunch. I went, telling myself it was for research, not lust. On the rooftop in Boston, I fell for him, and that never happens. It wasn't this great sensation, it wasn't a flashing moment. I just took it for what it was—a draw to this person, for our differences, for our similarities, to his intensity.

Me? I found myself right by his side, impressed by him, trusting of him, *What kind of mind f**k is happening to me?* I thought.

The mind f**ks began early on. I felt like I was in a time capsule with him; I had no feeling of the past or present. On our first day out, he told me I was charming—everything he said felt so raw, honest, genuine, and jagged. He had dark, brooding eyes full of passion, life, and secrets. I got sucked up right into it despite my usual reservation, despite what I'd been told, despite the lurking question.

Being surprised by my gaining interest, I felt that I had to do it right this time. I couldn't make the mistakes I made in my last relationship. I had learned from Dany, I had grown and changed. The kind of camaraderie between me and this new guy made me anxious, insecure almost. I hated not knowing why I was so drawn, especially to someone who had me so mystified and bewildered.

After our first date went effortlessly, he asked me out for the Fourth of July, which was two days upcoming. Two days away? A vacation? Together? What was this territory? Would it be smart to take off with someone after the first date? Could I uproot myself like this? I never agree without contemplation, and yet I found myself saying yes, knowing I'd be going regardless of what my brain told me. To make me comfortable, he welcomed my friends and left our time frame indefinite.

For the Fourth, I originally had plans with Jason, a friend of a friend, who went above and beyond for me. He was the one who contacted me out of the blue for a complimentary vacation, all expenses paid. At the time I turned it down, still trying to declare my dedication to Dany. I liked Jason, so we stayed friends and kept in touch. He made life feel so completely easy. One couldn't worry with this prepared, doting Libra. He was so nurturing, so easy to talk to, so willing to accommodate, and I couldn't find the connection enough to take us further. I didn't feel he was truly ready for it or me. Also, after Dany left me, I didn't think I'd love again, certainly not like that. Admire, yes. Date, maybe. Love, I still felt too guilty, fragile, and vulnerable.

Jason was wonderful to me, he helped me move into my new apartment, he even bought me a new laptop when mine was stolen, offered me work space by his pool, and then took me away one weekend for a spa trip. We shared an amazing time getting facials, going for a walk by the beach, walking around Maine hand-in-hand. He was trusting and dedicated. He knew about my long commutes and offered me his second car or the Infiniti to get there faster. I had no complaints. We laughed together, could have in deep talks, he listened, he cared, I could have been moved into the house and been the wifey within a week, and yet something held me back from anything beyond friendship.

I knew it was too fresh for me to move into a new relationship. I knew it'd take me awhile to get over Dany. I also knew Jason saw his own image of me versus who I actually was. Love and lovers bring out different sides to you, and I felt he was following the same footsteps of his past relationship.

Jason and I had made Fourth of July plans as friends to go to P-town, and Wednesday morning there, I was irrationally blowing him off over a text message, "Sorry, going to the Vineyard!"

It felt wrong. I was guilty, and yet I thought it was for the best. I get impulsive on my instincts, and all along I knew we'd never work out. All of our interactions were too smothering, I felt he held me to an image and that distracted him from seeing who I was or what we were in reality. Just like that, I was on my way with Danielle and Sonya to meet the guys at the ferry.

Dates to Remember - Gabrielle Anna

"Who is this guy?" Danielle probed. Her inquisition meant nothing to me. She was always inquiring about others. I had gotten used to her analysis. Gavin and his friend Nick were going to meet us in Falmouth and we'd be on our way to the island.

Date one on Monday, an island vacation on Wednesday. What effect did this bachelor have over me? I left everything behind, which was out of character for me. I felt confident in my decision. I brought a phone, but left my charger so I would be unreachable later on.

The trip was eventful. Each day was new, different, and refreshing. It had its pits and falls, but I was grateful to have gone. Martha's Vineyard was truly amazing. Gavin was charming; charming me, charming my friends, charming anyone in contact. How the f**k did he do it? I was immediately impressed with him and my friends adored him. He was respectful, intelligent, a listener, and had this air of freedom about him. We'd watch him give $100 to kids at a lemonade stand, buy crafty rocks from kids on another corner, a round of drinks for the two elderly ladies at the bar, and he'd do it naturally and quietly. There was never any awkwardness between him and all of us, or in any of our settings during the trip. He and I were like long lost companions.

On our second to last day, we were out at a bar and these older women thought we were married.

"No, we had our first date Monday."

The older woman later stopped me in the bathroom and told me he was the love of my life. I was peeing in the stall, and she came in and said, "Honey. He's the one. You two are it."

He'd walk around calling me his wifey and, for the first time ever in the name of humor, I'd carry on. He was unbelievably generous; he had a way of interacting with everyone on such a personal, special level. We read together at the beach, page by page in silence. We went on a bike ride together in deep conversation. We'd party at night then gather everyone for breakfast in the morning—it all felt so uncomplicated.

It was a group of ten of us, and his friends mentioned how different he was around me. There was such a feeling of family between all of us. God bless those Italians and their hospitality. He understood me, gave me space when I needed it and knew how to be with me otherwise. Sometimes his horns of jealousy would come up, and I'd ignore them. We were in tight living quarters so there wasn't much privacy for anyone, but when we could we'd sneak a kiss—under the fireworks, holding hands—little exchanges of intimacy. Is this what they call the honeymoon phase, pure infatuation, or could something more come from this mysterious crush?

On our ride back from the ferry, he felt I was pulling away from him as I rode home in silence, but really, I felt weird coming home. When we got home, I felt horribly attached to him. I felt ready to jump in. I wanted to be different. I wanted to merge our lives. I'd be a loyal partner of this Leo, defending him while he defended clients.

After a complicated relationship with Dany, I knew the value of a partnership, I knew where it could break or grow. After the ups and downs with us, I also felt a need for ease. As we got home, our lives seemed to go separate ways—him at work, me at work.

For the first couple weeks of us being home, we'd only run into each other at my work—he was obviously intoxicated. He'd say drunken "I love you" slurs intensely. Those odd behaviors I couldn't identify with—I knew he liked to drink and party, but with my homebody roots, could we assimilate?

Suddenly, I saw our living such different lives may not be so compatible. Him defending criminals, me defending. We'd been on awkward footing since he'd had family things going on after our return home.

When we first got back, I thought he blew me off so I freaked out. Another out of character move for me. I was embarrassed to later learn his sister was in the hospital and that his niece was enduring a traumatic experience. I thought he was trying to string me along, and my disappointment had gotten the best of me.

After that, I wanted to let him come to me. He'd come up in waves, an "I miss you" text, an unusual call—*What's going on with us?* I wondered. I tried to understand, but each time we talked, something was going on with him, each story crazier than the last. His life seemed so dramatic and busy and, like him, intense. It was a weird readjustment after Dany.

With Dany, I'd search for the abnormal, I'd bring drama and he was just continuously normal, stable, and undramatic. At first, I tried to hang onto hope with Gavin, but often felt disappointed in his up and down expressions. I now had to be on the other end of such behavior, and it was uncomfortable.

It became more sporadic. We tried a couple times to get together, but each time it felt like a mind f**k. When would I see him again? When would he call? I knew he wasn't lying to me. It was like a black cloud came over his life when we got back. His sister was in the hospital, his dad was in the hospital, his niece was going through her own things—all those traumatic events were proving to be true, and I saw how they were affecting him. It made me wonder why it was all happening now. Why his life was going to turmoil and why I was watching him get lost in the smoke.

Aside from that, he had his regular clients: Cons, the innocent, and drug dealers. As a defense attorney, he was always in crisis. Rapes, DUIS, murders, gang bangs—he'd take these calls so casually and calmly. He was intelligent with such intellect, with such a powerful presence, but I saw the crack. He was interesting to observe because he was so good and patient at his job. Then, when he'd drink, those brooding eyes would take on another life. I could see the energy he internalized from clients trying to be smothered down by alcohol. Could I deal with this? Did he want a woman to deal with this?

A part of me felt like he didn't trust women. My Leo lover—he could make anyone love him, deeply, but you'd find yourself lost. His love of life with hints of darkness reminded me of myself. We seemed to do well together—a kind of instant romance that grew all too rocky. Had we not had such different ideas about living, I'd be willing to try this out.

It amazed me what different types of romance with a person could bring up in ourselves. It's funny how, even when you think you've gotten down to the deepest kinks of yourself, untied some of your greatest knots, and then you meet someone who exposes you to yet another. I thought of how different these loves could be and what our draw to them meant. With Dany, our relationship was heart-wrenching for me. I became a woman, I had to face real issues—he was with me in a huge growth period of my life. He was a mirror to my deeply-rooted problems, and he'd bring them to the surface. I grew a lot from my first-time love.

Now Gavin was a shocking, quite different companion. He was persistent to me, he was engaging, he was loving, but the mystery about him started to close my open arms. If we'd had better communication when home, I would've taken a back seat to his colorful life. With Gavin... I gave him the reigns to lead but he only lead me in circles.

Weekend Debatable
Twelve Days Post-Vineyard

I made it to my usual haven, Starbucks. As my caffeine kick settles, I am finally able to write and reflect, while avoiding the real obligations set for today. I spent the weekend in Boston with my new fling. It was supposed to be one day, which turned into two, and then three. I could still be there if my real life wasn't longing for me to come back. That, and if my mother had not literally filed a missing persons report on me. She randomly has moments of mothering, but they are often extreme and unusual. Afterward, she'll go back to her usual self—aloof and self-absorbed. Last week, I tried to will him to give me some attention all week and weekend, and then this weekend, though ill-equipped, we became mates for four days. I didn't have the clothes or the right frame of mind for this type of companionship. I was also nearing a period—pre-period I am very blatantly socially awkward. It goes from irritated-by-everyone socially awkward, to nothing-to-talk-about-because-I'm-paranoid-and-insecure socially awkward, to so-horny-that-I'm-incapable-of-making-decisions-and-may-do-something-irrational socially awkward.

After a week of miscommunication—via text of course—my recent fling and I decided to go out Friday night. How convenient. I was looking for a reason to get out of work. What better excuse than in the name of love?

After an excellent and productive Friday of chatting in Starbucks, to a completed yoga class and some house cleaning, I felt great. I headed into the city for what was supposed to be dinner, unfortunately I showed up on my time versus real time. That meant 6:15 became 7:30. I arrived, stomach rumbling and gas gage nearing empty—

typical procrastination on my part. What I thought would be a dinner turned into catching up on the couch. He wanted to explain himself for his recent absence, and I sat there wide eyed. Then after he spilled his thoughts to me, he wanted to pick up his very savvy, Boston friends for a night out at a new bar. That also had me wide eyed. I hated bars. I found nothing appealing about standing in line waiting for a drink, pretending to be friends with the girls around you who are in fact just scanning your outfit, the guys that think within an hour or within two drinks they'll be able to take you or your boyfriend home. Ugh. Being a part of the IT scene was not my idea of fun. I wanted to go anyway as supportive female companion. So much for our romantic dinner that I had envisioned.

That's the thing—I never knew what I'd get with Gavin. One minute he wanted to join me on a bike ride, walk barefoot with me to fireworks and kiss my cheek on the dock, collect rocks with me with little kids and drink lemonade at lemonade stands. Then, the next minute, we were excessively bar hopping, giving me emotional "I love yous," and fighting with anyone who glances at me, declaring our love in drunken fits, engaging in complete gluttony of $1000 drink bills. We met his friends. They were a fabulous couple—I had to say, I genuinely liked them. Each was charming in his or her own manner. We all chatted and stood there, drinks in hand. I sucked down my first... then my second... then my third. *Why not?* I thought. I felt out of place and I hoped sucking down drinks could give me some ease or unity.

After leaving the bar, Gavin wanted to stay out for the last hour of the night. Betty, his ex-roommate, did too, but her boyfriend was smart and called it bed time for the two of them.

My boyfriend of the night had other intentions. It didn't become clear to me until later that his relationship with booze was going to prevail over any relationship we could have. We get to the club and he knew the manager because he got him off a drug charge once. Who knew district attorneys would have so many connections? There was something sexy, that I never quite considered, about knowing I was with a lawyer something kind of sexy about being with a lawyer who's got all the bad boys on his side. I didn't date bad boys, but I guess I'll date their attorney. We do a shot at the bar—I was stumbling-over-myself drunk. I think the last time I did a shot was beginning of college. He tried to be Rico Suave on the dance floor, and I was simply trying to find my feet.

As the bar closed, we found a taxi outside and headed back to his apartment.

We got back to his place and he was very clearly ready to ravage me with me passion. He is often exuding passion. It's an admirable passion due to its intensity. I have other intentions—if it wouldn't make me famished, I would even try to throw up to counteract some of this intoxication. I was unfamiliar with how to behave like this.

After falling off the couch, I told him I was too drunk to do anything sexual or even sexy for that matter. He, thankfully, didn't try anything, and after I rummaged through his snack cabinets, we drunkenly went to bed. I bit into a granola bar that tasted like sawdust. In the morning, we woke to snack remnants all over his bed. It looked like Hansel and Gretel were navigating his apartment.

After a 3:00 a.m. bedtime, we are up at 10:00 a.m. I had a few missed calls from Betty to spend the day on her boyfriend's boat. I wanted to back out, but I didn't want to seem boring.

He had a weird effect on me that made me question myself a little bit. I am submissive to no one, though I make small exceptions with him. I seem to continuously give him the reigns, which for me is quite unusual. At this point, I was thinking he's a potential. A few red flags have been waved, but I loyally defended this Leo. My ram qualities around him seemed to turn into lamb, and the lion in him leaves one captivated by his presence, by his quiet confidence. I rationalized any of his behaviors that I would typically write off. The sides I have seen to him are positive, so intriguing, so alluring that I defended him very dutifully—telling myself this time, things would be different. I will be different. I was not going to be the girl that drives her boyfriend crazy, I won't be the schizophrenic emailer, I won't be the "make him jealous" type that I see in so many females, no, I will just be me. I want to be faithful comrade and companion. I'm very dedicated once someone challenges me.

After my stomach made some ungodly noises, we both knew we weren't going to get far without eating. We went to a café down the street from him. I thought about the first day we had breakfast there and I pictured us sitting there in different seasons. I liked the walk over to it. I didn't even mind how often he wore shades to hide his hangovers. I liked the area he lived in. I was fitting myself right into this scene and it wasn't so out of my character to be so easily allured, so compliant. Usually this type of togetherness so early on made me feel suffocated, misread, or bored. With him, a lot feels natural. I felt hopeful and loyal.

We got breakfast and as we drove over to meet his friends, he took multiple calls. Each one was accompanied by luring invitations. I was impressed and almost confused by how many friends he had. There were invitations to a wedding, to Salisbury Beach, he and his siblings talked, and last night, he put me on the phone with his mother.

Small pieces of him reminded me of Saint Alexander. I wondered, *Is this a Boston thing? When you're in the city does your social life magnify?* It would make sense—after one bar last night, I woke up to three different females messaging me that next morning. I, apparently, gave out my number, and had dates lined up with each of them. A Starbucks date—so cliché of me—and a wedding invitation. Now that was wonderful.

As I watched Gavin interact so lovingly with each of his friends, I questioned my own social life. I found myself both proud of this busy social bee, and also felt a tinge of jealousy. I—the one who never got jealous—was. The unfazed guru I was could feel the ugly, green, jealous monster on my face each time this socialite took a call. Was it because I felt somewhat inadequate in that department? Did it make me somewhat insecure since I enjoyed being somewhat of a loner? Was it because I felt I had to compete with not just friends, but divas, couples, clients and those Boston who were savvy? Yeah, probably that one.

I entered into a carb oblivion as we pulled up to meet his friends. We stopped at a grocery store and he impressed me yet again. Way too much over-indulgence, but god he was good. His lawyer skills made him a great and refined listener. He had my Saint Germaine, chardonnay, coconut water, and came out asking how I wanted my sandwich, snack foods, sunblock, magazines to share. There was no room for me to say I was not comfortable and nurtured. He sure does a good job at "unconditional" love, though it was funny because I questioned if he'd ever truly felt that. Not that he didn't receive it, but if he knew he was worthy of it.

We drove over to the docks where the boat was, and we met a girlfriend of Betty's and another couple. The other couple consisted of a very metrosexual male named Marco who I swore I'd seen before, and a taller Eva Mendes look-alike. I said Eva Mendes, Galvin said Anne Hathaway. It was like I got a way hotter Snookie or a less hot Kim Kardashian all because I'm a short brunette. Marco and his date are the overly affectionate, well-groomed type who likely cheat on each other and probably openly. They may even both have spouses at home. We got on the boat and are nearing take off. I found my social skills severely lacking due to my hangover, pre-Mother Nature, and the fact that I couldn't even stand to look at alcohol though they were already cracking beers.

We started to sail off for our destination... Aquapalooza. I was about a minute in and already seasick. I wished I had a fair warning for that. I wouldn't have done shots last night—I would have gotten four or more hours of sleep, and I would be looking like a much better boat bitch. I had a bikini by chance, shaved but not really shaved also by chance, and no hat to keep me looking like a sun goddess. That was not how I'd like to picture myself on my first Aquapalooza. Even though I rarely wear makeup or care about an outfit, on some occasions I want to be feminine. Here, had I known or prepared, I'd be the cliché, cookie-cutter, boat bitch.

As we were sailing to our destination, Gavin and I read one of the juicy magazines he got me. Typically, I have no interest in magazines, but I liked how we read together. We did this at the beach in Martha's Vineyard, literally turning pages together, and there's something very comforting about that. It only took me almost three years later and about twenty breakups later with Dany to now be the mushy-gushy type.

Toward our end, Dany would often proclaim, "I'm going to make you such a good girlfriend for someone," I hated that he'd say that. It would crush my hope of turning us around, it would make me feel unfit—he often had this effect—and yet he was right. Our relationship refined my qualities. It helped me pluck ones that needed to be shed and groomed, and helped me blossom ones that were merely seeds. It helped me grow into who I wanted to be. He just didn't understand once that work was done, I'd hoped to be in a garden with him, but by then, he'd turned too cold.

I made friendly with the girl next to me. She was plain Jane looking and she told me she was a dietician. Once we tied up our boats with the others, I saw girls in bikinis, bachelors on the prowl—scanning—and lots of alcohol. How would I survive this day? I literally couldn't muster up any conversation. My stomach was in knots. I hadn't pooped yet. I feel a day is much more productive when a healthy bowel movement is made. My odds were not looking good.

The day progressed. I sipped alcohol here and there, hoping for a drunk to catch on without actual consumption.

Despite my anti-social behavior, Gavin catered to me, "Don't drink honey, just lay out."

He confessed his love for me again on the front of the boat, complimented me, kissed me on my forehead, catered to me all of the time. "Who are you?" I want to say. A part of me truly believed he was acting. This reformed bad boy couldn't be so smitten by me. I know I'm worth love and affection, but I just didn't feel like I was his type. I could already see I was not the type of girl he would go for yet, he treated me with such gaga eyes.

I was seasick at the front of the boat, sipping coconut water, and he was rubbing my feet telling me I looked sexy. If I wasn't so hung over, I'd try to make sense of this in my head, *No, everyone else on this boat is sexy. I can't even pull myself together enough to be cute right now.*

He kept checking in on me. Even his friends noticed and commented on how he put me on a pedestal. Would he like that with me or start to resent it? I don't do surface stuff in my relationships, I do psychoanalysis and some can appreciate that—some aren't ready to enter a dating relationship with a female Freud.

Usually, I can't stand when guys are so into me—especially so soon—but this one I didn't mind. There was a part of me that thought his years in the courtroom just made him a fabulous actor, but each time I tried to call his bluff, he proved me wrong.

After last week when I said he was lying about a sick sister and blowing me off for a family emergency, I came to find out it was true. I decided to bite my tongue from then on. He let me be, he stuck up for my oddities, agreed with me in conversation, told me how different I was, he was protective and jealous—typically in the right moments—and then spacious in others, and there was such a rawness to him that I but into that illusion. Despite my reservations, despite my being slightly jaded to hearing such things, despite, despite, despite. I felt myself going all in, instantly. Had I met my match in the established, older, persuasive, bad boy bachelor? Had I finally come close to figuring it out? He was a lawyer—they sway judges and courtrooms—he may have been wooing me along with it and I was not so easily swayed.

I was invited on a family vacation to Italy last month with Caeser, the Cheshire Cat—all inclusive. I said no as casually as turning down lunch. I was still trying to show dedication to Dany then, of course he'd never know or appreciate my waiting. That was the thing about Dany—he saw me, he just never saw who I had become, or the isolation I had to grow comfortable with in an attempt to keep us intertwined. He simply was too caught up in his past perception of me to meet me at where I was, even if it was for him.

The day was a drunken hot mess for all others on deck. The dietician went from one lap to the next. Between make outs, she mentioned a boyfriend. I watched her shot gun a beer, go vodka to vodka with Gavin, and scarf down nachos. By the time we got to a restaurant that night off harbor, she had fallen off the deck, passed out on the lower deck, had a breakup with the hottie captain next to us who was absolutely adorable and kept chatting me up, but I was ten drinks short of conversation and, without caffeine, I couldn't say anything remotely charming. In our toast of the night, she managed to actually smash two of her drink glasses. By 9:00 p.m. we pulled into harbor and I was still a mess. Most others were passed out and spooning on the lower deck with gelatos and booze still in hand. It was a great day, but I was exhausted from a lack of actual exertion of energy. I didn't work that way and I was envious of those who could balance both worlds.

Gavin offered to go out again, but thank god we each fell asleep on his couch during *Storage Wars*. A part of me wanted to go home and knew this togetherness may be too much for me. Five days in the vineyard together after our first date, and now two nights in a row after our reunion. I needed to redeem myself, not become roommate, bromate, or houseguest so early on.

Dates to Remember - Gabrielle Anna

Sunday morning we woke up, I missed church, I missed yoga, and I missed not being a gluttonous mess. When we finally got out of bed, he asked me to stay for the day. I was itching to do something to normalize myself, but I decided to be a hermit with him instead.

We walked over, hand-in-hand, to the café. His friends called us trying to get us on the boat again. God, his friends were fabulous. He said we'll be vegging all day together. Who was this guy? Drunken hot mess one minute, and doting, laid back boyfriend the next.

We ordered at the café. At this point, my mindful eating was shot, my body was a wreck, so I ordered whatever and we ordered a lot. "Just absolutely no milk," I say. "No milk, no peanut butter. And no cheese on my panini."

By the time we got back, and once I was already one bite invested, I ate it despite the cheese. It was unbelievably delicious regardless. I drank my smoothie without milk—I compromise on the Greek yogurt. Another bad choice for being lactose intolerant. I thought I could handle it.

We watched our first documentary. We watched a political documentary. As we eased into our third documentary, my stomach was all tied up. I sat uncomfortably through the third movie knowing I needed to leave, knowing I needed to poop, knowing nothing about me right then was sexy, and knowing lactose intolerance was a serious issue when ignored. I should've known this by now.

I sat through the torture in my stomach because I liked how he was giving me a history lesson. I love when men teach me—there's something so sexy about it, that is, if they know what they're talking about.

We shared a plate of cookies and watched a Sara Palin film. This USA advocator was quite impressive with all his liberal knowledge. Three historic documentaries and a comedy show later, and I was calling it quits.

He, apparently, was not. "A third night? Really? You want me to stay again?"

Then there he went, persuading me like the lawyer he was, and next thing I knew, we were each getting into our separate showers and saying we'd meet on the couch afterward for our fourth movie. I claimed

Dates to Remember - Gabrielle Anna

I was undecided on a sleepover. How did he do it? Was it me, or was it him? Were we companions in a past life? This was what went on in my head. I somehow doubt his was as active on such things.

Once I heard his shower go on in his bathroom, I knew I could only survive another movie if I pooped. I had to. It wouldn't be natural for me to refrain. I highly doubt men have to even consider this. We'd already broken ninety percent of first dating rules. Date one, and two wine bottles later, I stayed over. Date two, and he took me and two friends on a five-day vacation. Now, after over a week of having me on an emotional rollercoaster, I just agreed to my third day here. God, he was good.

That was it-I either needed to talk myself out of there, or I let myself poop at the bachelor pad. How the f**k did Alle live with a boyfriend and not poop? They lived together for a year and she would leave to poop, but not me. I ate dairy and I'm lactose intolerant. Unforgivable amounts of dairy. I didn't poop yesterday, and I absolutely had to.

God, this was so unsexy. I was a sunburned, no makeup, lethargic, pre-menstrual, full, and robust mess. He was in the other bathroom, bronzed, unaffected by the hangover, and with hair I'd still kill for. Okay, I'd do it.

At this point I was freaked by the noises my stomach made and felt today. I prayed it was quick and quiet. I sat on the toilet as delicately as I could, and I pooped. Hooray! I got in the shower, hoping to feel somewhat like a goddess again, and then it happened. It was like I opened the flood gates by letting my body poop. It was mad at me now. Literally, before I could even make it out of the shower, butt cheeks clenching, I pooped. In the shower. I had the liquid shits—thank you, Greek yogurt. Thank you, liquor. F**k! I couldn't even help myself.

At that point, I just let it go. Oh this was awful. I was mortified. I was picturing him coming in the bathroom now. I was thinking of all possible, awful scenarios that could occur. I was thinking of the cleanup here. What if the drain clogs? What if he comes in? What if he comes in and asks why the hell I was pooping in his shower? Oh my god, I'm actually pooping in his shower. Month one and this is what we've come to. This is like mommy status. I've advanced us way beyond our appropriate time progression for this possible relationship. This shit shouldn't happen 'til there is a ring on your finger and a baby in your belly.

Once I survived the trauma, I tried to collect myself. There was no redemption from there. God, did I feel better though. It had to be done. I would never be able to step foot into his guest bathroom again, but it had to be done. I couldn't be more grateful to know that he was moving soon. Whew. I came out and he tells me how sexy and flushed I looked. Seriously. I turned about three shades of crimson.

He grabbed us pillows to cuddle on the couch. He did some of his work stuff while we settled on a movie. I had to give it to him, while I sat there flustered, a part of me wanting to confess because it was so horrific, that if I didn't say anything, it would be burned into my brain.

He got to be the sexy, laid back lawyer. He was always dealing with clients and making family arrangements—a dependable guy on a Sunday. I loved even more how he involved me. I felt like I was let in on top secret information. He would ask my opinion on a case, let me listen in, ask me what I'd charge in court fees.

My dad should've included me on something when I was younger so I wouldn't be such a sucker for this. This is why I'm so into working men. I love watching them do it, I love being the sidekick. I love trying on their profession, yet I go to the extreme and date workaholics who later piss me off because they work too much. I haven't quite figured out how to get it right yet. I need someone who's appreciative of the clock but doesn't live by it. I need someone who works hard, but isn't enslaved by it.

We watched our movie. We slightly spoon. Then we went to bed and fell asleep like roommates. I woke him up in the morning for court. That was different. I made and poured him his coffee. I helped him shave and covered his pimple with my concealer. I helped him decide on an outfit for work. It was all a little surreal. We moved about like perfect housemates.

As we were out the door, he even said I could stay longer. He told me I could stay there and he'd try to get back from court early. Could I stay over a fourth night on a whim? I needed to get my shit together, otherwise I actually would. I used to loathe being submerged into someone's life. I hated inserting myself to theirs. I thought I'd miss my own potential and motivations. I politely declined and we went our separate ways. As I drove away, I wondered how long before I heard from him again. Which Gavin would call? Which Gavin was I more intrigued by? And, most importantly, will we or wont we be something more?

Time to Travel
Goodbye Crooked Apartment, Goodbye Mind F**k G.
August 22, 2012

For someone who is so cautious about her life, I seem to let my impulses excite me often on the most bizarre of times, but I go with it. Most of the time, it's like my body knows things before my mind or heart does. Last week, I didn't schedule myself for work, and then I just kept not scheduling, for no reason. All the while I thought, *I'm going to need to work.* Something told me I needed to travel.

The first invite was G, the Case A who had successfully mind f**ked me, G. I had just realized that, if all my other conclusions about him failed, he must be the due karma from when I stood Jason up for the Fourth of July. Whenever G saw me, he was in my face and then he left me in a whirlwind. I should have better foreseen this. Very few people really make me question myself, and that inadequacy I felt from our first interaction should have alerted me.

So, as protocol had it, last week he saw me, then sent me multiple, intense texts, intense follow up calls, and orders for a vacation together. What? Could we ever just have a normal catch up conversation or one day get-together? Perhaps even a consistent flow of communication? It seemed I was either hoping to reach him for a simple hello, or he was strategically trying to get me away when I least expected it. We haven't talked, and suddenly he wanted to go away together. Logic told me that he A: had a girlfriend, B: loved drinking more than dating, C: was just not that into me, D: was yet another eighty-hour work week man, or E: a mass-manipulator, secret woman-hater—the extremes truly varied here. I couldn't figure out his ups and downs.

Regardless of my wild assumptions, he saw me and begged me to take a vacation this week for the sake of our sanity.

"I felt sane until I saw you," I said.

He thought I was joking.

I was honest. Even then I said, "I don't know how to respond to this. We really can't keep playing house whenever it's convenient." But I supposed my small tinge of hope thought he meant it.

I slept over two nights later—it felt normal, but subdued. He kept putting me on that pedestal, "I kept your toothbrush in the holder, is that weird? I look at this picture on my phone of you sometimes when I miss you, is that okay? Whenever you want to come here after work, you can sleep over and I'll rub your feet. I feel so at ease and relaxed when I'm with you. I don't want to ever leave you!"

I nodded nonchalantly, baffled by the question, *Does he truly believe I want to hear this, or is this an actual confession?* He'd never given me a reason not to believe him, but he has given me quite a few to doubt.

The next day, he called off work—four or more court cases—so we could stay together. As I tried to leave, he had me agree to lunch. I guess it was just to drag out our non-companionship, to feed into a bliss he perhaps think women want to hear.

We had lunch by the water and he didn't take his eyes off me. Whenever we were together he stayed locked in. I got caught checking out more females in perimeter then he did.

We parted ways and I agreed to see him again, all the while knowing the cycle would continue with such an agreement. How did these patterns form with someone, and what was the best way to break them? The word of my "yes" was shallow, but I say it regardless.

As my non-work week approached, I thought to myself, *I'm going to have to work,* and I still didn't schedule. What non-vacation was holding me back? I pictured myself in my apartment. I'd have to work, so why was I so casually putting it off? I didn't work much anyway. Why couldn't I picture working two shifts that week? If I took off another week, I could go to Vegas with some coworkers—though that would probably leave me mischievous—I was, thus far, a Vegas virgin. As the hours got down to the grind, I wondered what I'd do with myself.

My Fiona Apple and Janis Joplin sing-alongs in the kitchen provided entertainment, but I couldn't dedicate a week of nothing for them.

Then it happened. Down to the grind, the night before I gave in to the duties and demands of work. Finally, beloved Gabriel—my Sagittarian friend since 7th grade—came through with a surprise text message. He spent almost the past month in Columbia and we hadn't seen each other or really talked since March. I'd always been impressed by his ability to balance his free spirited nature, and his responsibility.

"When are you coming to Miami?" he asked.

"Tomorrow, if it works for you," I challenged him to see if he'd dive in.

And, just like that, I found a $140 flight to Miami. I scrambled around my apartment, all the while knowing I just agreed to an 8:00 a.m. flight on a whim while doing karate and karaoke in my kitchen.

Surely this would work out better than my Jamaica trip. Martha's Vineyard was overall a victory, despite Danielle being voted off the island by every member of the group.

Here I was, people watching during my layover in DC. I was perplexed by all the miserable expressions surrounding me. How could everyone walk around carrying that much resentment? I rationally determined these individuals were going home, going on a vacation, or traveling for work, all of which implied they had jobs. Then why was there such disdain? It takes more energy to frown and be pissed off.

I sat there beaming, and I realized some people were even angry at me for being so happy. They were just looking for someone to direct their anger onto. A couple and a separate family were actually eyeing me as I ate my chicken taco salad—displeased, bothered by my idiotic contentment. I was simply beaming to go visit my long-time friend, and pleased that I found a vacation.

I practically wanted to hug the guy next to me just to ease some of his tension. A raging homosexual fought loudly on a phone call over treatment from a woman at work. I tried to find the most non-socially awkward engagement of physical affection I can give him, but fell short with my taco salad in my lap. Instead, I just offered him a smile whenever I thought he was going to look at me, but he was too caught up in the call to catch my gesture. As I tried to construct the weekend in my mind, a text came up. Kal—a chiro acquaintance—wanted me to take a road trip for two days and then head to NYC for the last one. He said it would help him tremendously to not have to travel alone. I didn't give that any attention—we were practically strangers.

It seemed the cosmic gods were conspiring to get me out of my own setting for a while. I knew I wouldn't be sitting at home in my crooked apartment doing karaoke, something was pulling me to go abroad. My horoscope told me this was my week for travels, but I questioned how achievable that would be. Thank you, Universe, for not leaving me single and alone in my apartment. They probably think I've sung Fiona one too many times after my break up with Dany. This vacation was best for me and for my neighbors.

Had I planned accordingly, I could have gone Miami to Boston to Maryland, back to NYC, and then a week in Vegas but I wasn't that much of a jet setter.

As I logged onto Facebook merely as a way to pass the time, I saw that mind f**k G blocked me. Was that because I had to think about us going away together? So much for our romantic vacation. It seemed I as no longer worthy of reading his political Facebook posts. Did he think I was skulking around his epiphanies via Facebook? I added him just to make sense of his mind games to settle my own sanity—he knew I loved psychology. Didn't he realize how stubborn I was when provoked?

I'd now love to tag myself next to some political figure and say nonchalantly, "Vacationing to the Whitehouse for golf with Obama." That would stir him. For my own kicks, I'd love to tag him in a picture next to Miami palm trees, and write "insert self here: with a tray of margaritas. There was a message in my inbox from Kris. We were Cape Cod companions from when I was four to about thirteen. Our grandparents were friends for years, so we'd play together. He'd tease me, I'd conspire against him with my Barbies—typical kid play. That is, until I got older and had a crush on him where I would consult with my dolls about whether or not they could make it to our wedding. Childhood friends are funny.

Dates to Remember - Gabrielle Anna

One of my last memories of him was when he'd come taunt me while I preformed nature rituals in his grandmothers garden. I supposed not too much had changed for me. It had been years since we talked, and here he was on the twenty-two, on my flight to Miami, inviting me to the Cape house for the weekend for his birthday via Facebook. What? Life has a funny way of getting its point across.

Another friend texted me about joining her on a work trip in Dallas. Seriously? She was going for work training and wanted to make the best of it with me. Though there was always a lure for all such destinations, I was completely at ease in my decision. I felt a strong pull to Miami, despite my previous assumptions. Gabe and I had known each other since I was adolescent and awkward, and no matter how far life has pulled us apart, we've always remained loving friends. Time doesn't faze or change our relationship. I am overly excited to see him and to experience life from his space for a while.

And when I thought the madness couldn't go on, I checked my inbox after a phone malfunction to hear a voicemail from dear Mike Jones. Spiritual comrade—super hot and cold, withdrawn, emotional, insightful, transcendentalist Mike Jones. He invited me on a trip to Newport to his friends' beach house .It seemed even if I had tried to be anti-social this week, I would've caved on something.

Off to Miami on a rash decision and I couldn't be more comfortable. I chuckled about the seeming coincidences of life, and for entertainment purposes, I fit myself into the different captions that could have transpired and taken me on another course.

This was a week for travels this single, white female who once, with shaky fingers, wouldn't venture past her familiar suburbia. Now, my footing was sure and confident, free in my decisions, knowing they'd lead me where I was supposed to be.

Chapter Eleven

Friend, Foe, or Just Say No

These excerpts span over the course of five years about dates, attempted dates, and the grey areas in the "are we dating?" stage. Each event is special in its own way, but not significant enough beyond a singular date or a lesson. These excerpts offer quick reminders, red flags, comical relief, or possible partners for some other. Some successfully became friends, some successfully dated my friends, some became stalkers, and some fade into the unconscious. Nonetheless, I would like to thank them all for their entertainment, and reference purposes.

"When I get lonely these days, I think: So BE lonely. Learn your way around loneliness. Make a map of it. Sit with it, for once in your life. Welcome to the human experience. But never again use another person's body or emotions as a scratching post for your own unfulfilled yearnings." —Elizabeth Gilbert.

Cardinal Sin of Dating or Blessed Blunder?
February 17, 2009

Last night, despite my reservations, I drove to Sal's house. Sal, the gym bachelor who many of us at the front desk flirt with, even though we heard he was a closet freak. He was usually quiet, so I was surprised when he was persistent in us suddenly hanging out. I warned him that I had the flu, but he continued to insist, this time with the lure of comfort foods. Guilt tripping and goodies, we were off to an interesting start. He made me soup and a grilled cheese sandwich with a salad. He could have done something not so cliché, but being sick, it all tasted the same anyway. My taste buds seemed oblivious, so possibly anything could have been in his favor. I'd been waiting for him to actually have a real conversation and face time with me, and of course he does it the week that I was practically bed-ridden from whatever epidemic or karma was hanging onto me.

I could tell he was a guy who didn't do well with rejection, one "no" and I'd probably have to wait a year before getting asked out again, so instead of making a rain check, I went.

All in all, we got along, but before I had a chance to be one of the coolest chicks he'd ever asked out during swine flu season, I committed like the cardinal sin of dating. Okay, maybe just the cardinal sin of first-time dating.

I farted.

F-a-r-t-e-d. Can you believe it? As the optimist I am, I believe this incident makes me memorable. Not exactly how I pictured being remembered.

That got me thinking—after the trauma passed of course—why is it so disgraced? Particularly for women? I wanted to meet one human being who doesn't fart or shit. Furthermore, when did burping become acceptable? A simple "excuse me" and it's pardoned. Is there ever a right time to pass gas? It literally took every ounce of my strength to keep composed when this happened, especially because I was mid-story. In my animation and storytelling, so it went. I was laughing so hard that it just slipped. I had this horrible cough, so I tried to hold in the cough and while my muscles were contracting, there it was. Unexpected, and to my dismay as well.

To make matters worse, after it happened, I didn't know whether to address it or just let it hang in the air like a black cloud lurking over us. After that, I was ready to send in the troops and go home, but he kept talking, talking, talking and wouldn't shut up. I didn't know if he just kept talking to block out the unforgivable fart, or if he meant to make genuine conversation.

I stayed three hours longer, running the incident over and over in my head every five minutes while trying to make out what he was saying. Did this mean he A: blocked out the incident immediately? Girls don't fart and just rejected it altogether? B: didn't want to embarrass me so pretended not to notice, C. was repulsed, and I'd be labeled fart girl, or D: thought it was funny and simply didn't care. It was probably a shame because even if he had dismissed the incident, it was now burned into my mind.

Every time that I saw him at the gym, I could hear the fart in my ears. I'd probably even develop some sort of weird phobia after this. My only thought was that he probably thought I couldn't keep my bodily functions in check.

Should I have come right out and said, "Don't worry, Sal, I won't do this again in public."

Would I now be banned from dates outside the perimeter of his house? I saw him more as a friend anyway, but it was just the mere fact that it was quite possible this discredited me, kind of like the girl who puts out too quickly.

I could see him talking about me, "She was a great girl, but she didn't meet the family because when she laughs, she farts, and we're all such funny people."

You know how guys are. They always take the situation differently and never fail to talk themselves up. I could be optimistic. I could start a feminist movement. Maybe he would respect me for being so au natural. I could just start farting on all my dates instead of parading around on false pretenses that there is a plug up my ass and, as a woman, I smell of vanilla and hormones. Oh, how I wanted to end those lovely beliefs some men hold us to where we somehow keep our physique and composure without pooping, and we bypass all bodily functions such as farting or burping. Ultimately, I feel if this happens, you can redeem yourself and turn it around and if you don't want to, it allows you leeway to silently exit.

When asked, would a man prefer a stage-five clinger, a you-can't-hang-out-with-your-friends-only-with-me, one who declares their love for and union with you on Facebook, or a woman who doesn't try to bottle up her bodily functions? That would alleviate the "you've changed!" expression so many partners make after living together or saying their vows. That would also alleviates determining the proper time frame in a relationship to exhibit fact that we, as women, are still human.

Eye F**ck, Mind F**k, No F**k
2009

It was the big day. I was teaching my first sensual dance class. I had this funny, anxious feeling that worked its way through my stomach and chest. Last night, I even dreamed I missed class today. One would literally have to hold me hostage to miss this class. Nerves and all, I was doing it, baby. I can and will let go of the old, conditioned, insecure brain. I instantly punch any negative thought that comes over me. Any insecurity that wants to surface, any negativity from my head will be crushed, I will literally Zumba all over them. While doing the Samba on any negative thoughts in my head, I was brought back to reality by a recent classmate admirer. I wore sweats and no makeup to class and there he was—this diligent, strange man-boy who continued to pop up in my nearby surroundings. He probably even sat in on some of my classes for observation. I won't write him off as a stalker, I'm fairly predictable so he'd be selling himself short. We may be, in fact, running into each other, but right now it was just plain distracting.

This man-boy has gotten the eye f**k down to a T. I literally felt dirty after he looked at me. Not dirty in a repulsed way, just dirty in that I could feel him undressing me out of my unflattering, don't-look-at-me pj's. Give a sistah a break or a lesson in acquiring this skill. It was a talent when they didn't lurk around to do it to you.

Being as awkward as I am, I wouldn't know what to do with that skill. There's a sex goddess in my head, she just prefers to remain in hiding. His creeping was potentially satisfying for my ego, so I wrote it off. I could only imagine what he'd do if he saw me looking hygienic. He'd probably lose his shit right there, or maybe have no interest at all. I couldn't identify his type yet.

Perception is such a funny thing. Yesterday I went into work au natural, but wore hat of course, because that's the best accessory for when you didn't feel like doing your hair or make up. And yet, a certain bachelor flirted with me all morning.

I wanted to say, "Are you serious?" Men and women are never on the same page; I want it and you're cranky, you want it and I'm cranky or feeling undesirable—thank you, estrogen. The days I went in thinking I looked like a diva and he passed me nonchalantly... Then yesterday I was bare-faced and he was following me around like a puppy. At dance class later, as the countdown was loud and slightly unnerving in my head, the Female Gym Master was set on wearing sunglasses, something with garter belts, and fake money. Would she ever give me a break?

I said, "Really? I'm not trying to train strippers, I want to teach a 'sexy dance.'" She continued to encourage that I go out there throwing fake money. She was technically my boss, so I'd accommodate, but I refused to accessorize beyond a boa. I couldn't teach a dance class while wearing shades on day one, I needed to build a relationship with the members first. Making it rain on day one could backfire or not, but I was not willing to take any chances.

    I was nervous enough as it was. I couldn't help but question her intentions. People can all be such manipulators; how could I get anything done in this vortex? While trying to study and visualize a successful class, eerie eye f**k boy—name and identity unknown—wouldn't let up.

Chapter Twelve

Dating Observations and Conclusions
The End of 2009

I didn't know when dating became so difficult. I was browsing the males in my life for speculation purposes and some insight into my own psyche. The results only lead me to conclude that rather than mating, I was going to be masturbating. I was both comforted and frightened by such a conclusion. On the plus side, I knew things would get done, however, on the not-so-plus-side, it was more fun to share this responsibility. I'm not a nymphomaniac in any sense of the word—I haven't even had that much sex in my life—however, masturbating I can speak on. I've put in my time on that one.

My real point is dating is never what it seems. It may be easy to hit it off with someone for an instant, but how often is that person actually what you imagined? I once read something that went kind of like this, so I'm paraphrasing: "Women go into relationships hoping men will change, and men go into relationships hoping women don't change." There's a lot of truth to that. It's not even that I see people with high expectations in mind, and still I feel a tinge of disappointment. It's not that there is lack of good men out there; it's just that there is lack of my desire to date them. I enjoy being single, but sometimes wearing this label is exhausting. Having to listen to bachelors pitch you on why you should be infatuated with them becomes quite repetitive. I'll let anyone talk about themselves, but these speeches are interfering with my own life. Are we surrounded by freaks in disguise? Are we all freaks in hiding? As long as my number doesn't circulate to any more of the wrong hands, I think I can handle it. Such examples are as follows:

Eric from the gas station asked me out every time I got gas there, not once losing hope or getting the hint. I finally caved one day when he tried to actually hold my gas hostage. I couldn't risk losing the one station in town that pumped for me and had reasonable prices, to a member at the gym who drank all my smoothies no matter how repulsive they taste.

These were cases where you know a number exchange was a bad idea, but you gave in anyway. I could've been mean, but I usually found something in everyone I met that gave them their sparkle. I love being able to see peoples' sparkle; I even want them to see it. But sometimes, if you gave any sort of kindness to someone, they want to suck you dry. I didn't want to explain myself and I didn't want to be subjected to such behavior.

The manipulation people have at their disposal has far advanced since ancient days. There's cyber stalking until someone caves, Facebook posting, persuasion, bribery, the list continues. Are we so depleted of our social kindness that when we receive it, we don't recognize it? The loving feeling I exude toward everyone often becomes miscommunicated. Must I be guarded in my appreciation for others' authenticity?

Now, before I make others out to be worse than they are, I have to establish the fact these are all eligible men. I believe you learn something from everyone you meet in your life, we just need to determine why they're being sent to us. Nevertheless, I am on overload. In no particular order, I am going to express why my hope for relationships diminishes.

There was Scotty. Each time I hear or say his name, I instantly think of the "Scotty Doesn't Know" song and for a second there, I really like him. My girlfriend Stacy was dating one of his friends so I decided to go over there with her one night when she needed to track the friend down and confirm his location.

Poor Stacy. Until she realized her worth, these boys wouldn't either. It was rare that boys in their twenties caught my eye, but Scotty did. He had this quiet confidence and sultry, dark skin.

The first night we met, he didn't even give me a double take; I like a challenge, so this intrigued me. Not even a look in my direction, not even eye contact?

The next time we went out—myself, again, as the designated friend—he wasn't so coy. He looked me dead in the eye and literally asked to lick my feet. Out of nowhere! We had all been sitting in the living room and he turned to me with the offer.

"Can you ... what?" I was put off and turned on all at once. The ability to make that line sound sexy was definitely something to be credited for. I really didn't want anyone to lick my feet, but he got me to consider it. He said it with such conviction. He looked at me with this erotic energy and I was dumbfounded. I just pinched Stacy's side and mouthed to her, "What the...? After that night, he really made an effort to keep in touch, but sadly I felt he was too much of a man-whore. I politely declined that night, but I left impressed.

There was Alexander. The ex. X is like the absolute perfect letter to describe past boyfriends. Those exes. I swear X was put in the alphabet just for this reason. Alexander could make any woman happy, except me of course. Anything I wanted he'd give to me on a platinum platter, with such a cool demeanor. Still, as much as I cared for him, he didn't give me that heart beating out of your skin feeling, that anxiousness you get before you see them. We had a relationship. It was fabulous, no doubt. It was refreshing. I was attracted to him, but his efforts to sway me didn't faze me. Some women love this, they feed into it. I do not.

He'd always try to talk me out of my own thoughts and it drove me crazy. "Alexander, I don't want to go there tonight."

"Yes you do, pumpkin squash butt. Let's just go, Gab. Come on."

It should've been a red flag to me that this constant persuasion would continue when he begged for our first dates. When I reached my breaking point, I stopped shaving, I made things as complicated as possible, I gave him the silent treatment, I ate off my plate and his, and still he didn't budge. My behavior had become borderline cruel. Even so he'd sit there smiling, almost as if he knew I was trying to sabotage us.

Then my inevitable guilt would kick in—guilt for being such a non-lover—so I'd justify or rationalize our staying together. We had a wonderful first date, then with the hype of the holidays and his sudden infatuation, we were the soon-to-be-married couple, literally. To break up with him meant to break up with his family too, and they were the family I'd always envisioned for myself and my future family. I suggest don't start dating in December—you can get completely blindsided. Christmas, New Year's, Valentine's... The hype will blind you.

There was Jazeir—his fate is undecided. He tried so hard to get me to do anything with him and I blew him off every time. Every time he asked me to hang out, I'd say I'd think about it, then I ignore him the day of. I'm not even sure why. I don't know what happened because he's sexy, he's older, he's built, he's active, and he manages a good job, an apartment—why was I avoiding him? We even hit it off when I got his attention, I guess I just grabbed too much of it.

Maybe I just liked looking at him and was disappointed that our terms couldn't be as simple as that. It was either because I couldn't understand what he's saying seventy percent of the time, or because some part of me felt he was still to boyish. I hated to refer to him as boyish, so we'll say man-boy.

Since the winter of this year, I as into men. You couldn't date one of Boston's most eligible bachelors and then start dating boys again. North End apartment to mother's basement, no way.

Chris Rock once said it best when he said, "Women can never go back in lifestyle, and guys can never go back sexually." Once you've dated a boyfriend with a car, there's a standard set for future bachelors. Girlfriend won't be picking your ass up anymore or carpooling with friends. For men, say you give them a strip tease over meatloaf, well, any time after that if you're making meatloaf, they can't be blamed for looking at you wide eyed awaiting their sultry dance.

If Jazier could emerge into manhood in the near future, it'd send me into frenzy. I'd bake for him, clean for him, turn into super girlfriend by default. Sadly, he couldn't help that he was twenty-three and I as mentally clocking in on an unknown age. Females generally mature faster, so that added years to my biological clock. And since I am such an old soul we could more years. I will continue to entertain the idea that perhaps we could have something, but my instincts know the truth. I'm not picky; I just don't need to dabble in mismatches. I guess I'll just watch him work out while I'm technically working. That seems like the safer, honest bet for each of us in this scenario.

Side note: an observation on couples. The couple across from me has distracted me and is actually starting to irk me. It was fine when they shared string cheese. It was fine when they shared Gatorade literally sip by sip. Now they're feeding each other cheese crackers. Before the girlfriend came along, I was somewhat convinced this bachelor was a homosexual, so the picnic they are having got old after snack number three. She looks as though she may bite into him next. Have I become too cynical? Is it wrong of me to notice that he was eyeing other men before she came back? I think he'd be much happier sharing string cheese with someone else, yet she seems oblivious to this.

Back to dating—there are the blind dates that friends try to set you up on, even though they're constantly complaining about their own relationship problems. Some dates are successful, some are excruciating, but we agree because it's fifty-fifty.

There was Paul. He was never considered a potential, ever. He was a frequent gym member who would come and pretend to work out so we would talk at the front desk. One day after my shift, I went for coffee with him as friends, and that was one time too many. He took that interaction far too seriously. He had a very dry sense of humor that, at one time, entertained me, but because I told him he was funny, he tried so hard to get me to laugh that it is uncomfortable.

He would stand there and stare at me until I was entertained. I'd just stare back at him blankly at every sarcastic comment he made; I swear he expected me to burst into hysteria. Each time he was around me, I felt like his body language was saying, "Laugh bitch, laugh!"

He knew we were only friends—I made that clear— but apparently friends should talk every day—not just by text, but on the phone. Apparently, I was committed to coffee three times a week, and I had to respond to his emails every hour on the hour, regardless of their rambling.

His new thing was to text me, "Can we talk for a sec?" That is the most unflattering line ever.

What was worse was when guys second guess themselves, "I'm annoying you, aren't I? You aren't laughing; I thought you said I was funny. Did my joke just offend you, Gab? You know I'm kidding right?"

Yesterday he said to me, "You know how you want someone to ask you out and he hasn't and I'm waiting for Lee to leave her husband for me?"

"Yes, Paul. That's an interesting way of putting it."

"Well, what if we get together, and then they ask us out because we're no longer available?"

I didn't send him a response. I was stuck in this predicament where he had a gym membership and he was free to come in whenever. By whenever, I meant my shift. I don't think I ever saw him actually lift a weight.

He'd had a mole removed from his back and, for close to two weeks, he said it was too fragile to work out, so he'd just come in, stand at the front desk, and stare at me. What's worse are guys who admit they have babies from the get-go and the guys who are constantly trying to prove they are fearless macho men.

Then there was Calvin—dun dun dun. I didn't think much about us anymore, I just tried to take things as it came. He used to make my stomach drop, that heartbeat-out-of-your-skin feeling had since been tamed.

One woman at the gym was convinced we're secretly dating, and as much as I loved her, I was out of excuses for the next time she asked about us and our non-relationship.

"You two have so much chemistry. You two look so into each other. Do you see how his eyes light up when he talks to you?"

"No Tina, I don't notice because my body is on f**kin' fire."

The more I had to explain that we were just friends to literally all observers there, the more the reality sunk in. The more I expressed how I was single due to my patiently waiting for him, the more I realized I would be single a long time. Two of my coworkers whom I love were constantly trying to figure us out.

I had the blunt facts. There was attraction—we've both admitted to it. I think I actually salivated in his presence and his smell made me kooky. We had developed a friendship, we talked on the phone before bed regularly, and our longest conversation I actually timed. Our longest conversation went from 9:00 to 3:30 a.m. Despite my efforts and conversational skills, he refused to ask me out. That fueled me one week then burned me out the next. I was so truthful with him that sometimes I couldn't decipher if he was meant to be my lover or my shrink. It was like sitting with a confetti cake, I f**kin' love confetti cake. How many times could I sit with it and not want to devour it?

Then there's the borderline stalkers from school, the guys you meet out one night and accidentally give your number to. The guys who get your number from someone you accidentally gave it to. The exes who randomly tried to come back around—of course only when you've decided you're over them. The guys from work who you have to see on a consistent basis so you give them you're number due to circumstance. The ones who have girlfriends—or wives for that matter—and flirt with you anyway, telling you anything to get your number. The guys who can't comprehend rejection so their tactic is to wear you down. The stage-ten clingers who can't let go. The friend of a friend whom you've got to be set up with. The guys who don't try hard enough—often the ones we admire!—versus the ones who don't stop trying. The guys who take the friend role. The guys who want to get with you just to say they did. Your date's best friend or brother who is either a skeez or a spy. The over-confident ones who feel you are privileged by their attention. The ones who feel entitled to your panties, and the ones who try to talk to you about anything when all you want to say is, "you'll never get in my panties."

And lastly, after all the non-potential bachelors, I've got an actual date coming up with Christian. Apparently when I took Carolyn's

Dates to Remember - Gabrielle Anna

6:00 a.m. spin class, a trainer saw me leave and asked her for my number and bio. I was going to say no to the date, but if he found me attractive under those circumstances, he's worthy of a date. He saw me noncaffeinated and sweaty, I'll take a chance. I haven't made my confirmation call yet, but I intend to see how it goes. Let's hope he's not one of those trainers who's obsessed with his body—or worse—how to better mine. I'll judge by his reaction when I order dessert. Dessert if our date goes well, and I'm testing the waters, a loaded cheeseburger and fries if our compatibility seems hopeless. (This certain bachelor ended up being Chapter Three—OCD, you saw our outcome).

Chapter Thirteen

BREAKDOWN, BREAKDOWN, BREAKTHROUGH
MAY 15, 2010

I'm either hormonal from a much-awaited period, or on the verge of a breakdown—no, optimistic thinking—breakthrough. I feel bored and stagnant with life right now. Tired of everyone's BS, my own included. I hate giving out negative energy, as it comes right back. Sometimes I feel people's energy can't touch me, other times I'm sucking up everything around.

My dad, who hadn't worked since December, was getting laser hair removal on his arms. My mother claimed it was my fault for taunting him in the 7th grade. What adolescent girl finds body hair attractive, especially on her dad, especially on her possible gene pool? They both justified his behavior by claiming it was a flat fee of $30. If that was the case I'd have gotten the procedure on my whole body, even where it didn't grow, just for caution. I'd have bought it for my friends even.

I wanted to feel reconnected with my mom again, but the relationship made me feel like I was constantly biting my tongue. Her newest thing was to constantly take what she wanted out of my room and put what she didn't want back in my room as some sort of bartering, as if I wouldn't notice. I may often be aloof but I noticed when a random thing was hanging from my ceiling that I didn't put it there.

She'd ask things like, "Gab I took that herbal face cream of yours. I love it. Do you mind?"

"Take the cream, but please take the random Bobo doll out of my room, too. I don't think it belongs there."

Family boundaries and relationship boundaries seemed to so easily become unclear. Aside from my dad's recent makeover, he'd verbally harass me for using GNC products. With all his free time, he started to think he was a Spartan or professional athlete. He couldn't make it to work because of a shoulder injury. He couldn't provide money for groceries I purchased so my brother and I could eat. We managed without his regard. Yet he could make it to work out and had an infinite supply of money for supplements. Was this a not-so-midlife crisis? I was tired of everyone getting mad at me for talking about the obvious.

I went to Rosie's and couldn't get out of there fast enough. I walked in on her spilling my most recent confidential news to two other people. That was an awkward moment. "Oh hi, that secret you'd been keeping was a secret!" I entered excited to see her as she'd be immediate relief from my family, and there she was, spilling my shit. I'll always think of her as a soul sister, but I couldn't bear to be around her right then.

I was left either to talk to myself on a long car ride or camp out in a bookstore. Perhaps I was on overload so I was irritable with all these dilemmas in my life. I was speculating when I'd get back in the dating pool again, or if I'd much rather speculate the rest of my life instead.

There was Javery, the coworker. I won him over the day I sang, word for word, Warren G Regulators. I didn't miss a beat or a line with it. With YouTube, I doubted I was the first white girl he'd heard rap, but he had since been quite attached.

I did this while tending to the front desk, made a sale, and then I went and jokingly asked one of the new trainers to spot me for a keegle. That very much amused Javery. I was simply trying to pass the time at the Vortex. We laughed a lot together. He said the most funny and obvious things. We got to be spectators together.

As precious as he was, I thought it too obvious he was looking for that special someone. That his male, biological, testosterone clock was ticking. He was under the impression we were getting married. It was a joke at first. However, after receiving our wedding playlist via email and being told I needed to meet some of his friends so we could decide the wedding party order, I realized that may be more serious than I'd originally thought.

There's Kareem, another coworker. He was known for being a man-whore. An adorable, reformed man-whore. It never bothered me, but it was all anyone talked about. He thought I didn't know about the married Brazilian chick he fooled around with in the back parking lot, so as he recently confessed his desire for us to be together, I had to say, "Not happening."

At the last gym he worked at, he was getting it on in the tanning bed; kudos, but I actually tanned in those. I was sure he could date a naïve girl like myself and have fun, but he was totally the type that gets gaga for your cookie and then either puts it in their jar for collection, or takes a bite and holds onto it. No thanks. My cookie wouldn't be going to any cookie monsters.

With his singing voice, there was a chance he could be the next Trey, but even that wasn't enough for me to fake a spark. I mentioned to him the other day that I had a fantasy of being with in a playboy and he said as my future husband, that concerned him.

"I don't feel totally comfortable," he claimed.

I then said, very honestly, "Playa please, you know if you make it as a pop star, you'll have girls spotlighting in your videos. So, please, let me express my sexual art through self-nudity versus degrading femininity for fame."

He laughed.

"Marriage in our future looks dim," I told him. I didn't tell him that if we weren't coworkers, perhaps I'd have crushed on him in a karaoke bar somewhere. I'm such a sucker for karaoke.

There's Dany, the perfect Sagittarian. Dany was recently thrown into the mix. He was fairly older than me, fairly far from me, fairly rooted in his ways from me—none of which helped our status. Still, I was interested. How? Why? I wasn't sure; Cupid works in strange ways.

Dany owned an upscale club which I found interesting and unfamiliar. Interesting not being the most encapsulating word, but this enigmatic life left me curious. There's such a black cloud around strip clubs, I couldn't help but be inquisitive. What went on in there?

Not that I am fazed by other people's opinions, but taking him home for the holidays could be difficult. When asked about his profession or previous children, his answer may pose concern. It could also lead to assuming that I must be a stripper, an impregnated stripper, or something kooky—people get creative. Others could have a field day with that one. I was fascinated by him so I hoped his positive qualities continued to outweigh the reality of our fate and time frame. He asked me out for our first date soon, at least, I think it's a date.

There's Christian, the OCD. Christian was, until I met Andy, the go-to booty call. We dated and never, not even once, had sex. Then we broke up and became booty calls to each other—go figure. Once we started to enter the grey area of booty call guidelines, I had to declare our end. Right before I went out with Dany, Christian and I were having sex and the sex went from good to hallelujah good. It's a shame he and I couldn't have started up a relationship, but it we already tried. See how funny life is?

Christian and I would have absolutely beautiful babies. And with his OCD and my maniacal motivation, we'd have an extraordinary house. And, to top it off, our sex life was good. There was nothing wrong with that picture. Nevertheless, I ended that odd circumstance and I was taking a chance on a strip club bachelor. If Christian wasn't so anti-children, maybe I would've considered our relationship status more thoroughly before moving on. I suppose, with time, his feelings could have changed, but apparently my procreation internal clock had her sights set on more active senses.

I needed to find a middle ground. I went from a bachelor who never wanted kids, to bachelor who had two kids before he met me.

And lastly, there's good ol' reliable, loveable Alexander. He wasn't in the picture. We'd been broken up for quite some time, but whenever I thought of relationships, he popped up.

I broke and texted him the other day. It was bad. Just a "Hi, making sure you're still out there." I don't know what came over me. I was missing the fun we had, the easiness. This was why we shouldn't have such easy communication at our hands. Poor Alexander. All I said was hi and he responded with how he tried to get me back for over a year, how he knew I was the one, and that the ball is in my court when I wanted to be loved. So mature, that Taurus. It melted my icy heart. I was hoping he'd respond and put me in my place, like telling me to move on, telling me he had a girlfriend or fiancé or lover. Or telling me that exes don't text each other hi for no reason. I was expecting that after getting pictures from him when he was in Vegas a week prior.

My hope is that this process is assisting in a breaking point. Breaks can be good. Re-energizing. Re-adjusting. Re-assessing. Instead of standing at a cross road for multiple paths, you can create your own. To walk alone, to walk together, to meet people on the way, and those you simply must leave behind.

J.D.: Just Don't!
August 9, 2011

My life is meant for reality TV. This past weekend's events alone beat out any "basketball wives" who aren't even wives. If people filmed Rose and me, they would never have to pay people to get drunk on TV and make light of themselves. They'd realize those of us who are trying to stay sane in an insane world makes for all the better entertainment. Where to start, where to start...

Friday was a couples day for Dany and me, even though we were at a standstill. I was unprepared for that day. The days when I was nurturing doting lover, he was too busy to notice. If only men realized how discouraging that is. Last week, I was on quite the independent kick, and Dany was in togetherness mode—perhaps it was his guilt talking from not spending time with me. I had already re-adjusted. I had already gotten used to my alone time.

I've always had good intuitions; however, since I got Reiki certified in May, my physical and emotional senses were heightened like crazy. Either my mind or body signaled to me and gave me this crazy awareness. Even when I didn't want to notice, I do.

Last week I wasn't feeling very connected to Dany, particularly after our time apart. How could I feel connected when he was telling me he loved me, but then I found Baby Mama Number Two's jewelry and whatever other objects of hers all over the house? How could I feel at home or comfortable in a space that had other women laying their territory all over it?

He asked me to get together on Tuesday, Thursday, and Friday. On Friday I caved and agreed, but I had an underlying feeling of casualness between us—of a broken trust. His Baby Mama Number Two tagged him all over Facebook. I had to explain to our fabulous group of coupled friends why I was constantly attending their affairs alone, or uninvited to the ones at Dany's house.

Christina called me twice in the past week to ask why I wasn't invited to two of Dany's recent occasions. He failed to understand why I didn't want to run into his arms on my "designated days." I spent the Fourth of July with Jacky and Jack as the only single person there. I knew them from my relationship with Dany, and yet they made more time for me then he did. He left for the yearly Vegas trip with half his staff and I was here, again uninvited. Still a Vegas Virgin. Maybe he wanted to keep me that way.

On Friday, whenever I attempted to leave, he convinced me to stay. We went out for lunch to this cute restaurant we spent a significant amount of time at. Then he convinced me to stay for an intense spooning and napping session. I woke up and my brain told me to leave. The "you're too comfortable" signal went off in my brain loud and clear it worked its way through my body. He had kept kissing me on the forehead saying he loved me, and as truly comfortable as I was in his arms, I suddenly felt this wave of disconnect. It was probably leftover remnants of my emotions from earlier due to the recent lack of trust and communication between us. He did feel like home to me, but his actual home started to feel very strange.

Being my impulsive, confusing self, I practically jumped out of bed, rounded up all my belongings, and then left. I was sure he sensed something was up but, as usual, his passive self just called me multiple times and asked if I was still dropping off the payroll later at his work. For him, that really meant, "Do you still love me?" He was probably expecting a breakup email, but I stopped writing novels to his inbox when I was upset.

When I did do my paycheck delivery, I had my full-blown drive on, this kickass, I'm-a-whole-lot-of-woman-get-out-of-my-way attitude that I got after a breakup. And yet, we had this close, intimate day.

My friend Mel wanted Dany and me to go out with her the following night, and when I went to ask him if he wanted to go, something in my gut told me something was up, so I didn't mention it. I asked him about the bike run Saturday, and he openly told me where they were going, so I didn't question it—I didn't even question my lack of an invitation. I was used to that by then.

That is how I knew I wasn't crazy. Had I been a crazy chick, I would've showed up at the chosen destination. I'm not crazy. Well, I'm crazy, but I'm not psycho. Despite my suspicions, I didn't send out the troops or spies, I didn't show up looking fabulous, nada. No Facebook creeping, no getting on a bike of my own and going out.

That night, I tuned my heat into my box at work. I love teaching Zumba, and gogo for that reason. When I'm dancing, it's the one time I can shut off my brain. No thoughts about past or present, I'm just totally consumed by the moment, by the energy. There was such an escape to music regardless of what my day was like.

On Saturday morning, I woke up emotional, but not uneasy. A person from my past kept calling me to hang out before he left town again. I decided to meet for our goodbyes, and he told me he was at some of my old friends' house. We had all gone to high school together, and I hadn't seen either of them in years.

Jason, whose house he was at, skulked around my Facebook while I was there, commenting on each of my go-go pictures and put on his best face to make me consider dating him. You're about five years too late, honey.

Aside from hitting me in the nose with a football and almost knocking me over during our backyard game, he was practically spoon-feeding me. He made me chicken parmesan, fried chicken, buffalo chicken, and too much to list. I wanted to be like 1: Find out a sistah's relationship status first before you bring out your best cards and carbs and 2: Women love to be fed, not fattened up. Fried chicken, chicken parmesan, cheese, and chips, that's all going to my thighs and I'm not turning down food you bring me on a golden plate.

Alijah, on the other hand, threw me for a loop, that's for sure. We hadn't spoken in six years, but he wanted to reconnect to apologize to me about how our friendship ended. That was fine by me.

The beginning of the day was fine. He offered a light apology for the past and we laughed about it. He was just as eccentric as I remembered, still with an edge I'd always sensed about him, but something felt different. I assumed it was because we'd both grown into different people, but it soon became clear to me it was much deeper than that.

I knew he hadn't had it easy. A couple of his mannerisms or comments left me unsettled, but I wasn't prepared at all for what was about to happen once the whiskey worked its way through his body. He showed me the backpack he was living out of, and he gave me a burnt t-shirt asking me if I would keep it forever because it was one of his most prized possessions.

F**k! I'm awful at accepting gifts. I'm even more awful at accepting a gift one asks me to keep forever. I was flattered and horrified all at once, especially not knowing why this shirt was so special.

I said, "No, really, you keep it," and he insisted. He then took my favorite headband off my head to put on his, and I knew he was keeping it. Second f**k. I loved that headband. I didn't so much love this burnt t-shirt that said "Whatever it takes," and had a story behind it that I didn't know.

My heart ached. My two thoughts were this, 1: If the shirt was important to him, why was he is passing it onto me? 2: This shirt meant nothing and he was buttering me up so he had a place to sleep the next two nights instead of finding someone at the bar or staying with old friends. As he drank a little more whiskey and I ate plate after plate, he then got all sentimental. Kisses on the forehead, holding my hands and not letting go, holding my face to stare in my eyes, telling me he loved me. There was the first "I love you."

I had to think fast. I don't like to say what I don't mean, so I said, "Oh, I love that song," and started making up lyrics. The second "I love you" I simply ignored but the third was much harder to let be.

This is why I spend so much time alone. I can't deal with decoding people's words, actions, body language, and my own thoughts and vibes. It's exhausting reading mixed signals.

By the time I got out of there, my nose was black and blue from the football toss, my favorite headband had been sacrificed, I as holding onto a burnt t-shirt like it was a sacred gift, and I eaten enough chicken to feed a small family. He even put that shit on mac and cheese, seriously.

Once I could depart, I drove straight to Rose's and I told her the story. She's the only individual I know who gives me appropriate reactions whenever I needed to digest events. She will make a great psychologist one day—all her friends have certainly given her enough practice. She told me she felt I should stay at Dany's, but something in my gut told me not to. Instead, I sent a friendly hello via text, but got no response. This is what I get when he doesn't want to tell me what he's doing and still not lie outright.

On, Sunday I woke up crazy emotional. I couldn't sleep Saturday and I couldn't stop crying Sunday. I rarely cry. Dany called me as I was in tears and a Pat Benitar song, and something told me not to answer. He left me his usual funny voicemail, but I felt upset toward him and I couldn't place why.

That night, JD who calls and texts me every day to get together asked me to meet him for dinner and to see a movie—I reluctantly agreed. I told him before, I liked him as a person, but that was it and he knew my circumstance. I had an hour before I needed to meet JD, and something told me to check Facebook. I f**king hate Facebook. It's a creepy social epidemic that's going to slowly be our destruction. Yes, I said it. I went online to discover Dany was on the bike run with multiple people, one being his ex, the baby mama—lovely. That explained my twisted stomach all morning.

I felt discredited. I felt minimized and disrespected. I felt like I wanted to swear off all men. There was no rationalizing here. As much as I knew she'd try anything to make me jealous—and I didn't blame her—as much as I had faith in him and his decisions, I had to trust myself. I know when something is unsettling. It didn't bother me she went. I don't believe in getting jealous or arguing or revenge, but I'm not Mother f**kin' Theresa. Had he told me she was going, I would have been fine, but to find out via Facebook creeping—no thank you.

The craziest thing, too, was to think that had I not Facebook stalked him, I wouldn't have known she'd been on the bike run and we'd carry on peachy-keen. What has our world come to? You can't get away with anything nowadays. I was especially bothered because, as much as he felt and showed, I tortured him the past year but I didn't lie. I was always up front with my mixed emotions and the growth I needed. I said I didn't see a future for us, so if he wanted to date, please do. I always communicated where I was at and my feelings so I wouldn't take advantage of him, but he persisted and persisted.

Now I was a truly changed woman in full relationship, put-your-ass-on-a-pedestal mode and you're taking your ex for bike rides and whatever else on weekends while I'm at Barnes and Noble in the relationship section to see how I can be a super girlfriend and sex goddess in one.

The other weekend, baby mama posted her and her girlfriend on his lake with the jet ski. I cracked, ego-flaring cracked. As much as I dislike childish behavior, I sent a sarcastic text to him. I referenced my Facebook find and stated that it didn't count as stalking when it was on one's newsfeed.

Maybe nothing did happen and he's at home unresponsive because he thinks I'm a psycho, but my calm demeanor only goes so far. I will not be a sucker. Of course the stubborn Aries side of me wanted to put on my best behavior after I found out this information and win him over just to piss off the other female, but I don't do phony. I'm much better at awkward. My expression is authentic on my face, regardless of when I don't want it to be so obvious. I made a commitment list to myself and I'm sticking to it. Yes, I was disappointed, yes to leave it unsaid irked me, but I am stronger then sinking to the crazy relationship level. I would not lose my shit over this and I was going to be the far-too-mature woman for my age, despite how easy it is to be irrational or the rush of being loco. Sometimes it's nice to give into emotions full-bodied, instead of resisting them. Following this, the last thing I wanted to do was go out to meet JD. Ugh. I wanted to go cry at Rose's; she would hug and listen, and maybe cry too. I wanted to go for a barefoot run in the trails—anything to allow my feelings some space. Between my off and on crying, I called JD to cancel. My heart was aching. He didn't hear me at all, but talked circles around me—the typical fix-it guy.

I told him what happened, I told him about Facebook and how I hate being in love and, of course, he felt his charm and dinner could cheer me up. I continued to warn him about how emotionally raw I was, and he said if we weren't laughing over dinner I could leave then. Fair enough.

I got to his house; that was my second time being there. The first time, I went by on our way to a charity bike run and there was a framed picture of me right by his front entrance. That was cause for conversation. When he met me at work going back, part of the event was taking pictures with members' bikes so I didn't say much about it. The second time I saw him, I agreed to do a charity bike run with him because I had already planned to donate for it.

That night, we went to Friday's, the dinner was nice but his intensity was tiring. "Do you feel our connection? I swear we-re connected—I'm not just saying that."

I fought back choking on my meal.

"Did you see I framed the picture of you from the first night we met?"

I wondered if he also recalled I was working the night we met and he paid for that picture.

"I'd never do to you what your boyfriend did, you're too special."

I cringed.

We left dinner and he tried to sway me to do this, sway me to do that. It was like déjà vu all over again of another ex of mine who never heard what I was saying. He'd always wear me down with alternatives and reverse psychology until I felt boring enough to say yes. Does "we're only friends" not mean anything anymore? Can there ever be an authentic friendship between the two sexes, or is one just trying to wear down the other?

On the ride back to my car, the night took a crazy turn. I could see flickering lights in the rear view mirror and a car riding close to us, but I didn't think much of it.

He started to get nervous and flustered, "Gabrielle, don't worry but my ex is behind us. Yeah, that's her."

"JD, why would she be behind us?"

We sat in silence, each following the car with our eyes. As we approached his house, the car was still right behind us. More ex drama, more baby mama drama. To think all these people are procreating. It seems that, to date boys in their twenties, I have to deal with their BS, and to date men in their thirties, I have to deal with their ex's BS. What happened to a happy medium and just dealing with mothers?

As we pulled into the drive way, she did also. She flew that door open and jumped out like a f**kin' ninja—all four feet eleven inches of her. My heart didn't even race—I was so shut off at this point.

"Handle your shit, JD while I make sure my new Kia isn't keyed, slashed, and peed on, whatever." God knows what crazy women will do, God knows especially what crazy Rhode Island women will do and we all know what a mad baby mama is capable of.

First, he asked me to stay in the car. I turned off the radio so I could listen, and I watched from the window as they bickered with each other. It started to get hostile between the two of them. I never like to see a man touch a woman viciously, so as much as I knew this girl was probably off her rocker, I opened my door and told him to never touch a woman and told them both to get it together.

"Why don't the both of you calm down, you're parents!"

They both turned, still in the moment. She very well could have clocked me right there, but again my crazy senses told me to hear her out as she stepped into my personal space bubble. She wanted to talk to me, so I got out of the car and it began. JD looked worried, I was not. I had a reservoir of crazy within me that just chooses to be afloat.

"He f**cked me last night, I want my money!" she blurted. Both of them were yelling all kinds of things.

He was trying to keep me in the car, "Angel, please don't listen to this, stay in the car, Gabriella."

Half-laughing said, "I don't care what you two do, we went to Friday's and now I'm going home. I have my own relationship to figure out. I have dealt with enough baby mama drama to disturb me." I knew I was not nearly caffeinated enough for this, and I was exhausted from my own tears earlier.

As I made my way to my car, she was saying something about his "big d**k," telling me to call her because she thought I was cool, him telling us both how I was his soul mate and I need to be strong and get through this because were connected.

"My angel Gabriella, I'm here for you as a friend because I know how deep our connection is. We've got to get through this."

I couldn't even formulate a response at that point. Was this real? As I stood there at the passenger door wide eyed, they next started arguing about child support. Between that and her yelling at him to tell me what he was hiding, he caved. Finally, he confessed that they'd had sex recently. He said how my friendship was so special to him and it hurt him to not be able to get close to me so he went to her for comfort. I literally thought I was in the twilight zone.

As he was actually on his knees pleading for my forgiveness, the baby mama flaring her hands in the air, clapping for him, I blocked out what they were actually saying. As I was trying to get him off my feet at my car door, I felt numb to all relationships. When I thought it couldn't get better or worse from here, three cruisers showed up—now it's a show.

The first cop came over and asked which one of us was the wife and which was the girlfriend—clearly he'd been in this scenario many times before. The second cop came up, knew them both, and nonchalantly tried to break it up like it was a regular thing. The third cop shined his light on me to get a look at me.

At this point I had managed to make it to my car and was half in it, but both cops had my door held open. The officers looked at me sitting in my car, trying to drive off.

"How old are you, honey? Nineteen?" one of them asked. The cop was shining his flash light on me so I was now the show for everyone, despite their smack down they'd just had in the drive way.

The cop with the flashlight still shining in my face came over and said, "You're beautiful. Why are you here? You should be dating guys in Providence having fun and doing your thing."

Interesting advice. No, I was thinking I should join the Peace Corps or move to Australia, especially after tonight. I was laughing hysterically now. The hysteria had hit me. After all my tears on the drive to Providence, I found myself in a laughing fit, just full of pressing emotions. I had JD on his knees holding my door open, spitting some soul mate stuff, I had the ex actually sitting on the hood of my car picking at her fake nails, and I had three cops there to regulate the situation.

The cop escorted me to leave as I fought back more laughter. I had a police escort just trying to leave a "quiet" neighborhood of Providence.

On the ride home, JD called multiple times. I eventually answered if only to cut this off. Between tears and confessing what our future could be, I half listened to, "Please be strong for us, Gabrielle. I know you're special. I know how mature you are, I know you can look past this. This house could be ours."

Not again. Look past what? Stick out what? Whew. He of course had to tell me how the cops told him he f**ked up and were asking about me also. Apparently he defended me and told them I was more than just looks.

I thought, *JD the last thing I want to be is your arm candy after all that drama.*

I tried to put our situation in perspective, "JD we met at work... I went to a charity bike run with you, we talked about doing another, that's the extent of it. You know my situation and now I know yours—all of yours."

And that is my life. Not even an explanation or sorry from Dany who clearly believes I should be forever punished for treating him insensitively, and a billion explanations from JD on how he is now empty and can't eat or sleep because of our fight.

"Gabrielle, I won't sleep. I'll never get over you. Give me a chance. When school starts again you can stay here, I'll drive you even!"

"J.D. last time you drove me anywhere, your ex and the cops showed up."

I later put JD in my phone for "just don't" to avoid any possible answering. Facebook was then deleted and on came the Googling of bikes and boats, for myself of course. As a future goal, I'd like to have my own Harley and a sail boat. That way I can never be lured by a bachelor with cool moving objects.

Chapter Fourteen

MAKEUPS AND BREAKUPS BEFORE EVEN A TAKE OUT
2010

I'm realizing my next significant other has really got his work cut out for him. As I was on my walk today, I wondered if maybe Rose and I would end up together after all. We complemented each other. We had the same foundational morals. She enjoyed kids but didn't want to birth one. I'd have our child while she was off being the bread winner in my maternity months. Then, we could run some extraordinary business together, and have a lovely awakened child. I wondered when the appropriate time would be to discuss that with her again. It came up before, but especially if I was going to be the mama, I'd like to be taken seriously in this talk. At the time, she was into the going-out scene, so our discussion had to wait. Once she was done with men who were too immature for her, I'd have to present my proclamation of love.

I'd like to focus on the over-aggressors I'd made some recent observations about. While I like when a man puts me in my place, he had to earn that privilege first.

Two weekends ago there was Qin. We'd caught eyes a few times at Barnes and Noble. I knew that I knew him from somewhere and would try to scan my brain for how. Then he finally said hi and offered me a seat. I politely declined the first time.

"No thanks," I said and sat two tables over, feeling his eyes on me for observation. Our second encounter was when I was on my way out, but he had pulled out the seat for me so I sat. It was reactive. He did it with such assurance, I almost couldn't help it. We made great conversation. It had a nice flow, truly. We talked for at least an hour and the conversation went nicely. He asked me to dinner—I politely said no, but settled on a maybe some other time. He asked for my number and I gave it to him but explained that there were rules to having it. I mentioned not to communicate with me via text, that it is best to call me if he decided to, that I had a busy schedule, and that the following weekend I had a friend's birthday party with Dany, so I probably wouldn't have my phone on me at all Saturday and we'd get in touch sometime Sunday. He texted me throughout the week, but I didn't think much of it. That was what they all did when they first tried to suck you in. I wasn't in much of a mood for conversation, so I'd simply remind him that I'd talk to him on Sunday.

On Saturday, he called me wanting to meet first at Barnes and Noble Sunday morning, and then do dinner that night. I didn't give him a response.

Sunday came around and by noontime I had two missed calls and multiple texts from him. The first text was the typical "hi are you ignoring me?" question. That was followed up by an ultimatum and *that* was followed up by an insult, a compliment, and a goodbye all at once. What a turn off.

I said, "Qin, I told you earlier this week I'd confirm with you Sunday on a plan. I also told you I wouldn't have my phone on me. I thought that was clear. Sorry you felt ignored, but it's best we don't get together. I'll talk to you if I run into you again at Barnes and Noble."

The poor guy tried to back track and texted me from the restaurant later saying, "I'm here, take your time."

I didn't give him an answer.

"When will you get here? Look forward to seeing you if you want to join me."

After not answering him again, he sent me another insult—something about women—and for the next twenty-four hours, I received texts about how his mom died, questions, phone calls, and apologies until we finally talked and I explained myself. How exhausting.

That, to me, was a major red flag. You just can't take things so personally. You can't bring past experiences into a relationship until there actually is one. You especially can't reference a dead family member and put me on a guilt trip. You can't abuse technology on someone just because we have it. And above all, what ever happened to simple conversation? Talk is not always a prelude to sex or dating. That was scenario one.

Dates to Remember - Gabrielle Anna

After that, there was Nicholas. He and I had an advanced English class together. I liked to talk to Nicholas so I did. He was interesting. He was quirky. He was a seat away from the guy I used to stare at, so conveniently we stumbled into each other. Now he was merely cramping my style.

He gave me a Starbucks card one day, so I took it. That was that. Don't give just to get. It was for a free coffee—ah, what a gesture! He saw me booking it to class, bag lady with her matcha tea habit.

For extra credit, my professor asked us to attend a seminar on campus and Nicholas asked me to go with him. Okay, sure. Naturally, we stopped at Starbucks first and he swiped his card ignoring my money on the table. I handed it to him and he pushed it away. I've learned not to fight guys anymore on this, it gets awkward. I was so over this dance. If you want to pay for me, do so. If you don't, you are not obligated to, but I refuse to say "No, no, I insist," if you had already insisted. We went to the seminar. It was awful. We decided to leave early and sit in the café for a while. He offered to buy lunch but I politely declined. The café felt like a happy medium. Again, we had great conversation. I seemed to be attracting the right people, but before you know it, I made one comment about a hookah bar and he text stalks me later that night for confirmation.

"When are you taking me out?"

Strike one.

"I won a million dollars on a scratch ticket, too bad you're not here."

Strike two.

"I'm at a hookah bar, just come out."

Strike three. The strikes just slowly racked up. Then, it was the inevitable insult, compliment, ultimatum, question, and goodbye. I had to do another breakup and make up before even entering a relationship or date for that matter.

My English class I couldn't avoid and I refused to change Barnes and Noble locations just because of the risk of an encounter. I would sit there with my oversized headphones before I relocated. I will get an A in

English class and, in the best case scenario, Nicholas will sit at another desk so I can sit next to the kid I stare at who I am happy just to stare at.

December 3, 2011

Today was my first holiday party of the season. Dany and I have not talked since Monday. We are apparently in our off season. I went stag, and although I have chosen that label, it couldn't have been any more apparent. That was so undesirable for the holiday season. I've never paid it much mind, but others do. The only other person who went solo was one other woman. I thought she was just single, not the Carrie Bradshaw kind of single, but the hoarders or cat-lady kind of single. To make matters worse, I was pretty sure my boss thought I wanted her husband. He's taken my class a few times and we carried good conversation, so her radar was on. I did sometimes get the sense he was flirting, so I couldn't blame her. For all of the one week that I had Facebook, he did Facebook me, but so what? I noticed a change in him ever since he figured out who my boyfriend was—perhaps the close proximity made him feel more connected, or perhaps just because he was married didn't mean he couldn't converse with other women. The stigmas with marriage are not flattering. No conversation with the opposite sex, even if you're quite the conversationalist. For better or worse, why not for better and better? 'Til death do us part—so you're telling me we spend all these years together here just to spend the afterlife apart. Well, if that's the case, we should all be more lax in a life of many lovers, then just meet our significant one in the afterlife.

I tried to converse with some of the kids closer to my age, but it was painful for me. I gave them my drink tickets as a peace offering—they acted like I was giving them the keys to a Benz.

The twenty-year-old front desk boy threw a little flirting my way, but I politely paid it no mind. If I did what I did to grown men, little boys would probably enter psych wards after dating me. It had nothing to do with my physical appeal—I don't put much effort into looks—it was everything to do with my existentialism. I think what draws anyone to me is my carefree attitude. Well, then they learn it is not just an outfit. It is my state of being.

How could I explain that I was literally born in the wrong generation and wrong chronological body? My mindset has always been about self-actualization, I now just have words and ways to accomplish it as an adult. The combination is deadly. Here was to another holiday where I was single and the love of my life continued to punish my past behavior by banning me from all family events. Bah humbug.

Chapter Fifteen

HORNY HOMEBODY
FEBRUARY 29, 2012

Oh the joys of being a woman. This morning, I woke up to my period and I couldn't have been more delighted. It's so easy to take for granted or to wish away a flow, but it is a huge piece of one's femininity. Each cycle reminds me I can let go, reminds me I'm here for a greater purpose and I can blame some of my rash behavior on hormones each month—I'm allotted complete justification for my bizarre behavior.

It explains a lot. The week before my period, I have set signals. A certain amount of days before, I feel so sexy, so sensual, and really powerful in my identity. At another point, I am really irritable, picky, indecisive, and can't be satisfied. One day, I will have very specific cravings that need to be met, the next I won't have an appetite at all. Then, the day before it's going to come, I am so tired I can't keep my eyes open. Then it never fails to show up. Right when I go from feeling like I'm on a high from drugs, I go to just feeling hormonally drugged. Then, sure enough, it arrives. During, whether it is the ironies of life or Mother Nature's sense of humor I am dysfunctionally horny. I could have the wildest sex on my period, but I eat sweets instead. It showed up this morning and now I was so lovey-dovey and I wanted to call everyone I'd recently offended in my hormonal state and make amends. I wanted to hug and pet any beings I saw and nuzzle them in my sore breasts.

This past weekend made perfect sense. I felt my space was so invaded. I had that feeling of set expectations from me which I often found emotionally draining. That's what I so struggle with in relationships. I think because I am so real when people interact with me, I bring a lot of their baggage to the surface—either emotions they want to have, or ones they often suppress. I can pride myself on that, but for years and years of my life, I have felt more like a vessel for people. While still working on my composition, I only have so much to give away. I find people want to mold you into their setting and I find myself trying to figure out how to least disappoint them.

Dates to Remember - Gabrielle Anna

Gabriel and I saw each other last week after years of time apart, being in different lives, growing into different identities. We went to dinner Monday night. After my many missed phone calls, he did the stopping by move. If it was anyone else, it could have been pushy. After knowing each other since 7th grade, you have love for them regardless of such behavior. Drop-ins are expected and okayed. He will always have a place in my heart because we were friends for so long.

Dinner would have been beautiful if it was left at that, but then, the next night, he blew me off for our yoga plans and the following days he cyber-stalked me. We had solid plans for a yoga class together, and I never heard from him. Then he knew I had work on Wednesday and he called me over and over. On Thursday, even while in Miami, he continued to cellphone-stalk me. On Friday he was supposed to go to New York and he got a hotel in Boston instead with the assumption I'd be working and—another assumption—I'd conveniently stay with him.

I certainly didn't blame him. We'd known each other since I first grew breasts. We basically watched each other grow up and he, off and on, had interest in me. It never quite worked between us beyond friendship because when he was single, I was intimidated and when he was in relationships, I was envious. I just never felt completely in the right space for it. We've always been close in our way. I told him Friday, after working two nights back-to-back the first night with open bar from 7:00-11:00, I wanted to do yoga and then veg out. I needed to recharge constantly due to spending any time in nightlife. He let that go, but still persisted with inquisitive texts bombarding me at all hours.

On Saturday, the phone calls started at 10:00 a.m. then from 11:00 p.m. to 9:00 a.m. the following morning, he called fifteen times. Fifteen times! If he had better stalking skills, he could have more subtly figured out my whereabouts. I go back and forth between a handful of locations. He justified it later by a drunken night in Boston, but nevertheless, when I'm in bunker mode, that behavior was not enticing. I'll always love him but I was in no spirit to join for his wild outings.

I isolated myself from poor Caeser all weekend too. We were companions in friendship, but I was hermitting. He of all people should understand that. It was somewhat wrong of me as we usually have weekly psychoanalysis chats via phone or iPad, or at his pad. At this rate, he may swear off all women. He probably wonders how the f**k we all change faces so quickly. He's one of the few people who can talk with me about a range of things, so I know he doesn't get it when I can't bear to talk.

It's not intentional. As honest as I am, honesty is so difficult sometimes. Boundaries, expectations, limits—I usually just barricade myself versus engaging in conversation. I was in alone-time mode for good reasons. This weekend, literally from Friday to Sunday, I was so horny that I had to barricade myself at home. There was no other option. I was having sexual fantasies. I was envisioning penises.

My period was absent last month and, to make up for lost time, it was apparently making a statement. I couldn't keep my hands off of myself, but as fun as that may be, it was not nearly satisfying enough. The more I get off without really being able to get it made me more and more cranky. I was like a cat in heat. I made chocolate pumpkin bread, I baked a cake, and I turned into a version of Martha Stewart all in attempts to be functional.

Caeser didn't understand. He just said, "Oh, so you're baking a cake again?" He tries. What's the more appropriate reasoning for when our hormones debilitate us? I can't think rationally when my body is thinking of procreating. The outside world is not safe on such timing. The last thing I want is for my scent and hormones to mislead. Those dangerous little things! Baking and "bating" are the better backups!

Short Lived

My ally, Danielle, and I have recently started taking Abdul's boxing classes. We used to box routinely, but being so much out of our regimen, we decided to take on a new challenge. I noticed very little in my environment, particularly men-wise. Those days were past me already. I've exceeded my pursuit for potential suitors at the ripe age of twenty-three, of course only after the wave of mind games with my ex. I finally realized I was waiting on what I already found. I made excuses for our failure. Had Dany and I been at a different time, if this, if that—but then you wonder if in all the "ifs," you align—what more could you want anyway?

That makes you question if life is about just growing with people, or if you loved them before you knew it. Back to Short-lived: This instructor made small attempts of conversation with me, falling short of impressive. He asked my name a couple of times, almost excessively.

"What's your name again, I forgot it?"

"Uhh, Gabrielle."

Ten minutes later, "You, what's your name again? Hit harder. You're not sweating yet."

"Uhh, it's Gabrielle."

The first mention of our engagement came from Danielle. She came into the girl's locker room, looking conspicuous as always. "He's been warned."

I was puzzled as I had no idea what she was referring to. "What did you do?"

"Gab, the kid you were boxing with was asking about you, like to me, to everyone. I warned him. It's for your best interest and his psyche. I figured I'd stop any efforts before they could start."

"Oh god, what did you say?"

"I told him forget it. I said you'd swallow him and spit him out. I also said you've seen someone off and on for like two years now."

Despite her choice of words, she was right. I felt bad for a second but what are friends for? Defending us from false romances. How thoughtful.

We thought the above would throw him off course. He later told me he liked a challenge, he fed off of it. I can now blame Danielle for adding to the bait. We should have considered this earlier on considering he was a fighter. They are fueled by beatings.

During the following classes, I'd look over and find him, his gaga eyes in my direction. Bright eyed, loving. Oh, not now! I'd brush off his comments toward me, though Danielle and I laughed at one of our favorite moments.

While I was cooling down the class in downward dog, he had to comment from across the room. He stumbled loudly on the words of how my voice was angelic. "You sound like an angel!"

I tried not to look over. With multiple sweaty fighters trying to breathe in downward dog, waiting at me to dictate their next move and Brad was behind me choking out the words, "You sound like harmony," I thought Danielle was going to croak.

In a not very yogi-like way, she punched me through laughter. His persistence continued. Danielle's efforts proved ineffective. Following gawking, awkward comments one makes while infatuated, it was all there. I kept quiet. I remained cool, distant.

On Saturday, Danielle told me she worked out with the guys. She said she was impressed with Brad and that he was a good fighter. It was my assumption we'd all work out together the following day.

"Okay, I'm in," I said, trusting her. When I found myself there the next day like a good doobie, Danielle was not. Damn it. I didn't feel comfortable asking Abdul to teach me jiu-jitsu unless he offered first, which he didn't. I didn't need his pregnant wife suspicious of me. I have enough baby mamas to watch out for.

The only other option was to wrestle with sixteen-year-old boys who not only looked lethal, but were likely hormonal. I couldn't justify wrestling with them. It seemed my opponent, teacher, and trainee would fall on Brad or I would be off to go get a latte. He was covered in sweat and probably just hormonal as the sixteen-year-olds. If it wasn't for Jerrid being the instigator he is, I would have quietly made my exit. Unfortunately, as I made a beeline for the door, Jerrid caught me and told me not to be a wimp.

"What, you're leaving? You girl!" This comment kept my feet planted, though my mind was at Starbucks.

Yesterday in our Starbucks corner, Danielle told me she knew of a kid here getting ring worm. This conversation was flashing red in my head. It was all too fresh. Even bigger alarms went off as I examined Brad's body for a quick check over. I identified an odd mark on his leg. Yup, ringworm.

Before I had a chance to question it, he knocked me down. *Shit. Are we working on jiu-jitsu? Right now? I'm subjected to it now, ugh.* I tried to cross it out of my head and did a few moves with him before saying I had to get going. Between his body odor, and my brain referencing to past *Dr.Oz* episodes, searching for a ringworm reference—I couldn't focus. I wasn't going to be able to work out.

After class, while Brad tried for conversation, I told him if he wanted to hang out, he could meet me at yoga. I didn't find this misleading. I invited two other people in that moment. It's rare people actually come to yoga. Not many want to willingly do poses in a room at 104 degrees. If they do come, it's rare they come back. Still, there are always those individuals that internalize any gesture and comment as a direct lead to your heart or pants.

The first class he was going to come to, he backed out of an hour beforehand. This didn't look good when you're trying to impress the ladies. For the second class, he wanted to ride up together. He insisted, but finally he agreed to simply meet at the studio. He showed up early—bonus point for him. I later found out, though, that he was high—minus that point.

After yoga, he forgot his wallet—minus a point. Money isn't the issue, responsibility, however, is. Not paying yogis is. We were parting ways and he was pushing going for something to eat. As we stood there it started to rain, so I just agreed. My stomach was rumbling and I was already late for my Italian friend, Johnny's, usual Sunday dinner extravaganza. I explained I like to be there for his Sunday dinners when I could, but he just stood there with me, in the rain. Frozen. Looking at me like anything I said was bypassing him until it was what he wanted to hear.

I then suggested we stop at a pizza place nearby. Danielle and I were regulars there, so it was convenient. I said she'd likely meet us. He insisted I followed him to his house for his forgotten wallet. Back and forth, back and forth via text even though we were driving on the highway. He was behind me, a call would have been sufficient.

We met at his house; I had Danielle on standby on the phone so I wouldn't be subjected to going inside. He ever-so-cheerfully came out moments later with a thing of hemp protein in hand for me. It was half full. A sweet thoughtful gesture—bonus point.

We went to the pizza place and ordered. Over salads, he watched me scarf mine down, all the while saying how filling those salads were and that he simply couldn't finish his—minus a point. At that moment,

I'd been eyeing my pita bread and contemplating the protein bars for dessert in my car. To hear him complain of an oversized salad was flat out foolish! Also, over salads, he told me his aspirations, dreams, and work ethic—two bonus points. I appreciated the motivation. He also discussed his colorful past. I appreciated the honesty, but again I found myself in counselor role. I was hoping some of his hostility would be let out in yoga. He was often highly over-caffeinated and somewhat hostile—not toward me, it just resonated.

He confided in me about how he absolutely doesn't believe in abortion, but if it didn't exist as a procedure, he'd have four babies. Two exes were lazy and got pregnant thinking he'd want to stay in the relationship. The other ex was his last ex and they both cheated on each other and she got pregnant a month after they broke up. Oh, these stories. These fertile women lately are irritating even me. There was like a three day window, maybe four day window to conceive once a month if you're fertile, if they're fertile—if, if, if—and all these women were pregnant. Come on ladies, no, come *off* I guess is more appropriate.

Just for discussion purposes, I asked him his star sign. I chose not to acknowledge other topics.

I said, "Seriously, what's your sign?"

"I don't know about that shit."

At this point I wondered if he realizes he has just sealed his fate between us, absolutely. He's a Capricorn, I love Capricorns and they love me, but we make better as friends.

I said, "Told you. We're meant to be friends."

He looked at me and comments about how weird girls are.

We finished eating, well I did. I felt he was sweet and optimistic, but still not compatible.

The following morning, I went to Abdul's class and at one of the stations, Brad was holding the pads to hit. The question of the ring worm came around and I remembered Brad being suspect.

Dates to Remember - Gabrielle Anna

When Danielle and I went to Starbucks afterward, we discussed the "warned." Being as frank as I am, I sent Brad a text and asked him outright whether or not he had it.

His response was, "I have ringworm. I've had it seven times. It's not that bad. I just got over it. It happens in gyms and to fighters. Your real concern should be body herpes or like staph."

Body herpes? Staph? I did not pay $120 a month membership to be worrying about either of the above. Shit! What are these men trying to do to me? As if I didn't miss my ex enough. They're practically sending me on my way to him wrapped in a golden bow. I'm constantly subjected to flashes about how I can't be subjected to the bizarre world of dating or even in these types of engagements. Why am I being warned of body herpes so casually? I think I get flustered with my ex because all the times I was telepathically trying to will him to save me, I'd get no response. I wanted to know I had someone by my side, and I couldn't figure out his passive-aggressive ways so I'd freak like the young adult I am.

Shortly after my conversation with Brad, I developed nausea and Danielle developed an itch. I didn't have these concerns when working out with fellow yogis. I didn't have these concerns with Mr. Jones sending me the P90X system in the mail for my being a hard worker. He also warned me so helpfully when I told him of my experience with Short-lived and what he said. He offered to send state troopers my way if need be—much appreciated, but no. I will take a trooper for my pending seatbelt ticket needing resolution, otherwise I'd just like a physician so I can stop Googling Web MD and forms of insanity.

Now, I admit, I am no princess of hygiene. At times, mine is definitely questionable, but I knew there were multiple reasons why I was not drawn to athletes. Yet another experience written off for novel purposes, however this one was quite short lived.

Conclusion

It seems love can be found in fragments of life. It's about the experience, not the outcome. My deep belief is our life stems from our thoughts and behaviors. Above all, I learned to believe in myself first and foremost. I learned what I set out in love—I needed to learn to give to myself and to accept as well. My hopes for others are to walk confidently and embrace both your feminine and masculine features. Love passionately. Love wildly. And most importantly, love yourself unconditionally. Don't be afraid to love those around you. Be inspired by those who are doing their best, and have compassion for those who are not. Have all the relationships you can—with your peers, with your family, with friends, with colleagues, with your body—take on and embrace all the relations in your path.

I found I needed to learn different things from different people; they either gave me something to give myself—a memory, a quality, to bring an issue to the surface—or a relationship in full. Each person and scene coming along as they needed to, even when I least expected it or was unprepared, often even unwilling.

For those that you find absolutely deplete you again and again, leave them behind. They came up for a reason, and you either need to let them pass by, or find the answer in yourself. For those who keep you coming back, let that sort of magnetism inspire you. Have the greatest relationship with yourself; mind, body, heart, and spirit so you always feel fulfilled. There's life in each entity, but ultimately they can only be most powerful if they're all connected. One must trust and have faith in the other. I wish you an expansive and dimensional relationship with yourself, and I wish you a loving relationship with others—whether you have multiple lovers or you find just one.

And may you always have love for your dates to remember, and wine and laughter for the ones to forget. Both are just as special.

Dates to Remember - Gabrielle Anna

҉About the Author҉

As a Counseling Psychology major, Gabrielle has a deep interest and knowledge in human behavior and inter/intrapersonal relationships. She prides herself on her versatile life and aims to share her experiences and insight with others. Education has helped develop clarity on her self—understanding and experiences have given her a higher understanding and compassion for others. Graduating from Johnson and Wales, she made the decision to work and continue her education, but kept her focus in writing. Ultimately, her deep passion is writing. Writing allows her creativity and personality to flourish. For Gabrielle, writing novels is not only therapeutic, but a way of connecting with people. Writing is a gift that we all have, but the passion to put the book forward is not there for everyone. For years, Gabrielle has had a burning desire to fulfill her books path and reach out to those who want to share in its fruition. She strives to be an honest voice and motivator for her audience. For more excerpts, follow her at: www.Gabrielleanna.com

CPSIA information can be obtained
at www.ICGtesting.com
Printed in the USA
FFOW02n1824260614
6047FF